THE BUCKET LIST
ROMANTIC ESCAPES

First published in the United States of America in 2026
by Rizzoli Universe, a Division of
Rizzoli International Publications, Inc.
49 West 27th Street
New York, NY 10001
rizzoliusa.com

Copyright © 2026 Quarto Publishing plc

All rights reserved. No part of this publication may be reproduced, stored in a retrieval system, or transmitted in any form or by any means, electronic, mechanical, photocopying, recording, or otherwise, without prior consent of the publishers.

Printed in Huizhou, Guangdong, China
TT/Nov/2025
2026 2027 2028 / 10 9 8 7 6 5 4 3 2 1

ISBN: 978-0-7893-4630-8
Library of Congress Control Number: 2025944283

Conceived, designed, and produced by the Bright Press,
an imprint of the Quarto Group
1 Triptych Place
London, SE1 9SH
United Kingdom
T (0)20 7700 6700
quarto.com

Publisher: James Evans
Editorial Director: Isheeta Mustafi
Managing Editor: Lucy Tipton
Editor: Ellie Stores
Art Director: James Lawrence
Project Editor: Anna Southgate
Design: JC Lanaway, James Lawrence, and Marcia Pedraza Sierra
Picture Research: Jane Lanaway and Charlotte Rivers
Picture Rights: Charlotte Rivers

The authorized representative in the EU for product safety and compliance is
Mondadori Libri S.p.A.,
via Gian Battista Vico 42,
Milan, Italy, 20123
mondadori.it

Visit us online:
Facebook.com/RizzoliNewYork
Instagram.com/RizzoliBooks
YouTube.com/user/RizzoliNY

THE BUCKET LIST
ROMANTIC ESCAPES

1000 Ideas for Couples' Adventures, Lovers' Getaways, and Out-of-this-World Honeymoons

KATHRYN ROMEYN
& KELLI ACCIARDO

HOW TO USE THIS BOOK

This book is divided into six chapters—North and Central America, South America, Europe, Africa and the Middle East, Asia, and Oceania. Countries are given at the start of each entry. For large countries, the relevant territory or state is also given. If you have a specific location in mind, simply turn to page 406 to search for it in the Index.

COLOR CODE

Each entry number in the book has been given a color that relates to one of seven categories, shown here at right, allowing you to select activities based on the type of experience you're interested in.

■ Cities and culture

■ Luxury hideaways

■ Something for both

■ Exciting adventures

■ Giving back, together

■ Wonders of nature

■ Making memories

Hot-air balloon, Lake District, UK

Contents

Introduction	6
1 North and Central America	8
2 South America	156
3 Europe	180
4 Africa and the Middle East	276
5 Asia	322
6 Oceania	376
Index	406
Picture Credits	414
Author Biographies	416

INTRODUCTION

Nothing bonds two people quite like the shared experience of travel. While this can be true on vacation with a dear friend or family member, the ultimate partner for a special journey is often your soulmate. Frolicking across the world with your forever companion can feel like wearing rose-colored glasses—their very presence imbues landscapes with more beauty, heightens the flavor of your meals and drinks, makes the stars twinkle brighter, and your exploits all the more thrilling and meaningful.

As a longtime travel journalist, I've been fortunate to take countless honeymoon-worthy trips around the planet, and I've come to recognize that romance, sexiness, and allure are subjective. Some couples spark most in a city, where an exquisite dinner is the ultimate seduction, while others are electrified out in nature, with only wild animals and wide open spaces around. It might be that giving back to a place or community gets your dopamine flowing—or maybe it comes from hopping onto a zipline or helicopter.

Of course, the more you see, the longer your bucket list grows. Whether for a special occasion such as a honeymoon or anniversary, a flawlessly orchestrated proposal, or for no reason at all other than wanting to spend quality time with your favorite person on Earth, there is an idea—or 1,000—in this book.

We've researched and traveled extensively to select 1,000 captivating experiences that span the seven continents. After all, there is magic to be found all over the globe, hand in hand with the person you adore. So as you prepare to take your own epic romance on the road, we hope you find this book a treasure trove of ideas with which to build a trip that deepens your love of the world and, of course, each other.

P.S. *The world is ever changing, with the safety and political issues of certain countries fluctuating, too. There are recent or ongoing conflicts in some of the destinations in this book, but they'll surely be ready for travelers again in the future. We didn't want to exclude these beautiful and romantic places, but we very much recommend checking government guidelines before booking your lovers' getaway.*

KATHRYN ROMEYN

Relaxing in Marrakesh, Morocco

1 North and Central America

2 Inn on the Lake

CANADA, YUKON

1 Gaze skyward at the northern lights in Whitehorse

With its silent forests and snow-blanketed peaks, Canada's vast northwesternmost territory is a dependable place to wonder at one of the most magical phenomena on Earth, the aurora borealis. In Whitehorse, book a glass chalet, a window-roofed cabin, or even a campsite adjacent to steaming hot springs, and rest up for nights spent under swirling spirals, rays, and curtains of neon light. The best time to go is mid-August through mid-April—ideally during a new moon.

CANADA, YUKON

2 Explore the wild Yukon from Inn on the Lake

Inn on the Lake's rustic log building makes an ideal base for discovering the unspoiled beauty of the Yukon. In the winter, cozy up with warming cocktails in the executive suite's two-person jacuzzi after a day's ice fishing or kick-sledding with your partner. For the long summer days there are canoes and kayaks to paddle on Marsh Lake, and mountain bikes to ride under the midnight sun. The inn has a romantic restaurant serving delicious fare from the boreal forest.

3 Hot Springs Cove

CANADA, BRITISH COLUMBIA

3 Follow a cold-water surf with a hot-spring dip

The dramatic environs of Tofino, on Vancouver Island, promise cold-water beaches lined with fog-shrouded pines. Wetsuit up, booties and all, for a private introduction to surfing. Out on the water, the rhythm of the Pacific and the misty backdrop of old-growth forest create a surfing experience that feels both raw and meditative. Follow your wave riding with a scenic boat tour bound for Maquinna Marine Provincial Park where you can warm up together in hot spring pools fed by geothermal waterfalls at Hot Springs Cove.

CANADA, BRITISH COLUMBIA

4 Take a tandem bike for a seawall spin

As urban green spaces go, Vancouver's Stanley Park—1,001 acres (405 ha) of lush rainforest, beach, and Salish Sea vistas—is unrivaled. Rent a tandem bike and pedal together the striking 5.5-mi. (9-km) circumference of the park, and maybe beyond, to Kitsilano Beach Park, with its soft sand and mountain views.

CANADA • **NORTH AND CENTRAL AMERICA**

5 Patio dining at SIDECUT Steakhouse

CANADA, BRITISH COLUMBIA

5 Fly through old-growth forest before settling down for a candlelit dinner

Combine an outdoorsy escapade with an intimate dinner for two at the sumptuous Four Seasons Resort Whistler, where the Winter Aprés Tour zipline allows a couple to experience high-flying thrills through snow-coated, old-growth forest on a series of ziplines illuminated with fairy lights. Return for a quick wardrobe change before settling down for melt-in-your-mouth A5 wagyu and fine wines over candlelight at SIDECUT Steakhouse.

CANADA, BRITISH COLUMBIA

6 Ride through powder at North America's largest ski resort

Snap into skis for an unforgettable morning gliding through an Ansel Adams photograph come to life at Whistler Blackcomb. The two-mountain resort comprises a picturesque 8,100 acres (3,300 ha) that provides terrain for every ability level. A trip during the festive season is especially memorable, with Whistler Village sparkling with more than 350,000 lights.

CANADA, BRITISH COLUMBIA

7 Helicopter to a once-in-a-lifetime ice cave lunch

Climb aboard a helicopter for an exciting flight to Whistler's otherworldly ice caves, where a Shangri-La Vancouver guide will lead you through chambers of blue en route to the ultimate five-course, wine-paired lunch. The package includes a photographer taking photos you can keep as mementos of the extraordinary experience. Fly back to the hotel for a spa treatment followed by a mixology session using glacial ice from your outing.

CANADA, BRITISH COLUMBIA

8 Forest bathe together before enjoying an intimate sushi dinner

Connect deeply to nature—and each other—on a meditative, guided Forest Therapy walk with the Indigenous-owned Talaysay Tours in lush Stanley Park. Take your heightened sensitivities from the supersensory session to two stools at RawBar in Fairmont Pacific Rim's Lobby Lounge, where succulent modern Japanese fare will treat your taste buds, and vintage James Bond flicks spice up the ambience.

Whistler Village

CANADA • **NORTH AND CENTRAL AMERICA**

9 Capilano Suspension Bridge

CANADA, BRITISH COLUMBIA

9 Get lost in the beauty and culinary scene of Vancouver

Take a wobbly walk over the 450-ft.-long (137-m) Capilano Suspension Bridge stretching across the Capilano River at a dizzying 230 ft. (70 m) in the air. The exhilarating experience is a perfect precursor to a glamorous dinner featuring the region's seasonal bounty at Hawksworth Restaurant. Retire to a glam suite upstairs in Rosewood Hotel Georgia, with libations from 1927 Lounge.

CANADA, ALBERTA

10 Pedal into a winter wonderland in Banff National Park

Choose the best and liveliest mode of travel for exploring Canada's first national park: electric fat bikes, which make light work of cycling, thanks to pedal assist. Join a tour group for your biking adventure through the mesmerizing Rocky Mountains, and you will find not just the famous photo stops, but also stunning secret spots in the backcountry that only a knowledgeable guide can reveal.

CANADA, ALBERTA

11 Skate and paint at Fairmont Chateau Lake Louise

Among the many activities available at this charming lakeside hotel, a fairy-tale skate across Alberta's Lake Louise has to be the most romantic. The time to visit is mid-December through mid-April. By day you will have the Victoria Glacier as a dramatic backdrop; by evening, a sky full of twinkling stars. Afterward, join a paint night at the hotel and create a keepsake canvas together.

11 Ice-skating on Lake Louise

NORTH AND CENTRAL AMERICA • CANADA

CANADA, CALGARY

12 Cocreate a sexy signature scent

Book a workshop at Milk Jar where you can each build a fragrance inspired by your love. Working with essential oils and natural extracts, you will each use your scent to create a candle and reed diffuser. Afterward, drop into the retro Vietnamese speakeasy Paper Lantern, an intimate bar with low lights, sharing plates, and an impressive cocktail menu.

CANADA, SASKATCHEWAN

13 Soak up the love in Saskatoon

Set out on foot to explore Saskatoon, Saskatchewan's largest city, which boasts a tempting culinary scene, a healthy dose of culture, and a vibrant nightlife. Then return to your suite at cozy-chic the James Hotel, where romantic gestures are the house specialty. Its "Soak Up the Love" package promises floating candles, bath bombs, and a bottle of rosé sparkling wine.

CANADA, SASKATCHEWAN

14 Snuggle up for a Plains Cree tepee sleepover

Venture northeast of Saskatoon to the UNESCO World Heritage Site of Opimihaw Valley, an important location for First Nations people, and be transported to another time and way of life during a one-night sleepover in an authentic Plains Cree-style tepee. Watch in wonder at Wanuskewin's interpretive programming about the park's famous conservation bison herd.

CANADA, MANITOBA

15 Journey across the surreal subarctic tundra

Ride an all-terrain Tundra Buggy through subarctic Manitoba's Churchill Wild, where wide-open skies meet icy expanses. Sightings of wolves and polar bears roaming freely in this remote and protected habitat are guaranteed.

CANADA, MANITOBA

16 Spy the northern lights and Indigenous artworks

With ethereal northern lights dancing overhead for half the year, Manitoba's a visual feast for nature aficionados. Couples also seeking culture can find it in the vibrant capital, Winnipeg, full of moving murals and public art projects by Indigenous artists.

CANADA, MANITOBA

17 Explore the romance of the wild

Take a Big Five Safari in the wilds of Manitoba. Amid the sheer beauty of Riding Mountain National Park and Churchill River, you will see black bears, bison, moose, polar bears, and beluga whales in the most pristine natural surroundings.

CANADA, ONTARIO

18 Sweeten your trip with a maple syrup workshop

Book a private Maple Masters Workshop at Alabaster Acres, which guides you through the various stages of making maple syrup from scratch. The experience involves a maple forest tour, sap collection, and bottling. Decide on the amount of syrup you want to produce—a lot, to give as wedding favors, just enough for a few gifts, or the perfect amount for pouring on breakfast pancakes back home on cozy weekend mornings.

14 Opimihaw Valley Heritage Site

NORTH AND CENTRAL AMERICA • CANADA

CANADA, ONTARIO

19 Toast with ice wine in Niagara-on-the-Lake

For intrepid oenophiles seeking something different from their wine, there's Niagara-on-the-Lake, likely Canada's most unique wine-growing region. Clink glasses filled with ice wine made from grapes that freeze on the vine to create an intense, concentrated dessert wine. Go in January to take part in Niagara-on-the-Lake Icewine Village festivities and stay at the Riverbend Inn.

CANADA, ONTARIO

20 Play footsie as you dine in total darkness

Feel your senses heighten and your sensitivity to touch turn on as you sup with your soulmate in complete and utter darkness. The pitch-black, three-course dinner at Ottawa's Dark Fork restaurant temporarily puts couples in a similar state as their servers, who are all visually impaired. Opt for three surprise courses, and allow the sensory journey to deepen your connection—to taste, to touch, and to each other.

CANADA, ONTARIO

21 Book a lakeside cabin at a Nordic resort

Snag a sleekly minimalist-yet-comfy cabin at Wander, a transcendent lakeside resort with its own extensive Nordic spa. Use the cabin as a base to explore local wineries offering behind-the-scenes tours. On your return, head to the subterranean spa for a nourishing body treatment or a traditional Finnish sauna before dining on seasonal dishes at the resort's restaurant, Gather.

CANADA, ONTARIO

22 Pair beaches and breweries on Lake Ontario

Stroll along the windswept beaches of Prince Edward County—an island in Lake Ontario—and explore the dunes at Sandbanks Provincial Park before cooling your feet in the shallows at Dunes Beach. Then, quench your thirst by hopping between cideries and craft breweries—such as Lake on the Mountain Brewing Company—to taste their famous Cream Ale and Country Brown brews.

23 Fairmont Le Château Frontenac

CANADA, QUEBEC

23 Canoe through ice then cozy up in a castle

Brave the challenge of ice canoeing on the St. Lawrence River, where you part paddle, part push your way across water filled with slabs of floating ice. Afterward, reward your physical efforts with a hot bubble bath for two in the claw-foot tub of a specialty suite at the magnificent Fairmont Le Château Frontenac, a castle-like hotel perched high above Old Quebec.

CANADA, QUEBEC

24 Picnic ahead of a floating couples massage

Pack some charcuterie, a baguette, and a bottle of wine to carry up the moderately challenging—and incredibly pretty—hike to the summit of Mount Royal for a picnic overlooking all of Montreal. After an active few hours, head to the floating Bota Bota spa-sur-l'eau, on a repurposed historic ferryboat, for a couples hydrotherapy circuit and well-earned massage.

NORTH AND CENTRAL AMERICA • CANADA

CANADA, QUEBEC

25 Celebrate love and new friends in Montreal's Gay Village

Stroll through Montreal's vibrant Gay Village, where love is always love. In the summer (and, for Pride, in August) the neighborhood's main street, Rue Sainte-Catherine, is festooned in pink and closed to traffic, making it even more irresistible to explore and support queer-owned businesses and the intense nightlife scene.

CANADA, QUEBEC

26 Admire fiery foliage around a heart-shaped lake

Take an easygoing hike around a portion of picture-perfect Étang Baker, known as Heart Lake. Every fall, the heart-shaped body of crystalline water is embraced by intense red and orange foliage as the leaves change color, which means it's prime time for an idyllic visit just ninety minutes away from Montreal.

CANADA, QUEBEC

27 Sail the St. Lawrence River toward Greenland in style

For couples with mixed interests, try Ponant's Le Commandant Charcot polar exploration vessel. Departing from Quebec, it sails gracefully toward Greenland, through river locks and ice and amid islands, with specialists on board giving talks on a range of subjects from geology and oceanography through history, architecture, and ecology.

CANADA, NEWFOUNDLAND

28 Road-trip to Newfoundland's seductively named towns

Let local town names inspire you on a road trip through breathtakingly beautiful Newfoundland. Seek out real places such as Heart's Desire, Tickle Cove, and Cupids. Sign up for a secret beach picnic orchestrated by Experience Twillingate complete with champagne on iceberg ice, delectable seafood, and a ready-made campfire.

CANADA, NEWFOUNDLAND

29 Immerse yourselves in the fantastic icescape of Fogo Island

Embrace the wildness of Fogo Island while spending time on the raw offshore isle of Newfoundland and Labrador, an artist haven that could be the backdrop of a Wes Anderson movie. A boat trip around the island will further envelop you in dramatic glacial scenery, complete with adorable puffins nestling along the rocky shores.

CANADA, NEW BRUNSWICK

30 Search for semiprecious treasures on the ocean floor

If natural marvels excite you, a legendary place between New Brunswick and Nova Scotia is worth seeking out. Bay of Fundy is home to the world's most dramatic tides—think water as high as a five-story building swelling in and out each day! Treasure hunters can walk the ocean floor at low tide, discovering semiprecious stones.

29 Fogo Island

NORTH AND CENTRAL AMERICA • CANADA

CANADA, NOVA SCOTIA

31 Cruise the rugged Halifax coast, slumber in sophistication

Enchantment is baked into the experience at Muir, Autograph Collection, a hotel designed, built, and decorated around the spirit of Nova Scotia. Rooms and suites feature subtle seafaring references and distinctive multimedia art commissioned from local artists. Relax at the hotel's wellness center, with its vitality spa pool and halotherapy salt room. Then, watch the sunset from one of the waterfront's many piers or on a coastline cruise on the hotel's 36-ft. (11-m) Morris yacht, *Little Wing*.

CANADA, NOVA SCOTIA

32 Jet boat into mind-boggling reverse rapids and whirlpools

Jump aboard a jet boat for a whirling, hair-raising ride around the Bay of Fundy, with its extreme tidal patterns. Prepare to get soaked, even with the provided life jackets and raincoats, as the captain navigates spectacular wonders that include the Reversing Falls Rapids, a place where the Saint John River crashes into rising tides and actually reverses its flow. Watch out for playful dolphins, too.

CANADA/GREENLAND • **NORTH AND CENTRAL AMERICA**

CANADA, PRINCE EDWARD ISLAND

33 Take a moonlit hot-tub soak in a treetop pod

Wellness destination Treetop Haven is set within 50 acres (20 ha) of forest on the virginal Prince Edward Island. Book a geodesic dome perched 9 ft. (2.75 m) off the forest floor among verdant foliage. Individually named for a bird you might spot depending on the season (blue jay, great horned owl, bald eagle, blue heron, and hummingbird), each tree pod is equipped with snowshoes in winter and private hot tubs for moonlit soaks.

CANADA, PRINCE EDWARD ISLAND

34 Dine on bivalves on Prince Edward Island

For a pair of seafood savants, consider Prince Edward Island your ultimate destination, thanks to its particular confluence of estuaries and bays. Exceptionally scenic, these waterways also produce world-famous bivalves. Enjoy the best mussels, clams, and oysters you will ever taste at dockside shacks or seaside restaurants—an experience that is as much about the flavor as it is the setting.

GREENLAND

35 Kayak alongside whales and icebergs

Enter the most wondrous white and blue dreamscape when you embark on a kayak and camping journey through East Greenland with Greenland Adventures by IMG. Even the best-traveled couples will be mesmerized by the arctic wilderness so quiet you will hear icebergs crumbling and humpback whales in the distance. Train together for the days of paddling to come.

35 East Greenland's white and blue dreamscape

GREENLAND

36 Surround yourselves in glacial wonder

Reserve a panoramic Aurora Cabin at Hotel Arctic, where icebergs are literally everywhere. Built on the mountainside, the cabins are almost entirely glass, mirrored from the outside. The glass is heated so that snow slides right off, ensuring you always have an unencumbered wraparound vista from your bed. The four-star hotel—the world's northernmost—sits on Disko Bay, home to the UNESCO World Heritage Site of Ilulissat Icefjord, whose name literally means "iceberg," and the planet's largest glacier.

36 Aurora Cabins at Hotel Arctic

GREENLAND

37 Live in your own nature documentary

Go from streaming *National Geographic* during home date nights to stepping foot into the world of arctic wildlife with luxury operator Black Tomato's inland Greenland experiences. From the safety of a RIB boat, filming polar bears, reindeer, and musk ox together will only be topped by the hilarious challenge of attempting to catch arctic char with your bare hands.

USA, ALASKA

38 Honeymoon on the scenic Alaska Railroad

Hitch a ride on a winter wonderland of a honeymoon escapade—or well-orchestrated proposal exploit—for a journey through ravishing landscapes on the Alaska Railroad. A wide variety of trains and routes are possible, ranging from two to ten days. Whichever you choose, marking the occasion amid such stunning scenery is bound to leave lasting memories.

USA, ALASKA

39 Hop aboard a small ship for a coastal cruise

For a US state with nearly 34,000 miles (55,000 km) of shoreline, counting islets and islands, it seems obvious that to explore, a boat is the best. Reserve a cabin for two on an intimate, all-inclusive small ship—ideally one with naturalists or marine biologists on board—and prepare to be absolutely floored by the beauty beyond.

USA • **NORTH AND CENTRAL AMERICA**

SEA KAYAK ESCAPADE

USA, ALASKA

40 Glide through glacial waters in a sea kayak

Slip into a sea kayak made for two for an unforgettable adventure through the surreal surroundings of Glacier Bay National Park and Preserve. Be brave and venture out on your own, or go with a guide—either way, expect an abundance of glaciers and craggy peaks, plus creatures that include black and brown bears, sea otters, and moose. Watch out for orcas and, in summer, humpback whales!

NORTH AND CENTRAL AMERICA • USA

USA, HAWAI'I

41 Show aloha to Hawai'i's precious environments and culture

Jet off to a Hawaiian island with a shared plan to enrich your honeymoon or vacation by joining the Mālama Hawai'i voluntourism initiative. Unite deeply with your destination as you lead your own beach cleanup, help resuscitate damaged wetlands, or help restore a forest. Certain hotels and resorts even say *mahalo* with special perks for guests.

USA, HAWAI'I

42 Learn hula, the Hawaiian language of the heart

You will look at those hip-shaking, grass skirt–wearing, dancing souvenir girls and guys differently after joining your love for a hula lesson arranged by Oahu's Four Seasons at acclaimed school Ke Kai O Kahiki. Both sexes perform the ancient art form that is Hawai'i's language of the heart—and a surprisingly intense one at that. Learning the graceful tradition may spark laughter and definitely joy.

USA, HAWAI'I

43 Forage for and fashion a traditional lei for your beloved

In Hawaiian culture, the most loving thing you could give someone is a lei you made yourself, ideally one composed of ti leaves and flora you personally foraged and hand-selected to make something more special than the sum of its parts. This classic symbol of love has become ubiquitous, but can be made more personal, so commit to carefully crafting a lei for each other from scratch.

USA, HAWAI'I

44 Kiss in the clouds above Kauai's jurassic Napali Coast

Leap into a private helicopter for an aerial survey of the lush Garden Isle's Napali Coast. If the otherworldly scene below—verdant cliffs, tucked-away waterfalls, sapphire swell lapping golden sand—looks like a scene from a movie, that's because it is (from *Pirates of the Caribbean: On Stranger Tides*, among others). Come down from the ride at Timbers Kauai Ocean Club for a dip in an infinity pool and a farm-to-fork dinner.

USA, HAWAI'I

45 Dine barefoot on the beach during a golden sunset supper

Request a table beneath Hau Tree restaurant's lantern-lit namesake and slip off your sandals to savor the feeling of sand between your toes. As the sun sets, sip tropical cocktails and order creative dishes featuring hyper-regional ingredients that include oysters, ahi (yellowfin tuna), and rainbow-hued caviar. Relax into a magical beach evening before sinking into bed upstairs at Kaimana Beach Hotel.

USA, HAWAI'I

46 Ooh and aah through a heavenly couples lomilomi treatment

A romantic vacation in the Polynesian islands would be incomplete without a couples massage featuring the signature Hawaiian version called lomilomi. A free-form massage technique, it provides peak pampering, with long, wavelike strokes and rhythmic tension-release techniques. For ultimate zen, book an outdoor treatment room with actual crashing surf as your soundtrack.

USA • **NORTH AND CENTRAL AMERICA**

44 Napali Coast

USA, HAWAI'I

47 Hide away in a chic Waikiki hotel

Opt for an oceanfront room at 'Alohilani Resort, where the view from your balcony of Waikiki's supernaturally turquoise seascape will imprint into your minds forever. From there, wander the beach, take beginner surf lessons, get a buzz going at the rooftop bar, and sample an Iron Chef's cuisine while admiring the setting sun.

USA, HAWAI'I

48 Start the day on a traditional sailing canoe

Seek serenity but also spinner dolphins, green sea turtles, and even monk seals on a calm morning out aboard a chartered Hawaiian sailing canoe. Hop into the saltwater holding hands for a glimpse at life under the sea. Oahu's west (leeward) coast is a particularly pristine environment to traverse on a craft inspired by the original voyaging canoes responsible for migration via astrological wayfinding.

USA, HAWAI'I

49 Plant a tree and then pop the question

Plant an endemic milo tree at Gunstock Ranch's nonprofit Hawaiian Legacy Forest. GPS technology will allow you to track how your tree is doing long after leaving Oahu. Book a Private Off-Road Planter's Experience and, after the planting, enjoy a bouncy ATV adventure up and down mountain trails. You will stop to picnic at a spectacular lookout point—the perfect setting for asking that all-important question.

USA, HAWAI'I

50 Follow an island safari with a sunset hug

Set out on a Lahaina Island Safari, organized by Black Tomato, for an action-packed day of hiking, snorkeling, and cruising Maui's most exciting highlights. The trip concludes above the clouds, with you and your partner gazing over the edge of the spectacular 3,000-ft.-high (900-m) Haleakala Crater while the sun drops.

USA, HAWAI'I

51 Witness the majesty of humpback whales

Savor a moment of shared awe as a humpback whale breaches just feet away. See the rainbow mist exhaled through its blowhole, perhaps even hear the mating songs. With snorkeling gear and a marine naturalist part of the package, a private charter with eco-aware operator Hawaiian Ocean Rafting guarantees sightings for lovers of these magnificent cetaceans.

USA, HAWAI'I

52 Make a keepsake for a lifetime of cooking together

Join third-generation Hawaiian blacksmith Neil Kamimura in his Hualalai workshop to forge a most personal chef's knife for you and your partner. Featuring materials such as bone, wood, and semiprecious stones, the beautifully crafted handle will be imbued with meaning. Back at Four Seasons Resort Hualalai, a knife-skills cooking class will set the two of you up for a lifetime of memorable meals.

50 Haleakala Crater

USA • NORTH AND CENTRAL AMERICA

USA, HAWAI'I
53 Retreat to an adults-only haven

Reserve a suite at a resort where romance is king. Hotel Wailea, Maui's 15-acre (6-ha) Eden, has a delightfully zen ambience. Find decadence during an in-room champagne breakfast, beauty on an outrigger canoe tour, and peace in a two-person sound bath. Borrow the vintage Porsche Speedster then drool over a seven-course tree house dinner.

USA, HAWAI'I
54 Feast over hula and storytelling

Embrace the spirit of aloha during Maui's most dynamic luau, or feast: the Ritz-Carlton Maui, Kapalua's Tales of the Kapa Moe Lū'au. Opt for VIP tickets and arrive early for an evening involving endless Hawaiian dishes and build-your-own poke. From beautifully costumed hula performers to a fire-knife dance, the entertainment is unforgettable.

USA, HAWAI'I
55 Indulge in a luxury wellness resort

Sensei Lanai is an adults-only retreat with the ambience of a traditional Japanese *ryokan*, or inn. After arriving, dedicate your trip to almost endless spa treatments and evening rituals in the wellness-haven spa *hales*, or homes, savoring chef Nobu Matsuhisa's famous fare for every meal, and soaking in secretive hot-spring pools beneath moonlight.

USA, HAWAI'I
56 Take a drive in a Mars-like landscape

Rent a 4x4 Jeep and drive a wild red dirt road through the otherworldly Mars-like landscape of Keahiakawelo (Garden of the Gods), where a sense of wonder invites climbing and playing on the amazing rock formations to be found there. To cool off, continue to a deserted beach only accessible in an off-road vehicle to dip into tide pools together.

USA, HAWAI'I
57 Plan the ultimate sunset dinner

It may seem early, but opt for a 5:30 P.M. booking at CanoeHouse, Mauna Lani's exquisite alfresco restaurant, to get the best of the setting sun. Beneath breezy palms, order from an exciting menu of Japanese-style plates that include scallop sashimi, lobster tempura, and wagyu tatiki. Be sure to look up from the mouthwatering dishes once in a while—you might just spot a humpback whale breaching.

USA, HAWAI'I
58 Sip cocktails amid the lava contours

Journey to Hawai'i Volcanoes National Park to walk atop an unearthly landscape of frozen-in-time lava flow that drops into the deep-blue Pacific. Bring along a blanket and some drinks and find a secluded, palm-shaded spot amid the once red-hot waves that now resemble striking, large-scale sculptures. Explore remarkable geological formations that include lava tubes, pit craters, and cinder cones.

53 Tree House at Hotel Wailea

31

NORTH AND CENTRAL AMERICA • USA

FLORAL WONDER

USA, WASHINGTON

59 Wander a fantastic garden of imaginative glass creations

Experience flowers in an entirely new way on a spellbinding walk among Dale Chihuly's wondrous glass sculptures at Chihuly Garden and Glass, beside Seattle's Space Needle. The Washington-native artist, who reinvented glassblowing and took it to new heights—and scales—has filled an urban green space with delicate yet vivid installations that are equal parts awe-inspiring and attractive. After admiring the 100-ft.-long (30-m) sculpture in the Glasshouse and watching a glassblowing demonstration, try the art form yourselves during a hands-on private class at Seattle Glassblowing Studio. Make your own masterpiece—or anniversary memento.

USA • NORTH AND CENTRAL AMERICA

USA, WASHINGTON

60 Ferry to the natural wonderland of Orcas Island

Book a ferry and embark on a wildly romantic beach camping getaway on radiant Orcas Island in the San Juan Islands. Fill your days with plush mossy hikes to lush waterfalls, diving into fresh mountain lakes, and night sea kayaking amid porpoises and bioluminescence.

USA, WASHINGTON

61 Indulge in downtime luxury following a Pike Place Market tour

Sample sweet treats during a Seattle doughnut tour or go for a chocolate extravaganza at iconic Pike Place Market, before walking off the sugar en route to your sleek Thompson Seattle hotel. Slip into fluffy matching bathrobes and relish in vistas of Puget Sound and Elliott Bay.

USA, WASHINGTON

62 Find some intimacy sipping cocktails in a Seattle speakeasy

Paper Fan Cocktail Bar, Seattle's most atmospheric eighteen-seat speakeasy above a noodle shop, was inspired by a 1960s love story of a paper fan seller in Hong Kong and an American soldier. Settle in to sip velvety, foamy cocktails and martinis kissed with tea and lychee.

USA, OREGON

63 Toast your way through Willamette Valley

Oregon is one of the celebrated wine destinations in the United States, producing world-class wines. Check into one of just eight gorgeous suites in Tributary Hotel in McMinnville, an exquisitely restored, hundred-year-old building where the concierge team will lovingly create bespoke experiences for you.

NORTH AND CENTRAL AMERICA • USA

USA, OREGON

64 Take a private sparkling wine tour

Book yourselves on the Masters of Sparkling tour at Oregon's legendary champagne-method sparkling wine house, Argyle, in bucolic Dundee. You will be privately shown hand-disgorging and dosage trials and will sample library vintages that were bottled in 1987, before enjoying a bubbly flight and charcuterie board.

USA, OREGON

65 Admire Japanese flora in the middle of Portland

Take a stroll through the world's most breathtaking and authentic Japanese garden outside of Japan itself. Become enamored with a proliferation of delicate cherry blossoms or red-hot maples, depending on the season, and visit the Zen sand and stone garden. Check ahead for cultural events held in the park.

65 Portland Japanese Garden

67 Minam River Lodge cabin

USA, OREGON

66 Fully unwind in a hotel with thermal springs

Escape into the lush environs of the sustainable hotel Cascada in the Portland arts district and do not leave until checkout. Spend secluded one-on-one time in the secret garden, relax and rejuvenate together in the underground thermal springs spa, and dine à deux in the zero-waste restaurant.

USA, OREGON

67 Get off-grid in untamed wilderness

The Eagle Cap Wilderness retreat, Minam River Lodge, cannot be reached by car. Many saddle up on horseback for the 8½-mi. (14-km) ride. Once you arrive, your stay is all about intimate time together: soaking in a wood-fired hot tub, savoring couples massages, and enjoying the untamed scenery side by side.

USA, CALIFORNIA

68 Find joy in the perfect Northern California day

Marry activity and tranquility at the seaside SCP Mendocino Inn and Farm. Start with an in-room breakfast, sauna, and cold plunge, then choose your own adventure—a farming and foraging culinary journey, perhaps. Return to aromatherapy massages and a private bonfire for cozying up under the stars.

NORTH AND CENTRAL AMERICA • USA

USA, CALIFORNIA

69 Embark on a vintage train car wine journey

Savor a day of luxuriously slow travel on a restored vintage Pullman rail car whose purpose is to wine and dine you as it rolls through NorCal's vine-laced landscape. The Napa Valley Wine Train is an elegant affair, so dress the part before stepping aboard for multiple courses served on white linen tablecloths and scheduled stops for winery tastings, too.

USA, CALIFORNIA

70 Take a gastronomic trip to Auberge du Soleil

Reserve a room on 33 acres (13 ha) of iconic dappled wine country at Michelin-decorated Auberge du Soleil. It is like arriving in the South of France, but with California's laid-back energy. Gastronomic experiences may include courtyard wine tastings, pastoral picnics in the olive grove, and multisensory dinners at long-starred the Restaurant with stunning views.

USA, CALIFORNIA

71 Set the stage for a proposal in Stags Leap

A stay at Napa's most intimate romantic hotel, Poetry Inn, in the Stags Leap District, means homegrown wine, a sumptuous setting, and a three-hour couples biodynamic spa spectacular dubbed the Epic. It just might spark a proposal.

USA, CALIFORNIA

72 Marvel at 8,000 species of flora

Spend a glorious afternoon perusing some 8,000 plant species from around the globe in the San Francisco Botanical Garden, a bountiful 55-acre (22-ha) portion of Golden Gate Park. Seek out a few favorite spots for taking memorable selfies.

USA, CALIFORNIA

75 Get a taste of overwater bungalow life

Inn Above Tide, a luxurious hotel in Sausalito, is practically perched atop water. Rent the City Lights suite, which comes with a king bed, double-sided fireplace, deck, and impressive San Francisco city views.

USA, CALIFORNIA

73 Take a selfie with a massive heart sculpture in Sonoma

Head to Sonoma's Donum Estate for extraordinary wine paired with delectable canapés, and visit its sculpture park featuring monumental works by a who's who of the international art world; many of the sculptures are playfully interactive. Take an intimate guided tour of this astounding collection interspersed with the estate's certified organic grapevines. Among the artworks are a Louise Bourgeois spider, a prismatic, rainbow-hued pavilion, and Richard Hudson's gigantic reflective heart.

USA, CALIFORNIA

74 Plan your Sonoma pilgrimage around biodynamic cuisine

Gourmets will find paradise in the heart of Healdsburg, Sonoma's quaint town with major Michelin shine. Exactly twelve weeks out, reserve one of five consciously crafted rooms in the Michelin three-keyed SingleThread Inn—where breakfast is an extravagant Japanese or Sonoma spread. The booking also guarantees a dinner slot for two for ten courses of seasonal biodynamic magic.

73 Donum Estate

USA • **NORTH AND CENTRAL AMERICA**

USA, CALIFORNIA

76 Road trip on California's legendary coastal highway

Track down a vintage convertible for a throwback spin along California's quintessentially scenic cruising route, Highway 1. Make the road trip even more romantic with an overnight stay at the cliff-top Post Ranch Inn in Big Sur, legendary for its breathtaking views of the coastline.

USA, CALIFORNIA

77 Amble through a valley of heavenly blooms

If awe-inspiring panoramas and abundant flora appeal, plan a romantic jaunt to Calla Lily Valley (just off Highway 1 near Big Sur and Garrapata Beach) between mid-January and mid-March. Walking among the bright white blooms is as heavenly as can be.

USA, CALIFORNIA

78 Strip down on a hippie weekend in Big Sur

Sign up for a clothing-optional weekend at the Beat-era not-for-profit holistic educational center Esalen Institute. The naked liberation and empowering, meditation-based activities may even inspire a transformation as a couple.

78 Esalen Institute

USA, CALIFORNIA

79 Stroll on purple sand together

In Big Sur, witness some of the world's most uniquely colored sand during an extra-special beach walk at Pfeiffer Beach, where eroding manganese garnet from neighboring hills creates streaks of stunning purple sand. If visiting in winter, stay on to watch the sun burst through the monumental sandstone Keyhole Arch.

USA, CALIFORNIA

80 Cozy up to grandeur at the gateway to Yosemite

At Yosemite National Park, book into the Relais & Châteaux hideaway Château du Sureau. Young children are not allowed at this ten-room country resort in the Sierra Nevada foothills, but even so, opt for über-private Villa du Sureau. The generous nineteenth-century, European-styled accommodation has a Roman spa, steam shower, bar, and Steinway piano.

80 Yosemite National Park

USA • **NORTH AND CENTRAL AMERICA**

USA, CALIFORNIA

81 Learn the ropes at cowboy camp

Capture the rugged appeal of Yellowstone with a five-star, three-day cowboy camp experience at Los Olivos' the Inn at Mattei's Tavern. Practice your saddling, roping, and riding skills and put them to the test with real cattle. At night, treat yourselves to s'mores at a private firepit, before hopping into a sumptuous four-poster bed.

USA, CALIFORNIA

82 Watch dolphins from your balcony

At the Surfrider Malibu, slip into your balcony hammock or cozy up on the rooftop to watch surfers and dolphins dance in the waves of the very first World Surfing Reserve right out front. Borrow a couple of paddleboards for a side-by-side ride of your own.

USA, CALIFORNIA

83 Book an ocean-view beach house

Santa Monica's Fairmont Miramar Hotel & Bungalows has beach-chic accommodations with sun-drenched balconies and a two-person soaking tub, nestled among the palms. The hotel's secretive, eight-seat sushi bar Soko is worth a visit.

82 The Surfrider Malibu

NORTH AND CENTRAL AMERICA • USA

BEACH CLUB WEEKEND

USA, CALIFORNIA

84 Book the best of Malibu at Calamigos Guest Ranch

Spend a weekend in Malibu, checking in to a luxurious cottage or bungalow at Calamigos Guest Ranch, a 250-acre (100-ha) estate that hosts many a fine wedding. Start with craft cocktails on the sand at the Beach Club and then see who can make the best pizza to bake in the outdoor oven. Later, climb into your patio bathtub with a bottle of wine and gaze up at trillions of stars.

USA, CALIFORNIA

85 Indulge like Marilyn Monroe at a Beverly Hills landmark

The legendary Beverly Hills Hotel was a home away from home for beloved and frequent guest Marilyn Monroe—why not make it yours too? The storied circa 1912 hotel's Bungalow 1A carries on as an ode to the star. Reserve the suite for amenities themed on Monroe's life and movie career and soak up the romance as you slumber together by the living-room fire.

USA, CALIFORNIA

86 Shop 'til you drop on Rodeo Drive

Rodeo Drive promises high-end shopping for international luxury brands. Have fun trying on impressive ensembles for each other and pick out the best for a sparkling evening at Spago, chef Wolfgang Puck's signature restaurant. Amble "home," if you wish, to an oasis-like room at Waldorf Astoria Beverly Hills, right in the city's heart, and change into plush robes for a balcony snuggle.

85 The Beverly Hills Hotel

USA, CALIFORNIA

87 Play all night at a glam private bowling alley

Check into Pendry West Hollywood on the Sunset Strip, just minutes from notorious music venues and comedy clubs. The decadent suites are all velvet and mirrors, but the best perk by far is in the basement. Plan a night in and, after dining at the rooftop restaurant, Merois, head down to the most fabulous bowling alley and bar you have ever seen, reserved only for guests.

USA, CALIFORNIA

88 Dial up the romance at the Hollywood Bowl

Buy a private box to watch your favorite artist or band at the fabled Hollywood Bowl amphitheater and arrive early for a preordered, three-course meal prepared by a celebrity chef. Served on your very own private table, it makes for the ultimate romantic gesture before settling in for a night of swaying along to the songs that have soundtracked your relationship.

NORTH AND CENTRAL AMERICA • USA

USA, CALIFORNIA

89 Get hot and bothered together at a bikini bar

Take your better half to an Eastside LA institution, Jumbo's Clown Room, to cheer on talented, provocative dancers in risqué themed ensembles performing to legendary tunes. Stroll back for a nightcap in your Cali-meets-Mediterranean room at the boutique Cara Hotel.

USA, CALIFORNIA

90 Swim downtown in your own private indoor pool

Skinny-dip in a fantasy suite at Downtown LA Proper Hotel with your very own 35-ft.-long (10-m) swimming pool inside. A tremendous ceramic art installation runs the length of the pool and interior design by the inimitable Kelly Wearstler makes the suite completely one of a kind.

USA, CALIFORNIA

91 Get intimate with architectural masterpieces in Downtown LA

Appreciate an architectural masterpiece by Frank Gehry with a Downtown stay at Conrad Los Angeles, where you can gaze at Gehry's exceptional Walt Disney Concert Hall from the comfort of your bed. Take a walking tour of the neighborhood or wander the exciting cultural hub sans agenda.

USA, CALIFORNIA

92 Go clothing-optional at Palm Springs' gay men's resort

Begin with a ride up to 8,000 ft. (2,400 m) above the modernist desert city on the Palm Springs Aerial Tramway for a glittery evening of cocktails, before returning to the luxurious gay men's idyll, Descanso Resort, for a clothing-optional night of swimming in a heated saltwater pool.

USA, CALIFORNIA

93 Say "I do" at an opulent Palm Desert villa

Invite your closest friends to a sweet wedding weekend or anniversary celebration at your very own private resort for up to eighteen adults. The luminous location is the fully staffed Kempa Villa, which stretches over five lush acres (2 ha) with a pond, massive fire circle, and multiple bars.

USA, CALIFORNIA

94 Go fancy camping in a Joshua Tree Airstream

Rent a fully equipped vintage Airstream for a weekend of fancy camping in the Joshua Tree desert. AutoCamp Joshua Tree is a laid-back luxe resort with a refreshing swimming pool, yoga classes, and campfire music sessions set among the Dr. Seuss-like namesake trees and huge boulders for scrambling on.

USA, CALIFORNIA

95 Tantalize your taste buds in San Diego

At the Fairmont Grand Del Mar, Addison—San Diego's first three-Michelin-star restaurant—is a gastronomic gem led by chef William Bradley. Feel like kings or queens as you sink into plush armchairs and have your every need met during a mind-blowing dinner. Afterward, return to your poolside suite for a nightcap.

94 The Joshua Tree desert

USA, IDAHO

96 Trace the glittering diamonds of the Milky Way in Central Idaho

Witness next-level stargazing together at the country's first Gold-Tier Dark Sky Reserve. Perfect for couples, this unforgettable activity in Central Idaho offers a rare chance to see a naturally starry sky away from harsh city lights. With expert-led tours, this bucket-list experience lets you connect with the cosmos in a truly magical way.

USA, IDAHO

97 Spend a day together at the iconic Sun Valley ski resort

Book a mountainside lodge at Sun Valley, the country's first destination ski resort. After a morning of playful skiing on Dollar Mountain, spend the afternoon in the spa or strolling Ketchum's Main Street before returning to your cozy lodge for a fireside glass of champagne. Round off your slow-paced day dining by candlelight at the historic Sun Valley Lodge.

96 Central Idaho Dark Sky Reserve

USA • **NORTH AND CENTRAL AMERICA**

98 The Ranch at Rock Creek

USA, MONTANA

98 Embrace the art of Montana living

Explore, relax, and indulge at the ultra-luxurious Ranch at Rock Creek. Whether you are saddling up, hiking, biking, painting, or simply enjoying an evening in, playing board games in the Silver Dollar Saloon, every moment is one to remember at this all-inclusive hideaway. The best part? Counting night-sky constellations from a private cedar hot tub in your canvas glamping cabin.

USA, MONTANA

99 Pan for sapphires at Montana's oldest mine

You have already found a real-life gem—now is your chance to uncover sparkly blue sapphires together at Gem Mountain. Learn all about the panning process before selecting a stunning stone to hold sentimental value for years to come. This is an added bonus if you happen to be celebrating your fifth (or forty-fifth) wedding anniversary, when sapphires are traditionally given as gifts.

USA, MONTANA

100 Take a safari over Yellowstone National Park

For adventure-seeking twosomes, combine photography and paleontology with a one-of-a-kind experience in Yellowstone, on a helicopter tour over the park's 10,000+ geothermal wonders. Capture aerial shots of Grand Prismatic and Old Faithful from a bird's-eye view, before making your way back down to solid ground for a dinosaur fossil dig and romantic overnight at Montage Big Sky.

USA, WYOMING

101 Enjoy the views while soaking for a good cause in Jackson Hole

Escape to Astoria Hot Springs Park in Jackson Hole for a steamy side-by-side soak in healing thermal waters. With six serene pools located along the Snake River, this natural oasis was built with conservation efforts in mind, as well as relaxation. One hundred percent of ticket sales go toward preserving this special space (which you can have to yourselves if you opt for a full buyout).

USA, WYOMING

102 Float on the Snake River then indulge in a couples spa treatment

The breathtaking beauty of Grand Teton National Park is best experienced on a private float trip for two, bobbing along the scenic Snake River with nothing but a rugged mountain range and lush landscapes in the backdrop. Post-float, unwind with a couples spa treatment at Hotel Jackson, where expert therapists ensure total relaxation, and a deep state of bliss is the only thing on the agenda.

102 Grand Teton National Park

USA, WYOMING

103 Breathe deep, love deeper at Caldera House

Retreat to the mountains for holistic healing with your partner at Caldera House. With the Grand Tetons as your backdrop, reconnect mind, body, and spirit on a three-day wellness escape featuring forest meditation, intuitive soul readings, and a nourishing in-suite cooking class.

USA, WYOMING

104 Head out on an animal-spotting safari

Whether you set out at sunrise or sunset, a private wildlife safari in Grand Teton National Park is the ultimate way to spy bison, elk, and mountain goats in their natural habitat, while marveling at the park's unspoiled terrain.

USA, WYOMING

105 Book a farm-to-table stay in the Wild West

Capture the spirit of the Wild West with a stay at Brush Creek Ranch. During your vacation choose from a range of culinary classes hosted by the Farm, including pasta-making, burrata-stretching, and wagyu grilling.

NORTH AND CENTRAL AMERICA • USA

USA, NEVADA

106 Trade Venice for Vegas at the Venetian

Who needs a flight to Venice when you can hop on a gondola inside the Venetian Las Vegas? You will swear you have been transported to the Floating City once you are drifting along charming canals, singing gondoliers in tow. To cap off the evening, the Venetian rowboats glide across a lagoon at the front of the hotel, where you will be treated to spectacular views of the Strip.

USA, NEVADA

107 Catch a state-of-the-art concert at the Las Vegas Sphere

When it comes to concert venues, nothing compares to the futuristic Sphere in Las Vegas. With its cutting-edge technology, audiences are fully immersed in a 360-degree visual experience while watching their favorite performers onstage. With stunning visuals and enhanced sound, a show here feels uniquely personal and unforgettable at the same time.

USA, NEVADA

108 Elope with Elvis at the iconic Little White Wedding Chapel

Whether you are planning to tie the knot, renew your vows, or just drop by to watch other couples get hitched, there is nothing like a white wedding—with Elvis officiating. Aside from making fun memories that will last a lifetime, you will also get to enjoy the quirks of one of Vegas's most famous wedding chapels.

USA, NEVADA

109 Play high rollers for the night at the LINQ in Las Vegas

Book a private cabin for a slow spin on the Las Vegas High Roller, the world's second-tallest observation wheel. Reaching a height of 550 ft. (168 m), you can customize your package to include photography, flowers, champagne, and music, as you embrace all of Vegas at your feet.

USA, NEVADA

110 Toast to love in a sky-high Vegas suite

Skip the slots and go all in on romance with a stylish suite at the Cosmopolitan or Waldorf Astoria Las Vegas. Think twinkling Strip views, deep soaking tubs built for two, and room service champagne. After dinner at Top of the World, retreat to your private perch above the city for a night that feels straight out of *Ocean's Eleven*—minus the casino heist.

108 Little White Wedding Chapel

NORTH AND CENTRAL AMERICA • USA

USA, NEVADA

111 Raise a glass to true *amour* atop the Eiffel Tower

You will always have Paris (the Vegas version) after dining at the stateside Eiffel Tower Restaurant, where you can enjoy a three-course feast of ice-cold seafood and melt-in-your-mouth beef Wellington medallions followed by decadent desserts. Think Grand Marnier soufflé and classic crème brûlée. To really impress your date, upgrade the evening with a VIP helicopter flight over the Strip first.

USA, NEVADA

112 Declare your love in the middle of the desert

Nestled in Nevada's majestic Mojave Desert, the natural wonder Red Rock Canyon presents the perfect terrain for grand gestures. With its towering red sandstone peaks, dramatic Keystone Thrust Fault, and ancient Native American pictographs, the canyon offers a sensational setting for down-on-bended-knee proposals and impromptu photo shoots with your special someone.

USA, NEVADA

113 Take your love to new heights with a high-altitude picnic at Lake Tahoe

The frontrunner luxury hotel on the lake, Edgewood Tahoe offers a scenic stay with cozy villas, private hot tubs, and crackling fireplaces. These accommodations were designed for staying in, but an alpine-inspired picnic awaits when you do decide to venture out. With cheese and charcuterie, sparkling wine, and a mountaintop vantage point, you will start to see why life is better on the lake.

USA, ARIZONA

114 Stage an epic engagement shoot

Capture your special moment in the otherworldly landscape of Arizona's Antelope Canyon, where millions of years of erosion have sculpted swirling sandstone walls bathed in vibrant yellows and golds. Horseshoe Bend Slot Canyon Tours will pick you up and guide you to the most photogenic spots. Visit at midday to see shafts of sunlight pierce the canyon, illuminating its orange-hued walls.

USA, ARIZONA

115 Feel the mystical energy at Boynton Canyon

With colossal red rock formations in every direction, Boynton Canyon is an unparalleled site for romantic photo ops. Follow a 6.5-mi. (10.5-km) trail for awe-inspiring views of Arizona's striking desert landscape. Pause at the site of the Boynton Canyon vortex, said to radiate a rare balance of masculine and feminine forces. Let the mystical energy sweep over the two of you, creating an overwhelming sense of harmony.

USA • **NORTH AND CENTRAL AMERICA**

FULL-ON ADVENTURE

USA, ARIZONA

116 Thrill then chill with a heart-racing adventure and serene soak

Take your love to new heights, quite literally, by embarking on the Via Ferrata—which means "iron way" in Italian—course that involves steel cables and ladders embedded in rock, plus sexy helmets and harnesses, and highly trained guides. The exciting feats couples might take on include multiple peaks to scale and summit, and a 150-ft.-high (46-m) walkway that puts you far above the Sonoran Desert's saguaro cacti and famously healing, natural mineral-rich hot springs, a guaranteed salve for any resulting soreness. The course is available at the acclaimed—and aptly named—historical resort Castle Hot Springs, which challenges as well as it cossets adult-only guests. The potential pairings are plentiful: axe throwing and wine tasting; slot canyon exploration and watsu therapy; paddleboard yoga and dark-sky stargazing; hiking and a plein-air painting class. The inclusive offerings also include pickleball, sound bowl meditation, and crave-worthy farm-to-table fare highlighting seasonal bounty from the resort's 3-acre (1.2-ha) organic farm.

USA, ARIZONA

117 Learn the art of astrophotography

At Under Canvas Grand Canyon, gather around a cozy firepit and use telescopes to learn the art of astrophotography. In between capturing stunning images of the cosmos and creating keepsake photos of the night sky, you will bask in the beauty of this protected haven. It is the perfect evening for couples seeking a celestial escape.

USA, ARIZONA

118 Take a helicopter ride to the Grand Canyon

Fly to the Grand Canyon from Las Vegas, on an adrenaline-pumping helicopter ride, gliding over rugged desert terrain before descending into the heart of the canyon. As you approach, watch the expansive walls and winding Colorado River unfold below. After touchdown, take in the remarkable landscape in peaceful solitude—together.

USA, ARIZONA

119 Get cozy on a stargazing excursion

Stargazing knows no bounds under the velvety Arizona sky, at the iconic Trailborn Grand Canyon hotel. This Western-inspired boutique retreat offers a custom blend of adventure and romance, with the Grand Canyon's South Rim just a short, scenic railway ride away.

USA, ARIZONA

120 Stay at Frank Lloyd Wright's desert home

Design lovers will swoon over a romantic evening at Frank Lloyd Wright's Taliesin West, his Arizona masterpiece and a UNESCO World Heritage Site. Nestled in the Sonoran Desert, the property reflects Wright's visionary work and commitment to organic architecture. After a candlelit dinner, retreat to your cozy, artfully designed room.

USA, UTAH

121 Take the scenic route to a mountaintop picnic

Make your way through the snowy wilderness surrounding the Lodge at Blue Sky, Park City. Your destination: a secluded mountaintop yurt, where a crackling fire, hot toddies, and cozy fondue for two await. The next morning, wake to a campfire breakfast in an 1800s-era cabin nestled deep in the mountains.

USA, UTAH
122 Share a moonlit kiss among hoodoos

For the most magical of full-moon hikes, head to Bryce Canyon and walk the 8 mi. (12 km) Fairyland Loop Trail. Under the moon's glow, the park's otherworldly hoodoos come alive. As you wander through the towering crimson spires, the serene desert air feels like a dream.

USA, UTAH
123 Renew your vows under a natural stone arch

Arches National Park serves as prime real estate for a vow renewal, featuring over 2,000 stunning natural stone arches, towering pinnacles, dramatic rock fins, and iconic balanced rocks. As the evening light gently fades, the park's untamed beauty reveals itself, with the rugged desert landscape creating an outstanding setting for a truly unique commitment ceremony.

123 Arches National Park

129 Cloud Nine, Aspen Highlands

USA, UTAH

124 Tune into the rhythm of the land at Camp Sarika

Surrounded by the rugged beauty of Utah's desert, Camp Sarika at Amangiri offers an elegant approach to slow living in temperature-controlled tented pavilions with private plunge pools and firepits. Join your partner on the Sarika Mindfulness Path—a half- or full-day experience designed to deepen your connection to the land through meditation, breathwork, and yoga.

USA, UTAH

125 Indulge in unlimited activities for twosomes

With close proximity to two national parks, Under Canvas Moab promises an unrivaled glamping experience. The safari-inspired camp has an impressive range of activities that let you connect with your partner. Start your day with sunrise yoga, scavenger hunts, and guided hikes, then end the night with s'mores, stargazing, and live acoustic music.

USA, COLORADO

126 Unleash joy in a puppy yoga class

Who can resist canine cuddles and nose nuzzles? Join a rescue puppy yoga class for forty-five minutes of pure joy, and maybe even a lifetime of love. Those who attend are encouraged to stick around after, with a view to potentially adopting a puppy and taking it home with them. Rescue Puppy Yoga holds events in venues across the state.

124 Camp Sarika at Amangiri

USA • **NORTH AND CENTRAL AMERICA**

USA, COLORADO

127 Get hooked on a couples fly-fishing trip

Test your skills (and patience) on a Cast & Taste adventure for two, where Colorado Angling Company guides will teach you the art of world-class fly-fishing in Vail Valley. Once you have reached the day's limit, watch as a team of private chefs prepare a gourmet cookout from a cozy log cabin, perched on a private stretch of trout-filled water.

USA, COLORADO

128 Give lovebirds who lounge new meaning

For a glamorous night of caviar and champagne, reserve a table at Aspen's most stylish lounge, the Jade Room. As part of the Snow Lodge Music Series, you can enjoy performances by world-renowned DJs and artists in the intimate setting of the lounge, or catch larger headliners in the Après-Ski Courtyard. Dripping in jewel tones, the Jade Room radiates fizzy, fun energy and all things fabulous.

USA, COLORADO

129 Après the Aspen way at Cloud Nine

After a day of skiing on Highlands mountain at 12,392 ft. (3,777 m), there is no better way to celebrate than with an alfresco alpine lunch at Cloud Nine. Famous for its champagne showers, table dancing, and Swiss classics that include fondue, raclette, and strudel, this après-party spot is as iconic as it gets!

132 Breckenridge sleigh ride

USA, COLORADO

130 Sing along to your favorites at an alfresco concert at Red Rocks

The legendary Red Rocks Amphitheatre is one of the most iconic music venues in the world, known for its phenomenal natural acoustics. Set amid mammoth red sandstone formations and flanked by two 300-ft. (90-m) monoliths—Ship Rock and Creation Rock—the venue provides a truly romantic backdrop for any performance.

USA, COLORADO

131 Snowshoe to a candlelit foodie feast in a yurt

Embark on a powder-soft snowshoe adventure to a candlelit, gourmet feast in a cheerful yurt at Tennessee Pass in Leadville. Savor exquisite dishes prepared by top chefs, surrounded by the peaceful beauty of the winter forest. Afterward, journey back through the woods under the mesmerizing glow of the moon.

USA, COLORADO

132 Snuggle on a snowy horse-drawn sleigh ride

Grab the tartan throws and get ready to bundle up on a horse-drawn sleigh ride through the enchanting snowy forest of Breckenridge, Colorado. Wrapped up in blankets, and with a flask of hot chocolate to keep you warm, you will glide through a winter wonderland, enjoying the serenity of snow-dusted trees and the gentle jingle of sleigh bells.

USA • **NORTH AND CENTRAL AMERICA**

USA, COLORADO

133 Follow snowmobiling with a romantic spa day

Head to the mountains of Telluride for a snowmobiling adventure before joining your partner for a Mountain Love Journey spa treatment at Madeline Hotel. Designed specifically for couples, the four-step ritual starts with a body scrub and ends with a relaxing massage. In between, an indulgent, foamy mineral bath follows a steam shower infused with aromatics.

USA, COLORADO

134 Book an eco escape in the Colorado capital

Deepen your love for the planet at Populus, Denver, the country's first carbon-positive hotel. With its "One Night, One Tree" program, a tree is planted for every overnight stay in partnership with the National Forest Foundation, supporting reforestation efforts. Populus also champions sustainability with zero-waste dining, eco-friendly interiors, and a low-carbon concrete footprint.

134 Populus, Denver

136 Ghost Ranch

USA, NEW MEXICO

135 Revel in ranch-style romance at Vermejo Ranch

Spanning 550,000 acres (222,500 ha) across northern New Mexico and Colorado, Vermejo is the largest privately owned ranch in the United States. With snowcapped mountains, nineteen fishable lakes, abundant wildlife roaming the property, and luxurious accommodations (book Casa Grande, a 25,000 sq. ft. [2,300 m²] stone mansion, or the Costilla Fishing Lodge, a more secluded option), there are numerous enticing options for active duos.

USA, NEW MEXICO

136 Fall in love with New Mexico's diverse landscapes

Experience the "Land of Enchantment" at Ghost Ranch, Georgia O'Keeffe's creative compound and retreat center. Enjoy a private, intimate tour of the artist's Abiquiú home and studio before retreating to the Rosewood Inn of the Anasazi, one of Santa Fe's most alluring hotels, located in the heart of Historic Square. It's a perfect getaway for art lovers and romance seekers alike.

USA • NORTH AND CENTRAL AMERICA

USA, NEW MEXICO

137 Rise to the challenge of exploring deep, dark places

Descending 750 ft. (230 m) into the vast, dark, limestone caves of Carlsbad Caverns National Park is not for the faint of heart, but with a partner by your side, the journey is even more thrilling. And the reward of witnessing the stunning stalagmites below is worth every step.

USA, NORTH DAKOTA

138 Check in for an Old West storybook stay in Medora

Embrace the historic charm of Medora, where you two can cuddle up at the Rough Riders Hotel, trot along golden Badlands trails, and channel the spirit of the Old West over bacon-wrapped steaks at Theodore's Dining Room. End the evening with a kiss beneath the stars in the nearby national park.

USA, SOUTH DAKOTA

139 Stay at South Dakota's premiere resort in the Black Hills

With uninterrupted views of the Black Hills, Shortgrass Resort is the state's best-kept all-inclusive secret. Stay in plush Danish-style bungalows with heated floors for cooler months and private decks come summertime. You will find miles of flower-filled trails to explore together and scenic spots for picnics.

USA, NEBRASKA

140 Encounter nocturnal sounds and sightings on a full-moon hike

Nebraska's Fontenelle Forest comes alive on a scenic hike through the woods, under a full moon and with the sounds of owls hooting in the trees. As you meander through winding trails and wetlands, you will learn about the nocturnal creatures that call the forest canopy home. After your stroll, curl up by the bonfire for s'mores.

139 Shortgrass Resort

NORTH AND CENTRAL AMERICA • USA

USA, NEBRASKA

141 Witness spring in bloom at Lincoln's Sunken Gardens

Pack a gourmet picnic for two and set off on a spring outing amid the vibrant blooms of Lincoln's nearly century-old Sunken Gardens. Once a neighborhood refuse site, this stunning garden is one of Nebraska's most cherished public spaces, featuring rotating art installations, tranquil koi ponds, a serene waterfall, and offering a peaceful retreat for nature lovers.

USA, KANSAS

142 Score front-row tickets to the Kansas City Symphony

Head to stunning Helzberg Hall at the Kauffman Center for the Performing Arts to see a film like never before, with the Kansas City Symphony performing the score live. See an all-time favorite like *Jurassic Park*, *Home Alone*, or *Hocus Pocus* with unreal acoustics accompanying movie night. The synergy of cinema and live music creates an immersive, one-of-a-kind evening.

USA, KANSAS

143 Devour a plate of BBQ then go elegant at the Mercury Room

Hit Joe's Kansas City Bar-B-Que for one of the best in the state, freshly smoked out of a gas-station-turned-restaurant. Joe's is known for its no-frills setting and flavor-packed brisket, along with slabs of ribs and pulled pork sandwiches. Afterward, cue the lights at the Mercury Room, where the cocktails are always served ice cold under the bar's twinkling ceiling.

141 Sunken Gardens, Lincoln

USA • NORTH AND CENTRAL AMERICA

USA, OKLAHOMA

144 Check into a nostalgic Victorian mansion for the night

Spend a most romantic night at Bradford House, a Victorian mansion-turned-boutique hotel nestled in the heart of Oklahoma City. This beautifully restored historic gem dates back to 1912 and blends old-world charm with modern luxury, offering elegant rooms, cozy lounges, and an inviting atmosphere. Sip tea on the wraparound porch, or savor tempting tipples at the gilded bar, before catching a black-and-white movie in the courtyard.

USA, OKLAHOMA

145 Share some shrieks at OKANA resort's massive waterpark

Things are bound to get a little wet and wild at OKANA Resort's sprawing waterpark, the fourth-largest pool in the United States. Brave one of the twisty-turny water coasters or relax at Soothing Springs, an adults-only hot tub where kids are not invited to the party. When you are ready to shift the mood to serenity, enjoy a couples massage at the spa, or upgrade to a 150-minute ritual for two.

USA • **NORTH AND CENTRAL AMERICA**

USA, TEXAS

146 Check into Hôtel Swexan for a luxury stay

This Michelin Key stunner in the heart of Uptown Dallas combines luxury and hospitality with an unwavering Texan spirit. Book the Grand Swexan suite with private sauna, oversize shower, and lavish two-person tub—it is the perfect lovers' retreat. Start your evening of romance with cocktails at Pomelo, the hotel's breezy rooftop bar with 180-degree city views.

USA, TEXAS

147 Take a stroll on San Antonio's River Walk

Meandering through San Antonio's charming River Walk feels like a one-way ticket to a quaint European village—no passport required. As you stroll, pause to admire the whimsical beauty of the Grotto, where sculpted caves echo with quiet magic. Then, wander over to Pearl, a historic 1883 brewery, and settle in for a refreshing drink.

USA, TEXAS

148 Pose for quirky engagement photos

Artsy couples will have fun making engagement photos in the desert town of Marfa, where surreal landscapes, cinematic light, and iconic installations set the scene. Dress for the mood and switch up the looks—sleek minimalism for poses among Donald Judd's sculptural forms or vintage Western against sun-bleached adobe walls.

USA, TEXAS

149 In Houston, bike the Bayou before unwinding at Cidercade

Nothing sets the mood for a day of fun like cycling side by side—or better still by tandem. After soaking in the scenic views while cruising Buffalo Bayou Park, shift into play mode at the adults-only Cidercade where hard ciders, craft beers, and a plethora of nostalgic arcade games create the ultimate atmosphere for friendly competition.

USA, TEXAS

150 Stage a romantic city scavenger hunt in Austin

Nothing sparks playful connection like a clue-filled adventure. Craft a custom map that winds through your favorite shared spots—think coffee shops, bookstores, or art galleries—and have the last clue lead to colorful *Tau Ceti*, Austin's tallest mural.

USA, TEXAS

151 Let music lead the way on a seductive, low-lit evening together

Vinyl records set the tone while music-inspired cocktails add a creative twist to the night inside Austin's Equipment Room, a glowy, hi-fi sanctuary tucked beneath Hotel Magdalena on Music Lane. Intimate and effortlessly stylish, it is the perfect place to let the soundtrack shape your evening.

148 Quirky photo opportunities in Marfa

NORTH AND CENTRAL AMERICA • USA

USA, TEXAS

152 Find a breath of calm beyond the city

Swap Austin's vibrant urban energy for a peaceful afternoon of hidden swimming holes and cascading waterfalls along the Barton Creek Greenbelt. Or, slow down with a meditative forest bathing walk through Zilker Botanical Garden—a serene oasis that invites quiet connection.

USA, MINNESOTA

153 Seek adventure then seclusion at Minnesota's stunning Cuyuna Lakes

Spend a romantic getaway at Cuyuna Lakes. Known for the crystal-clear waters, these former mine pits offer a unique scuba-diving experience, perfect for couples seeking something unforgettable. Explore the underwater landscapes, then overnight at Cuyuna Cove, where tiny cabins offer comfort, seclusion, and serious stargazing potential. Whether you are diving below the surface or cuddling up fireside, Cuyuna delivers a one-of-a-kind blend of adventure and intimacy in the heart of nature.

USA, MINNESOTA

154 Pair lunch at a pizza farm with a distillery tour in the Twin Cities

Spend a laid-back afternoon in the Twin Cities with the perfect pairing: a farm-fresh pizza lunch followed by a spirited distillery tour. Start at Two Pony Gardens in Long Lake or Squash Blossom Farm, where seasonal, wood-fired pizzas are served in a relaxed, rustic setting. Then, head to Tattersall Distilling in Minneapolis to sip small-batch spirits and get a behind-the-scenes look at the craft.

USA, WINCONSIN

155 Follow a horseback ride in the wide-open spaces of Wisconsin Dells with a visit to a lavender farm

Start with a picturesque horseback ride through rolling hills and wooded paths, allowing you to slow down and connect with nature—and each other. After your ride, make your way to New Life Lavender Farm in Baraboo, where you can wander the flowering fields, pick your own sweet cherries and vibrant lavender sprigs, then pose for dreamy photos surrounded by fragrant purple blooms. Pick up a jar of the farm's cherry and lavender jam before you leave, for spooning onto warm, buttered muffins at breakfast time back home.

USA, WISCONSIN

156 Reignite romance at Kohler spa

Water takes center stage at this premium spa. Unwind in thermal suites complete with saunas, cold plunges, and hydromassage pools. Or, indulge in the RiverBath for Two, where riverlike currents and soft, colored lighting surround you, followed by a full-body exfoliation and moisturizing treatment to detoxify and hydrate.

155 New Life Lavender Farm, Wisconsin

NORTH AND CENTRAL AMERICA • USA

USA, IOWA

157 Visit the *Field of Dreams* movie site

Go at dusk. Even if you have not seen the film, you will be swept up in the magic as golden light washes over the cornfields. Bring a blanket and settle in for a romantic picnic as the sun sets, then linger a little longer to stargaze beneath the wide-open Iowa sky—it makes for a dreamy, cinematic moment.

USA, IOWA

158 Fall in love all over again in Madison County

Step into the timeless romance of *The Bridges of Madison County* as you stroll across iconic covered bridges like Roseman or Holliwell—the very spots that inspired Francesca and Robert's passionate, fleeting love story. Dial up the charm with a picnic by a babbling brook or explore abundant local farms and picturesque galleries nearby.

158 Roseman, Madison County

157 Dyersville, Iowa

USA, ILLINOIS

159 Discover centuries-old bathing rituals

Indulge in the ultimate couples escape at AIRE Ancient Baths, where time-honored bathing traditions create a deeply therapeutic experience in a tranquil underground space. Wade through thermal baths of varying temperatures, before immersing yourselves in a thirty-minute red wine bath rich in antioxidants. A candlelit couples massage is the final treat to melt away tension.

USA, ILLINOIS

160 Settle in for a sleep-cation in a Chicago hotel

Spend a weekend in bed in the Windy City, where the Park Hyatt Chicago's mindfulness-focused suites feature Bryte Balance Smart Beds designed for deep relaxation. These high-tech amenities use embedded sensors to monitor heart rate, breathing, and movement, enabling you and your partner to snooze in sync and wake up truly refreshed.

162 Gateway Arch, St. Louis

USA, MISSOURI

161 Take a horseback ride amid a canopy of flowering dogwoods

For a romantic rendezvous in the Ozarks, look no further than Big Cedar Lodge, where you can spend your days riding the trails of nearby Dogwood Canyon Nature Park. Known for its waterfalls and limestone bluffs, the 10,000-acre (4,000-ha) nature park is particularly stunning in spring, strewn with abundant wildflowers.

USA, MISSOURI

162 Admire the St. Louis Gateway Arch from a charming riverboat

Hop aboard a traditional Mississippi paddleboat tour past the iconic sixty-three-story Gateway Arch for a night of old-school charm. This floating party features dinner, live music, and dancing under the stars as you cruise along the river. With city lights twinkling and the paddlewheel turning, this a lovely way to experience St. Louis from the water.

USA • **NORTH AND CENTRAL AMERICA**

163 Plaza Café, Crystal Bridges Museum of American Art

USA, ARKANSAS

163 Blend calm with culture in the Ozarks

Spend the day at Crystal Bridges, a museum that celebrates American art. Explore galleries exhibiting works by prominent artists and stop for lunch at the Plaza Café. Afterward, explore the museum's 5 mi. (8 km) of nature trails through the Ozark forest, wandering through beautiful gardens with natural streams and art installations.

USA, ARKANSAS

164 Dig deep for gems at Crater of Diamonds

Team up for a one-of-a-kind treasure hunt at Crater of Diamonds State Park—the only place in the world where you can dig for real diamonds in their original volcanic source. If you happen to strike gold (or sparkle), turn your find into a custom jewelry keepsake of your adventure together. An engagement ring perhaps?

USA, LOUISIANA

165 Vibrate on a higher frequency at Jazz Fest

If music brings you together, there is no better place to sway than Jazz Fest. This eight-day celebration draws artists from around the world, filling New Orleans with blues, gospel, zydeco, and, of course, jazz. Immerse yourselves in the joyful atmosphere that sweeps through the city, inviting you to dance close and feel every note together.

USA, LOUISIANA

166 Relive childhood thrills and chills with a romantic twist

Start the evening with cocktails at the Carousel Bar that's been twirling in New Orleans' Hotel Monteleone since 1949. After the dreamy, slow-spinning ride, huddle close for a spine-tingling ghost tour through the French Quarter's shadowy streets, aglow with the flicker of gaslight and brimming with eerie lore.

USA, MISSISSIPPI

167 Hit the highway on the ultimate Blues Trail road trip

Blues lovers can cruise the legendary Mississippi Blues Trail. This self-guided road trip is a 170-mi. (275-km) master class in blues history and the genre's origins. From juke joints to clubs, churches, and cotton fields, every stop tells a story.

USA, MISSISSIPPI

168 Food crawl your way through a top culinary city

Embark on an edible tour of Southern flavors at Oxford's best spots, led by chefs recognized by the James Beard Foundation. For a romantic evening, dine upstairs at City Grocery for refined fare, or keep it cozy at Saint Leo, a wood-fired gem known for Neapolitan-style pizzas, a stellar wine list, and a warm, intimate vibe.

USA, MICHIGAN

169 Spend a leisurely day roaming Detroit's green Belle Isle

This 982-acre (400-ha) oasis is a go-to for romantic moments—including proposals—thanks to its sweeping views of Detroit and Canada. Stroll through lush parkland into the Anna Scripps Whitcomb Conservatory, a stunning greenhouse alive with vibrant flora, then cap the day with a kiss by the James Scott Memorial Fountain, a city landmark gifted by a local family.

USA, MICHIGAN

170 Fall in love with Michigan's art coast in Saugatuck

Soak up the sun at Oval Beach, known for its powdery soft sand and Lake Michigan vistas, or gallery hop down Butler Street, the main thoroughfare. The artsy, inclusive town of Saugatuck is one of the Midwest's most LGBTQIA+ friendly destinations. It promises a good time for all, especially those looking for a drag show or cabaret performance.

170 Oval Beach, Saugatuck

NORTH AND CENTRAL AMERICA • USA

Americana Idyll

USA, MICHIGAN

171 Step back in time on Michigan's car-free Mackinac Island

A picturesque destination that evokes a bygone era, Mackinac Island's streets have been car-free for more than a hundred years. Nestled in Lake Huron between Michigan's Upper and Lower peninsulas, this slice of Americana invites you to slow down and savor the moment, starting with a horse-drawn carriage ride past idyllic cottages, blooming gardens, and scenic bluff views. Mosey through the Grand Hotel's secret garden, a Bavarian-inspired hideaway bursting with color and romance. Cool off with a cone from one of the island's ice-cream parlors, then head to Fort Holmes for stargazing under a sky full of sparkle. Don't leave without sampling Mackinac's world-famous homemade fudge, available in nearly every flavor imaginable.

NORTH AND CENTRAL AMERICA • USA

USA, INDIANA

172 Get away from it all with a folksy stay at Robinwood Inn

Fairy tales come true in Brown County at the Robinwood Inn, where the stand-alone folktale cabin offers a cozy woodland retreat just a half mile from town. Built in the 1930s and lovingly restored, it blends rustic charm with modern comforts—think poplar beams, oak floors, and a grand stone fireplace. Plus, there is a hot tub for a soak together in peaceful, storybook serenity.

USA, INDIANA

173 Bake something sweet together at Macaron Bar, Indianapolis

Book a private macaron-making class in Indianapolis. You and your partner will mix, pipe, and fill these dainty French delights, choosing from fun flavors like Espresso Cardamom, Fruity Cereal, and Earl Grey Tea. Not only do you get to nibble warm macarons fresh from the oven, but you'll also take a box of your handmade treats home with you at the end of the class.

USA, KENTUCKY

174 Drift off to dreamsville inside a museum hotel

Louisville's avant-garde 21c Museum Hotel offers a sleepover like no other. Set within a former bourbon and tobacco warehouse, its art-immersive rooms and plush beds are perfectly poised for situational slumber parties. In the morning, you will not even have to leave the building to enjoy the museum hotel's bold display of contemporary art.

174 Cyclone Room at 21c Museum Hotel Louisville

USA • NORTH AND CENTRAL AMERICA

USA, KENTUCKY

175 Role-play during a murder mystery dinner

Revel in a night of candlelit intrigue as the two of you step into character to help solve a whodunit at the famed Kentucky Castle. The theatrical evening promises fabulous costumes, whispering in corners, and much exchange of flirty glances.

USA, KENTUCKY

176 Eat, drink, and be merry on a bourbon trail

Indulge in a bourbon-soaked sojourn at the Trail Hotel on Whiskey Row. Sip cocktails in a secret speakeasy, unwind at the swim club, and savor the charm of this spirited getaway. Did we mention the bourbon butler?

USA, TENNESSEE

177 See synchronized fireflies spark love

To witness nature at its otherworldly best, head to Great Smoky Mountains National Park in June. This is prime time for a spectacle that sees fireflies light up the forest, flashing in unison to find their perfect match.

177 Fireflies in the Smoky Mountains

USA, TENNESSEE

178 Sample tequila, honey, and five-star luxury at a farm retreat

Just outside Franklin, Southall blends refined romance with low-key luxury in a nature-forward setting. Discover the connection between agave and apiary during a personalized tasting for twosomes, then kick back with included perks—from yoga and guided hikes to sound baths, beekeeping talks, and kayaking. With farm-to-table fare and nightly turndown service, this five-star stay is as easygoing as it is elegant.

USA, TENNESSEE

179 Book two VIP tickets to a concert at the Grand Ole Opry

Treat your lover to a peek behind the curtain of country music's most iconic stage with VIP access to the Grand Ole Opry. Before the show, you will enjoy a backstage tour through memorabilia-adorned dressing rooms, cocktails in the private circle room, and if you are very lucky, a meet and greet with the night's performer. This is a rare chance to experience the heart of the Opry from the inside out.

180 Noccalula Falls along the Alabama wine trail

USA, ALABAMA

180 Sip your way along the Alabama Wine Trail

Nestled amid the foothills of the Appalachian Mountains, the North Alabama Wine Trail offers rolling vineyard views and boutique wineries pouring the state's finest vintages. On your scenic sip-and-stroll route, sample everything from crisp whites to bold reds, and end the day with a candlelit dinner overlooking the vines.

USA, ALABAMA

181 Geek out at the wonders of space

Embrace your inner space nerds at Huntsville's US Space & Rocket Center, where a weekly Cocktails & Cosmos event blends starry skies with liquid libations. For a more exclusive experience, book a private dinner beneath the *Saturn V* Apollo moon rocket. Whether you are toasting under constellations or dining beside a piece of history, it is sure to be an evening that is truly out of this world.

USA, OHIO

182 Reserve a pair of box seats to an NFL matchup

Football fans will enjoy the comfort and elevated experience of watching a matchup from a private suite at Ohio Stadium. From this vantage point, you will have panoramic views of the field, access to upgraded food and drink options, and a more relaxed atmosphere away from the crowd. Whether you are celebrating a big play or discussing a close call, this is a lively and engaging way to spend time together.

USA, OHIO

183 Head to Pride Inn in Columbus for an inclusive weekend of fun

Check yourselves into Pride Inn for a heartwarming weekend supporting LGBTQIA+-owned spots like the Plant Gays and the Little Gay Bookstore. In the evening, head to District West for a cabaret show. This is a fun, feel-good getaway where pride, community, and entertainment bring everyone closer.

USA, WEST VIRGINIA

184 Take a nostalgic, slow-paced trip through West Virginia

Wander the picture-perfect main row in Lewisburg or Berkeley Springs, two of West Virginia's most delightful small towns. Pop into a vintage soda fountain for a hand-stirred cherry cola, catch a classic movie at a century-old theater, and spend the night at a historic inn. The whole vibe feels like a sepia-toned postcard.

USA, WEST VIRGINIA

185 Dare your mate to a date night with a dose of fright

Spooky season or not, West Virginia's Paranormal Trail is a must for ghost story lovers. Follow the haunted path through eerie sites and historic haunts, uncover chilling local legends, and earn prizes along the way. But stay close—you never know what (or who) might be lurking just around the next bend.

184 Bramwell Street, Berkeley Springs

USA, VIRGINIA

186 Savor aphrodisiacs during a coastal getaway on the Chesapeake Bay

Located in the historic town of Irvington, Tides Inn is a serene, seventy-room waterfront resort in Virginia's Northern Neck region. With elegant Southern coastal charm and a commitment to sustainability, it offers more than just a pretty view. Summer is prime for immersive, hands-on experiences, like the Chesapeake Gold Oyster excursion, where you will boat out with the resident ecologist to harvest, sort, and grill oysters fresh from the bay. Or meet the "beautiful swimmers" of the Chesapeake—blue crabs—while learning to cook your catch.

USA, VIRGINIA

187 Let the wine experts at Keswick Hall craft a personalized tasting for two

Sip your way through award-winning pours and take in sweeping Blue Ridge views on a bespoke excursion curated by this luxurious countryside retreat. Nestled in the heart of Virginia wine country, along the scenic Monticello Wine Trail, Keswick Hall has easy access to plenty of nearby vineyards. Whether you are seasoned wine aficionados or curious beginners, your day can be as relaxed or refined as you like, with private transportation and custom tastings, making this an unforgettable, vine-filled adventure for couples.

USA, NORTH CAROLINA

188 Uncover secret desires during a couples intimacy retreat

Explore deeper connection and rediscover passion during an intense retreat in Asheville, led by Xanet Pailet—a nationally recognized intimacy coach and best-selling author of *Living an Orgasmic Life*. Set against the serene Blue Ridge Mountains, this customized retreat guides partners through sensual touch, mindful communication, and erotic massage to build trust and reignite intimacy in a supportive setting tailored to you.

USA, NORTH CAROLINA

189 Snorkel in clear mountain rivers and streams

For those who love to dip their toes in newfound waters and explore nature in unexpected ways, consider a one-of-a-kind adventure in western North Carolina. The Mountain Snorkel Trail is an immersive activity that allows you and your partner to explore clear rivers and streams teeming with native fish and aquatic life. It's ideal for curious couples who want to swap ocean waves for freshwater wonders.

USA, NORTH CAROLINA

190 Set sail at sunrise for a fun fishing, crabbing, and shrimping trip

Nothing says romance quite like casting off at sunrise, with the light catching the calm ocean waves and a gentle salt-kissed breeze filling the sail. In the Outer Banks, this is what you can expect when you book a charter from Oregon Inlet Fishing Center. Sign up for a morning of hands-on fun catching crustaceans and local fish with a seasoned captain guiding the way—it's a coastal caper you won't soon forget.

190 Corolla Park, Outer Banks

USA, SOUTH CAROLINA

191 Sip, sparkle, and swoon surrounded by grandeur at Hotel Bennett

For clinking flutes of bubbly with your love, there is no better spot in Charleston than Camellias inside the grand Hotel Bennett. Inspired by twinkling Fabergé jewels, this pretty-in-pink champagne lounge stuns with its etched-mirror ceiling and crystal chandelier, creating a one-of-a-kind setting for sipping in style. For a more intimate vibe, head up to the hotel's rooftop terrace and toast with cocktails against sweeping city views.

USA, SOUTH CAROLINA

192 Lean into true Southern hospitality at the Dunlin

Just 20 mi. (32 km) outside Charleston, the Dunlin blends authentic Lowcountry living with bucolic landscapes and charm to spare. Set along the banks of the Kiawah River, mint-green gingham tapestries echo the surrounding marsh, while riverfront cocktails are best enjoyed to the tune of distant Carolina wrens. Soak up the scenery from your in-room tub, then rock gently together on a front porch swing.

USA, GEORGIA

193 Scuba dive in the largest aquarium in the United States

Ocean-loving couples will enjoy scuba-diving at the larger-than-life Georgia Aquarium in Atlanta, home to one of the world's biggest single aquatic habitats. Explore the venue's awe-inspiring Ocean Voyager exhibit—built around a 6.3-million-gallon tank—where whale sharks, manta rays, and hundreds of vibrant tropical fish glide gracefully all around. Both certified divers and first-timers can take the plunge.

USA, GEORGIA

194 Fuel your need for speed with an adrenaline-pumping drive

Head to Atlanta's Porsche Experience Center where you can take the wheel of a powerful sports car and tackle a thrilling 1.6-mi. (2.5-km) track designed to test you or your partner's skills with hairpin turns, straights, and a low-friction circle. Whether you are seasoned drivers or curious rookies, it's a high-octane date idea that blends luxury, excitement, and serious bragging rights in one epic ride.

195 Chippewa Square, Savannah

USA, GEORGIA

195 Share key lime pie and ghostly whispers in historic Savannah

On a visit to the much-loved city of Savannah, start with a show at the historic Savannah Theatre, then wander through the city's charming cobblestoned streets lined with oak trees draped in Spanish moss. Stop by the iconic Gryphon Tea Room to share a generous slice of key lime pie. Cap off the night with spine-tingling ghost stories for a memorable end to your day.

NORTH AND CENTRAL AMERICA • USA

197 Disney's Magic Kingdom Park

USA, FLORIDA

196 Hit your target at a premium golf club

Fuel your playful side with a day of friendly competition at Cabot Citrus Farms, where you can cheer each other on through such thrilling activities as axe throwing, clay shooting, and archery. Afterward, wind down with a quiet game of golf on one of the property's world-class courses. Whether you are aiming for bull's-eyes or perfect putts, this outing promises the ultimate combination of high-energy fun and laid-back leisure.

USA, FLORIDA

197 Whirl, twirl, and wish upon a star at Disney's Magic Kingdom

With matching Mickey ears optional, dive into a fairy-tale day at the Magic Kingdom, whizzing up and down rollercoasters and spinning together on the Prince Charming Regal Carrousel. Afterward, share a sweet treat before hopping aboard a private pontoon cruise across the lagoon, where the spectacular fireworks light up the night sky.

USA, FLORIDA

198 Golf on two private championship courses by day, share s'mores by night

An exclusive retreat near Florida's scenic Highway 30A, Camp Creek Inn offers just the right blend of sporty adventure and effortless charm, framed by tall pines and lush, emerald-green fairways. Spend your days teeing off on two private championship courses. Then, after perfecting your swing, unwind with cocktails and classic s'mores under the stars.

USA, FLORIDA

199 Glide through grassy Everglades waters then dine at a legendary grill

Sign up for an airboat ride through Florida's legendary Everglades, where you will navigate narrow waterways and open marshes, spying native wildlife along the way—perhaps even an alligator or two. Afterward refuel with fresh seafood and stone crab claws at the one-and-only Camellia Street Grill in Everglades City.

199 Everglades

USA, FLORIDA

200 Share an epic, sky-high adventure

Strap on harnesses and take the ultimate leap together at Skydive Space Center in Titusville, Florida—home to the world's highest tandem skydive at 18,000 ft. (5,500 m). You will free-fall side by side for a full, heart-pounding ninety seconds before your parachutes open and you float gracefully back to Earth. It is an unforgettable way to conquer fears and celebrate milestones together.

USA, FLORIDA

201 Spend the weekend at a beachfront hotel

Make the Miami Beach EDITION your home base for a weekend of fun. Head to the Basement for ice-skating and bowling under color-changing lights with a live DJ. For when you get hungry, reserve a table at the Matador Room, the hotel's signature restaurant by Michelin-starred chef Jean-Georges Vongerichten. Order dishes like sweet pea guacamole and the dry-aged ribeye—perfect for two.

USA, FLORIDA

202 Join a sip-and-paint experience in the dark

Found in Miami or Orlando—and several other US cities, Neon Brush is a one-of-a-kind workshop where you can unleash your inner artist with glow-in-the-dark paints under blacklight. A booking includes your choice of boozy beverage to help your imagination run wild and great music adds a party vibe. Dress in your brightest whites or neon gear to really light up the room.

USA, FLORIDA

203 Pair a bachata dance class with a Cuban sandwich in the Magic City

Sign up for a bachata lesson and DJ-spun evening at Ball & Chain in Miami's Little Havana. Even beginners will have a blast dancing the night away. Afterward, head to Sanguich De Miami for the legendary Cuban sandwich, a flavorful combo of marinated and roasted pork, garlic, spices, and homemade bread.

USA, FLORIDA

204 Soak up the sun (and the scene) on Miami's legendary South Beach

On South Beach, snap a few selfies together beneath the iconic colorful lifeguard towers, then check into the illustrious Surf Club in Surfside, where Frank Sinatra and Ava Gardner once honeymooned. Now a glamorous Four Seasons Hotel, it boasts chic oceanfront bungalows and world-class dining from renowned chef Thomas Keller.

204 South Beach lifeguard tower

USA, FLORIDA

205 Vacation in style at SLS South Beach

Choose between a decadent Philippe Starck–designed suite with mirrored ceilings made for mischief—or a rock and roll penthouse oozing Lenny Kravitz's signature swagger.

USA, FLORIDA

206 Swim with dolphins

At Palm Island's Dolphin Research Center the two of you can swim alongside playful dolphins, experiencing their grace and intelligence firsthand. After, dive deeper into the world of dolphin science through hands-on activities to learn more about these fascinating creatures.

USA, FLORIDA

207 Channel Ernest Hemingway in Key West

Explore the writer's charming home, where you can meet his famous six-toed cats. This is the ultimate romantic escape for bibliophiles, offering an insight into the life of the man who penned one of the world's most impactful love stories, *A Farewell to Arms*.

USA, FLORIDA

208 Hop aboard the Gay and Lesbian Trolley Tour

Embark on a journey to learn about Key West's LGBTQIA+ history and hear the stories that shaped this welcoming community while soaking in the island's vibrant sights, from colorful streets to historic landmarks. After the tour take a selfie together on the Pink Triangle's rainbow crosswalk. End the day catching a drag show at Aqua on Duval Street.

USA, NEW YORK

209 Feast on art and culinary excellence

Explore the Storm King Art Center, where monumental sculptures rise from rolling fields in an immersive art experience. Afterward, savor a two-Michelin-star dinner at Blue Hill at Stone Barns, a farm-to-table beacon in the heart of the Hudson Valley. If you plan to linger longer, book a stay at Glenmere Mansion, a Gilded Age estate-turned hotel.

USA, NEW YORK

210 Unplug and fully disconnect at the Point

Leave behind TVs, Wi-Fi, and cell service to immerse yourselves in wholesome activities together. Built as a nineteenth-century Rockefeller Great Camp, the Point at Saranac Lake invites couples to treat the estate as their personal playground. Enjoy ice-skating, kayaking, and private boat lunches, before retreating to your log cabin for a nightcap in PJs beside a wood-burning fire.

USA • **NORTH AND CENTRAL AMERICA**

207 Hemingway Home and Museum

USA, NEW YORK

211 Forage, sip, and unwind in the Catskills

Escape to Eastwind Oliverea Valley, a Scandinavian-inspired, hygge-minded boutique hotel tucked away in the Catskills. Start your stay with a guided foraging walk through the woods, gathering wild herbs and edibles, then unwind with a cocktail tasting crafted from local ingredients. With newly built Lushna cabins and suites, private saunas, and hammocks perfect for stargazing, Eastwind's minimalist-luxe vibe makes it an effortlessly romantic spot to relax with your partner.

USA, NEW YORK

212 Roll back time at the Rainbow Rink

Lace up your skates for some retro fun together at Buffalo's iconic Rainbow Rink. Dress to impress for themed nights that include Skate & Burlesque, 1980s throwback parties, or an R&B rager. Glide across the floor beneath colorful lights, grooving to the beats of nostalgic tunes. Whether reliving your favorite era or discovering a new one, this is an all-in-one interactive activity with aerobic workout.

USA, NEW YORK

213 Tour Niagara Falls, the honeymoon capital of the world

Discover the romantic appeal of Niagara Falls, where you can experience breathtaking views on land and water. Feel the mist as you get thrillingly close to the falls, or stroll scenic trails. For a dreamy stay, consider iconic honeymoon hotels such as Red Coach Inn, Niagara Falls Marriott, or the historic boutique hotel Giacomo.

USA, NEW YORK

214 Enjoy a stay in LGBTQIA+ friendly Fire Island Pines

Ferry over to Fire Island, the iconic queer haven where sandy beaches, lively boardwalks, and endless celebrations await. Spend your days soaking up the sun and the nights catching a drag show in Cherry Grove. Don't miss Low Tea at the Blue Whale in the Pines, either—a beloved local tradition that sets the tone for the evening ahead.

211 Eastwind Oliverea Valley

215 Palm Court, The Plaza

USA, NEW YORK

215 Capture a moment in time while staying at NYC's The Plaza

Spend an afternoon in Central Park, where talented portrait artists line the paths ready to sketch lovers' likenesses. It is a timeless, romantic souvenir to bring home. Afterward, meander back to your hotel for a leisurely afternoon tea beneath the stained-glass dome of the Palm Court, surrounded by elegant furnishings and greenery.

NORTH AND CENTRAL AMERICA • USA

USA, NEW YORK

216 Enjoy gentle morning exercise in New York's Central Park

Start your day with a peaceful Central Park yoga class, where the urban buzz fades into lush greenery and hushed calm. Afterward, continue the tranquility with a romantic rowboat ride across the park's picturesque lake. Enjoy an alfresco lunch at the Central Park Boathouse, soaking in the views and savoring a moment of quiet bliss with your love.

USA, NEW YORK

217 Channel your inner Audrey with breakfast at Tiffany's

Step into Truman Capote's fantasy world with a real-life breakfast at Tiffany's. Savor a delightful morning spread of croissants, coffee, and freshly squeezed juice, all while surrounded by beautiful baubles and a canopy of suspended Tiffany blue boxes. Wander to the first-floor showroom to explore a stunning array of sparkling gems—and perhaps even try on engagement rings.

USA, NEW YORK

218 See the city sparkle from the top of the Empire State Building

Take a guided tour of the Empire State Building, followed by a celebratory toast in the Green Room. Then, request your favorite song from the saxophone player on the eighty-sixth floor, watching New York City thrum with electric energy beneath you. Time your ascent for dusk to see the city really sparkle.

216 Central Park Lake

217 Tiffany's on 5th Avenue

USA, NEW YORK

219 Visit the Museum of Sex while staying at the nearby Fifth Avenue Hotel

Have a blast being amused—and maybe aroused—at the Museum of Sex, where exhibits breed cheeky fun, especially on the Tunnel of Love ride. Afterward, retreat to your suite for a night of passion at the nearby Fifth Avenue Hotel, a romantic haven for lovers, dripping in chandeliers and jewel-toned interiors.

USA, NEW YORK

220 Hop on the aerial tram to Roosevelt Island for stunning sunset views

Take the aerial tramway over the East River to Roosevelt Island for a hand-in-hand, self-guided tour of the tiny island. Finish with a ride up to the eighteenth floor of the Graduate by Hilton hotel to sip Manhattans in the Panorama Room overlooking the Big Apple's glowing skyline.

NORTH AND CENTRAL AMERICA • USA

USA, NEW YORK

221 Embrace exhibitionist showering at the Standard, High Line

Leave your inhibitions behind and indulge in a stay at the Standard, High Line, renowned for its scintillating spaces, including a German beer garden and the rooftop discotheque Le Bain. In your room, clear glass separates the bed from the bath for a sensual shower experience. For a titillating twist, book the Liberty Suite, featuring a dramatic round platform bed and teacup bathtub for two.

USA, NEW YORK

222 Spice up date night with a cooking class

Book yourselves in for a cooking class at Platform by the James Beard Foundation. The hands-on experience will teach you and your partner essential skills to create memorable meals together at home. From mastering new techniques to exploring fresh flavors, you'll both leave inspired and confident to whip up delicious dishes for many intimate nights in. Take note of what really resonates with your partner's palate and save the recipe for later.

USA, NEW YORK

223 Dine under the bridge in Brooklyn

Enjoy a dazzling dinner at Brooklyn's famously romantic River Café, tucked beneath the arches of the Brooklyn Bridge with sweeping views of the Manhattan skyline. Housed in a former coffee barge, this fine-dining landmark has charmed guests since 1977—ideal for a first date or a ten-year anniversary. Do not miss the Signature Chocolate Brooklyn Bridge dessert—rich, artful, and best shared on one plate with two spoons.

225 A Hudson Valley Orchard

224 Coney Island

USA, NEW YORK

224 Kick off a summer weekend at Coney Island

For the months of June, July, and August, Coney Island hosts a free fireworks display every Friday. Hop on the Q train and take it to the very last stop, then step into a retro dream, where you can ride the iconic 150-ft.-tall (46-m) Deno's Wonder Wheel for a stunning bird's-eye view of the city. Roam the boardwalk as fireworks light up the sky, capping off your perfect summer evening together.

USA, NEW YORK

225 Escape to the Hudson Valley for a cozy fall weekend

Once the leaves turn crimson and gold, grab the apple of your eye and escape to the Hudson Valley for a cozy, cider-scented weekend. Meander through the historic pick-your-own fruit orchards of Rose Hill Farm in Red Hook, a beloved, family-run spot dating back to 1798. Come nighttime, share wood-fired pizza and crisp pours at Twin Star in New Paltz.

NORTH AND CENTRAL AMERICA • USA

USA, PENNSYLVANIA

226 Book an exclusive heirloom experience

Located in the heart of Philadelphia, the Rittenhouse five-star hotel offers refined elegance, world-class service, and bespoke experiences. The Heirloom Concierge service comes with a custom-made gold locket crafted by Bario Neal jewelers, designed exclusively for you—a unique keepsake for you and your partner to cherish.

USA, PENNSYLVANIA

227 Create your own Damascus steel rings

Celebrating an eleventh anniversary? Since steel is the traditional gift after eleven years together, head to the Barefoot Forge, where you can join skilled artisans in a hands-on workshop to craft a timeless symbol of your love through the art of metalworking. The experience offers a unique chance to forge meaningful treasures that will last forever.

USA, PENNSYLVANIA

228 Share a stimulating, fast-paced foodie evening

At Ambra in Philadelphia, enjoy a wine-paired dinner for two at the Chef's Counter, starting with light snacks and a spritz, and concluding with handmade desserts and amaro. Each course is thoughtfully narrated by executive chef/owner Chris D'Ambro for an evening filled with flavor and storytelling.

231 Cherry blossoms in Washington, DC

USA • **NORTH AND CENTRAL AMERICA**

USA, MARYLAND

229 Check into the five-star Inn at Perry Cabin

Maryland's most romantic inn is one of the East Coast's finest retreats. Savor luxury and adventure with sailing lessons, or perfect your croquet game after a rum tasting. Surrounded by lush gardens, every day feels like a holiday on the Miles River.

USA, MARYLAND

230 Shuck 'n suck on a Chesapeake harvesting adventure

For the ultimate oyster harvesting voyage, hire a local fisherman to take you around Maryland's renowned waters, famous for their aphrodisiac mollusks. After gathering your fresh catch, savor the ultimate combo—slurp down your haul alongside a chilled glass of champagne—preferably on a sandy knoll somewhere.

USA, WASHINGTON, DC

231 Get a double dose of cherry blossom beauty in DC

Washington, DC is famous for its blooming cherry blossoms, peaking between the last week of March and the first week of April. Stroll beneath these fragrant flowers with petals falling around you. Then, head to the couples suite at Salamander Spa, where their Cherry Blossom Body Ritual will leave you refreshed and glowing.

NORTH AND CENTRAL AMERICA • USA

USA, DELAWARE

232 Cross state lines on a romantic ramble together

At White Clay Creek State Park, winding trails guide you through lush forests and across state lines into Pennsylvania or Maryland. The novelty of crossing borders by foot makes for a rewarding day date, surrounded by the quiet solitude of nature. Pack a picnic and find a shady perch to share a beautiful meal together along the way.

USA, DELAWARE

233 Pair a ride in a heritage railroad car with a stay in a boutique hotel

Climb aboard the Wilmington & Western Railroad for a nostalgic ride through Delaware's picturesque Red Clay Valley. The 10-mi. (16-km) route passes historic sites such as Greenbank Mill and Brandywine Springs Amusement Park, crossing farmland along the way. Afterward, unwind at the Quoin Hotel, a boutique hotel with an opulent speakeasy and Wilmington's only rooftop bar.

USA, NEW JERSEY

234 Learn to sail on Barnegat Bay

Set sail with Barnegat Bay Sailing Charters, which offers personalized lessons and charters from Cedar Creek Marina in Bayville. After mastering the ropes, unwind at a nearby tiki bar, where you can kick back with potent fruity cocktails and tropical island vibes.

COASTAL ROMANCE

USA, NEW JERSEY

235 Write your own seaside love story

Whether sitting side by side in Adirondack chairs on the lawn or barefoot with sand between your toes, Cape May's Congress Hall is as storied as grand American resorts come. Set sail on the *A.J. Meerwald* for oysters and refreshing wine, or indulge in a couples treatment with a massage that mimics the rhythm of the sea.

USA • **NORTH AND CENTRAL AMERICA**

USA • **NORTH AND CENTRAL AMERICA**

USA, VERMONT

236 Hunt for leafy hearts in Stowe, then hop on the Gondola SkyRide

Take a whimsical leaf-peeping excursion through Stowe's fiery fall foliage, searching for heart-shaped leaves among the vibrant reds and oranges. After your stroll, hop aboard a scenic gondola ride up Mount Mansfield for awe-inspiring views from the top. Share a warming fireside drink at a historic inn or explore the charming village filled with local boutiques, covered bridges, and artisanal chocolate shops.

USA, VERMONT

237 Spend a weekend with your flame at Twin Farms

Take a twilight stand-up paddle around Twin Farms' private lake, where the evening light dances on the water. Then settle in for a decadent five-course, wine-paired dinner, where seasonal farm-to-table dishes are matched with rare vintages. Nestled in a secluded setting, Vermont's most romantic hotel also features cozy cabins with hot tubs and an impressive art collection showcasing works by David Hockney and Jasper Johns.

USA, NEW HAMPSHIRE

238 Follow a playful paintballing date with a night of karaoke

Channel your inner Kat and Patrick by reenacting the paintballing scene from *10 Things I Hate About You* at Laconia Paintball Park. After the action, explore the town's lively downtown area and serenade each other at a local karaoke bar. Whether you are belting out love songs or laughing at each other's performances, you are bound to have a date full of laughter.

USA, NEW HAMPSHIRE

239 Glamp it up in an A-frame tent in the heart of the White Mountains

Hidden among the pines, Lumen Nature Retreat redefines roughing it, with A-frame cabins that blend Nordic style with mountain charm. Spend the day sledding down snowy trails or watching flakes fall on your porch, cider in hand. When the chill sets in, fire up the barrel sauna. With moody forests and starry nights, it is an unplugged getaway for every kind of couple.

USA, MASSACHUSETTS

240 Reconnect and recharge together in the Berkshires

Canyon Ranch offers world-class wellness retreats, and its Berkshires outpost—modeled after Marie Antoinette's Petit Trianon at Versailles—is one of the best. Spend a few restorative days indulging in luxurious spa treatments, nourishing meals, and mindful activities designed to spark connection. Workshops titled Love in Balance and Deepen Your Bond are tailored for couples looking to strengthen their relationship.

236 Stowe, Vermont

NORTH AND CENTRAL AMERICA • USA

USA, MASSACHUSETTS

241 Spend a wintry evening in Boston, starting with a skate on Frog Pond

Boston may be known as "America's Walking City," but, come wintertime, swap your sneakers for skates. New England's oldest rink, Frog Pond, is the perfect spot to glide hand in hand under twinkling lights. Afterward, head to the Newbury Boston for martinis and snacks at Street Bar. Then take a romantic evening stroll through Beacon Hill's snow-dusted cobblestoned streets, surrounded by charming brownstones.

USA, MASSACHUSETTS

242 Explore Provincetown's dunes before heading to the Boatslip's legendary Tea Dance

Discover the stunning Provincetown dunes, part of Cape Cod National Seashore, before dressing up for the Boatslip's iconic Tea Dance. A Provincetown tradition for nearly fifty years, this lively event honors the Sunday Tea Dance tradition that began in New York's LGBTQIA+ community in the 1950s and 1960s. It is a must-see celebration of joy, inclusivity, and coastal fun.

241 Beacon Hil, Boston

244 Mystic, Connecticut

USA, MASSACHUSETTS

243 Plan a memorable stay on Martha's Vineyard

Soar above Martha's Vineyard on an exhilarating vintage Biplane MV ride, where daring dives will have your hearts racing. Then decompress at Winnetu Oceanside, the coastal-luxe resort perched right on South Beach. Later, relax with a romantic dinner at the Dunes where seasonal, fresh ingredients from the island's local farms, harvesters, and fisheries shine.

USA, CONNECTICUT

244 Set a nautical theme for a stay in Mystic

Once a sleepy seafaring village, Mystic has blossomed into a lively port brimming with stores, restaurants, and hotels. Take a sunset sail aboard the 81-ft. (25-m) schooner *Argia*, then check into the Delamar Mystic, clad in nautical details and old-world maps. Of course, grabbing a slice at Mystic Pizza is a given before heading home.

USA, CONNECTICUT

245 Cuddle up at Sycamore Drive-In

Watch a double feature the old-fashioned way—from the comfort of your car. Open since 1948, this retro gem dishes out frosty root beer floats, crispy onion rings, and classic burgers delivered right to your window by carhops in vintage uniforms. Consider it pure, comfy Americana under the stars.

NORTH AND CENTRAL AMERICA • USA

USA, RHODE ISLAND

246 Feel the heat at Providence's WaterFire

This multisensory art installation is a must for first-timers to America's smallest state, often called "Little Venice." Stroll along the glowing waterfront as woodsmoke from eighty fires lining the rivers perfumes the air and gondolas drift past. Witness the city morph into a dreamscape of firelight, warmth, and whimsy.

USA, RHODE ISLAND

247 Tour Newport's Gilded Age mansions

Step into the grandeur of Rhode Island's legendary summer homes, where sublime suites and sprawling gardens set the stage for a day of excess and romance. After touring the Breakers, retreat to the Chanler at Cliff Walk, a Gilded Age mansion that's been given a glamorous makeover into a seaside hotel, perfect for sleeping like royalty.

USA, MAINE

248 Prepare for cuteness overload, puffin style

Mount a classic Maine lobster boat for a breezy cruise in search of Atlantic puffins—the irresistibly charming seabirds that mate for life. As you drift past rocky islands and salty waves, keep your eyes peeled for these loyal little lovebirds bobbing along the coast.

247 Gilded Age mansion, Rhode Island

USA • NORTH AND CENTRAL AMERICA

USA, MAINE

249 Get your hands dirty on a lobster shack crawl

Embrace the cheesy bibs and ramble through Maine's iconic seaside lobster shacks. This crustacean extravaganza fit for foodies celebrates the state's famously sweet, tender bounty. If you need a nudge in the right direction, try Young's Lobster Pound, where you can feast on fresh-caught tails beside Penobscot Bay.

USA, MAINE

250 Hole up in a well-appointed houseboat

White Barn Inn's luxe retreat, the Cora Houseboat, floats right on the Kennebunk River. The decor was styled by celebrated interior designer Jenny Wolf—expect a chic dose of subtle blues and beiges. After checking in, make a beeline for the rooftop deck, your stylish perch for soaking up Maine's seaside charm in total privacy.

USA, ALL OVER

251 Take a spontaneous road trip

Pick a destination neither of you has been to before, cue up a custom playlist, and hit the road together. Whether starting on the East or West Coast, chasing a dot on the map—windows down, snacks in hand, and a shared sense of adventure—makes for the ultimate romantic getaway.

250 The Cora Houseboat, Maine

USA, ALL OVER

252 Work side by side doing your part for a more beautiful coastline

Join a Surfrider Foundation dune restoration project on a coastline of your choosing and contribute to the preservation of coastal ecosystems. By participating in dune planting and cleanup efforts together, you will help protect vital habitats for local wildlife and combat erosion at the same time. It is a rewarding experience that combines outdoor adventure with environmental stewardship—sand underfoot, sun on your face, and a sense of community as you make a real impact on the nation's beaches.

USA, ALL OVER

253 Travel in first-class style in a luxury suite in the sky

Book a first-class ticket not just for the destination, but for the indulgent journey itself. Think private suites with closing doors, gourmet meals, and next-level onboard service aboard Emirates 777 Game Changer first-class suite (flying from Chicago), Etihad's the Residence (flying from New York), or La Première experience by Air France (flying from Los Angeles, Miami, New York, San Francisco, and Washington, DC). With lie-flat beds, oversized TVs, and total privacy at 30,000 ft. (9,150 m), they are like hotels in the sky.

USA, ALL OVER

254 Swap homes and immerse yourself in another couple's world

Opt, perhaps, for a week in a charming beachfront abode in Santa Cruz. Or seek out a stylish apartment in a bustling city like San Francisco. Here is your chance to experience a different way of life! Kindred offers you the opportunity to swap homes, explore new surroundings, relax in someone else's space, and discover hidden gems that make these destinations unforgettable. This is the perfect way to step into someone else's life and experience their favorite places.

USA, ALL OVER

255 Embark on a seven- or ten-stop round-the-world flight

Nothing brings soulmates closer together than a continent hop. Regardless of which major hub you start from—perhaps JFK or ATL—this plan-as-you-go journey allows you to explore diverse cultures, cuisines, and landscapes all in one trip. With each stop offering new experiences, you will savor the thrill of jet-setting across the world. From European capitals to bustling Asian cities, your dream destinations are just a flight away. Pack your bags, choose your route, and prepare to check off a lifetime's worth of bucket-list goals.

252 Walk together along a beach you helped clean

256 Two-person catamaran cruise

PUERTO RICO

256 Charter a catamaran for a two-person sail to Icacos

Set sail for the uninhabited cay of Icacos, a hidden gem just off Puerto Rico's east coast. This tiny, under-the-radar paradise is the perfect place to reconnect as you snorkel turquoise waters and loll on powdery white sand. With no crowds in sight, it is just you, your partner, and the raw island beauty (plus tide pools teeming with crabs, fish, and baby sharks). Many private charters include optional stops for hikes and beach picnics, making the experience as relaxed or active as you like.

PUERTO RICO

257 Work up an appetite wing foiling, then cook a feast together

Take a wing foiling lesson for two, where you will glide above the water on a hydrofoil board while harnessing the wind with a handheld inflatable wing. After working up an appetite, head to La Cocina Gourmet Culinary Center in San Juan to cook a Puerto Rican lunch together. Using fresh ingredients, you will learn to craft traditional dishes like mofongo (mashed fried plantains) and arroz con gandules (rice with pigeon peas)—an interactive way to savor the island's rich flavors.

PUERTO RICO

258 Book an adults-only stay located directly on the beach at Condado Ocean Club

With floor-to-ceiling ocean views and a sleek, modern vibe, this chic spot on Condado Beach was made for romantic getaways. In-room perks—bath bombs, champagne, candles, and a cheeky romance kit—set the mood for connection behind closed doors. Outside, spend sun-soaked days lounging on the deck, dipping in the infinity pool, and retreating to your private cabana for more stolen moments together.

258 Condado Ocean Club

NORTH AND CENTRAL AMERICA • CARIBBEAN

PUERTO RICO

259 Make a splash in El Yunque National Forest

For an unforgettable couples' adventure, hightail it to El Yunque—the only tropical rainforest in the US National Forest Service—where cliff jumping, rope swinging, and zipping down a natural waterslide turn the lush landscape into your personal playground. Afterward, unwind at the St. Regis Bahia Beach Resort, set on a former coconut farm between El Yunque and the Espíritu Santo River Preserve. With sweeping rainforest views, 483 verdant acres (200 ha), whitewashed accommodations, and an above-par eighteen-hole golf course framed by swaying palms, this romantic refuge is deeply rooted in nature.

259 El Yunque National Forest

US VIRGIN ISLANDS

260 Scuba dive in sync through the labyrinths of Buck Island Reef National Monument

Glide through the underwater wonders of Buck Island Reef National Monument, diving among coral labyrinths and hidden grottos. This protected marine sanctuary bursts with vibrant reefs and thriving sea life, where every turn unveils a new surprise and set of eyes. It is a shared journey that brings you closer to each other and the mesmerizing world just below the surface.

260 Buck Island Reef National Monument

262 The Cove Eleuthera, Bahamas

BERMUDA

261 Share a kiss beneath a moon gate, then escape to a candlelit cave spa

Embrace a cherished Bermuda tradition that sees newlyweds sharing a kiss beneath a limestone moon gate. It is said to bring luck and lasting love to the marriage. Afterward, slip away for a dreamy couples massage at Natura Spa. Hidden inside a candlelit cave with its own tranquil lagoon, this enchanting retreat feels straight out of a fairy tale.

BAHAMAS

262 Find tranquility together at the Cove Eleuthera

Inspired by the Blue Mind Theory, which suggests that proximity to water fosters a calm, meditative state, Eleuthera's hidden gem, the Cove, offers its Blue Mind package for couples seeking serenity. Enjoy a two-person picnic on the Floating Sea Lounge, enjoy a day of kayaking, or unleash your inner Picasso with oceanscape painting sets. Nestled between two pristine white sand coves, it is the ultimate escape.

BAHAMAS

263 Opt for quiet Bahamian luxury at the storied Potlatch Club

Set on an unspoiled 7-mi. (11-km) stretch of pink sand, the Potlatch Club was once a glamorous getaway for New York socialites and A-listers such as Greta Garbo and Paul McCartney (who honeymooned here with Linda in 1969). Lovingly restored in recent years, the eleven-key hideaway now welcomes a new generation of honeymooners. Oceanfront villas have rose coral stone floors, whitewashed walls, and artworks by local artists.

BAHAMAS

264 Pack your tennis whites for a sun-soaked vacation at the John McEnroe Tennis Center at Baha Mar

At Baha Mar's John McEnroe Tennis Center, couples can enjoy friendly matches, take tips from seasoned pros, and maybe even spot the tennis legend himself on the court. With world-class facilities and a lively yet laid-back vibe, Baha Mar is the consummate spot to sharpen your swing and break a sweat together—all with a touch of McEnroe magic.

263 The Potlatch Club, Bahamas

NORTH AND CENTRAL AMERICA • CARIBBEAN

265 Nurse sharks in Compass Cay, Bahamas

BAHAMAS

265 Capture moments of each other swimming with friendly nurse sharks

Animal lovers will thrill at the idea of gliding alongside docile nurse sharks in crystal-clear shallows. These gentle creatures move with slow grace, offering a surprisingly serene encounter. There is no danger involved—Compass Cay's sharks are famously well-fed and behaved. And you will walk away with a story to retell for years to come. Just don't forget your GoPro.

TURKS AND CAICOS ISLANDS

266 Follow thrills on the water with a couples massage workshop

COMO Parrot Cay is a private island resort set on 4 mi. (6.5 km) of sugar-soft white sand. Spend the day kayaking through flourishing mangrove forests where herons and egrets thrive. Afterward, get closer at the spa with a couples massage workshop, learning hands-on techniques that will leave you more in tune with each other's bodies.

CARIBBEAN • **NORTH AND CENTRAL AMERICA**

269 Spotting stingrays in Grand Turk

TURKS AND CAICOS ISLANDS

267 Take your love under the sea on a charming submarine tour

Known for their balmy weather and laidback ethos, the beguiling Turks and Caicos Islands also boast an underwater world that turtles, rays, and tropical fish call home. The Undersea Explorer semi-submarine tour by Caicos Tours allows you to admire marine life 5 ft. (1.5 m) below the surface—no swimsuits required. Plus, you will get to hear a pirate tale and witness a surprise appearance from Bella, the resident mermaid.

TURKS AND CAICOS ISLANDS

268 Sneak away to a sexy hotel set on a nature reserve

Turks and Caicos Islands' main archipelago, Providenciales, has long drawn lovers. For a truly secluded experience, head to Amanyara on the remote northwest coast. Set within an 18,000-acre (7,000-ha) nature reserve, its sleek pavilions overlook azure waters—an ultra-private Caribbean escape that is pure perfection.

TURKS AND CAICOS ISLANDS

269 Retreat to Grand Turk

Take a rendezvous to intimate Grand Turk with your partner for a blend of island history and off-the-beaten-path beauty. Wander colonial-era streets, then settle in a quiet cove where you might glimpse stingrays gliding by or share a peaceful ocean paddle—just the two of you, far from the crowds.

NORTH AND CENTRAL AMERICA • CARIBBEAN

TURKS AND CAICOS ISLANDS

270 Venture to Salt Cay for unique wildlife encounters

From striking tropical birds to majestic humpback whales, this sleepy, sun-soaked island is a haven for nature lovers, especially during whale migration season. Take a boat tour to snorkel near these gentle giants and, if you are lucky, hear their haunting navigation songs echoing through the deep. With its untouched charm, Salt Cay offers a rare immersion in the rhythms of the natural world.

272 Viñales Valley, Cuba

TURKS AND CAICOS ISLANDS

271 Create a lasting legacy on a coral restoration expedition

Give some of your time to the Turks and Caicos Reef Fund. Together, you will help plant new coral on the reef, playing a small but meaningful role in preserving the islands' fragile marine ecosystem. As you connect over a shared passion, you'll be giving back to the dazzling underwater world that makes these islands so magical with a unique and purpose-driven outing.

CUBA

272 Learn the art of cigar rolling in the Viñales Valley

Cuba evokes dreamy visions of rum-soaked nights and vintage attire. Venture 100 mi. (160 km) west of Havana and discover Viñales—a misty, mountainous heartland steeped in tradition. Among sweeping tobacco fields, where time moves slowly, take a hands-on lesson from local cigar rollers, before lighting your freshly rolled Cubans and heading off on horseback, twirls of smoke trailing behind.

CUBA

273 Checkmate your partner in Cuba's chess capital, Santa Clara

Skip the crowds of Havana and head to Santa Clara, Cuba's true chess capital, where the game is more than a pastime. In this culture-rich city, plaza tables host quiet battles daily. Settle in, lock eyes over the board, and let the intensity build. Whether you are aiming for checkmate or just savoring a flirty rivalry, it is a uniquely Cuban blend of strategy and local tradition.

CARIBBEAN • **NORTH AND CENTRAL AMERICA**

A Night in Havana

CUBA

274 Blend art, salsa, and Cuba libres on a night out in Havana

When in Havana, salsa. Take a private lesson at Casa de la Música and find your rhythm in the birthplace of this sultry dance. Afterward, sip a lime-kissed Cuba Libre at O'Reilly 304 or El Floridita, then dive into Havana's creative core at Fábrica de Arte Cubano—a former oil factory turned cultural powerhouse where art, music, and nightlife pulse under one ever-evolving roof.

NORTH AND CENTRAL AMERICA • CARIBBEAN

CUBA

275 Indulge in a bespoke itinerary for the Cuban tour of your dreams

Let the experts at Abercrombie & Kent craft an authentic journey through Cuba's most captivating corners. From the pastel-hued streets of Havana to the cobbled alleys of Trinidad, you will discover the island's vibrant culture, compelling art, and bold flavors. Highlights might include cruising in a vintage convertible, sunset cocktails along the Malecón, private dinners in *paladares*, and behind-the-scenes access to Havana's thriving music scene.

CAYMAN ISLANDS

276 Descend to a stunning drop-off at Bloody Bay Wall Marine Park

Explore the technicolor corals of Bloody Bay Wall, one of the world's premier wall dives, where the drop-off begins at just 20 ft. (6 m) and plunges more than 1,000 ft. (100 m) into a deep blue abyss. After your adventure, snorkel over to Owen Island. Though a bit tricky to reach, it is worth the journey once you have a rum cocktail to sip and a quiet beach to enjoy.

CAYMAN ISLANDS

277 Savor culinary mastery by Eric Ripert

For foodie couples heading to the Cayman Islands, indulge in culinary brilliance at Blue by Eric Ripert at the Ritz-Carlton, Grand Cayman, where dishes such as foie gras and conch sashimi are reimagined by the three Michelin-star French chef in a breezier, island-inspired setting than his NYC landmark, Le Bernardin. Craving a more intimate experience? Arrange a private alfresco dinner prepared by Ripert himself at Starfish.

CAYMAN ISLANDS

278 Soar above a turquoise dreamscape

Take a flyover of the Cayman Islands, where the water is so crystalline you can spot coral reefs and shipwrecks from the sky. The ride offers panoramic views of all three islands and the dazzling blues that make the Caribbean so legendary.

JAMAICA

279 Join a floating reggae dance party

Book a sunset "floating party" catamaran cruise, departing from Montego Bay. As reggae rhythms play and rum cocktails swirl, you will be dancing barefoot on the deck in no time. Visit the Caymans' Seven Mile Beach and don snorkels for a chance to cool off when the cruise makes a stop at a protected reef.

JAMAICA

280 Live out a love story at GoldenEye, Bond-style

There is no more stylish sanctuary than GoldenEye, where Ian Fleming penned the iconic spy series—and where his typewriter still rests in the original Fleming Villa. This hideaway has welcomed everyone from Truman Capote and Bob Marley to Grace Jones and Bono . . . and now, the two of you.

276 Bloody Bay Wall

281 Martha Brae River, Jamaica

JAMAICA

281 Float on a bamboo raft for two

Glide through the lush heart of Trelawny Parish on a handmade bamboo raft down the tranquil Martha Brae River. As you gently steer your way through the jade-green waters, enjoy the quiet rustle of jungle leaves and birdsong overhead. It is an unhurried way to soak up Jamaica's natural beauty.

DOMINICAN REPUBLIC

282 Lean into luxury at Eden Roc Cap Cana

Settle into a private oceanfront bungalow at Eden Roc Cap Cana, where romance meets indulgence. With your own pool, dedicated butler, and golf cart for exploring, this is the kind of escape that makes the rest of the world disappear. Sun, sea, and seclusion—paradise made personal for just the two of you.

DOMINICAN REPUBLIC

283 Catch the trade winds in Cabarete

Cabarete is a kitesurfing haven, offering more than three hundred days of steady trade winds annually. Kite Beach is renowned for its beginner-friendly conditions, with a protective reef creating calm waters near the shore and waves farther out for advanced riders. Whatever their level, twosomes ready to fly will find the friendly environment an ideal place to learn the ropes together.

CARIBBEAN • NORTH AND CENTRAL AMERICA

DOMINICAN REPUBLIC

284 Live like fashion royalty at Oscar de la Renta's Tortuga Bay

Set within Punta Cana Resort & Club, this luxury hideaway was envisioned by the late legendary Dominican fashion designer Oscar de la Renta, and features beachfront villas crafted with his signature grace and tropical glamour. De la Renta designed some of the world's most iconic wedding gowns, so do not be surprised if the romance here feels suspiciously aisle-worthy.

BRITISH VIRGIN ISLANDS

285 Let loose aboard the legendary floating bar Willy T on Norman Island

Sip rum cocktails and be as carefree as you want to be on the infamous Willy T. This floating bar and grill is pure Caribbean fun—bold, boozy, and a little wild. And who knows? You and your partner may even walk the plank together—just make sure to grab the bar's famous conch fritters first.

BRITISH VIRGIN ISLANDS

286 Re-create your own *Love Island* moment on Necker Island

Having hosted everyone from the Obamas to Lady Diana, Richard Branson's original private island resort is the epitome of a seductive escape. With 74 acres (30 ha), seven beaches, tropical forests, and organic orchards, it is one of the few remaining privately owned islands in the region. Enjoy complete privacy, candlelit dinners, and a local flock of flamingos.

285 Willy T, British Virgin Islands

CARIBBEAN • NORTH AND CENTRAL AMERICA

BRITISH VIRGIN ISLANDS

287 Hit the open water for a sea fishing adventure

Try your luck chasing elusive bonefish around the flats of Anegada or venture into deeper waters in search of barracuda and wahoo. A private charter with Ocean Surfari BVI or Anegada Adventures comes with all the gear and no experience is required. After reeling in your prize, head to the Wonky Dog or Potters By the Sea for a true catch-and-cook dinner, where the chefs will prepare and plate your fresh haul.

BRITISH VIRGIN ISLANDS

288 Ride the waves and and chase the wind in Virgin Gorda

Dive into an impressive lineup of stimulating watersports, from stand-up paddleboarding and wakeboarding to wing foiling, kitesurfing, sea bobbing, tubing, and waterskiing. There is no shortage of ways to make a sporty splash together. Whether you are chasing adrenaline or just craving time on the water, these action-packed moments are best shared in Virgin Gorda.

BRITISH VIRGIN ISLANDS

289 Book an all-inclusive yacht charter with the Moorings

Discover the British Virgin Islands in effortless style. With a private captain guiding the way, you will be taken to hidden coves and pristine beaches only accessible by boat. Choose from the Moorings' sail, power, or fully crewed charters to match your preferred pace. When you start to feel peckish, let the yacht's chef pamper you with gourmet meals.

ANGUILLA

290 Take a romantic journey for the senses

Cap Juluca, A Belmond Hotel, is an architectural masterpiece on the powdery sands of Maundays Bay—one of the world's most exquisite beaches. While it is tempting to lounge all day on your sun-drenched terrace or in your private pool suite, don't miss Guerlain Spa's Romance Journey. This sensual experience includes a couples massage, a soothing scalp ritual with wild herbs, and ends with champagne and truffles.

ANGUILLA

291 Record a love song at the AMA Center

At Malliouhana Resort, give it your all, recording a romantic duet with your one true love at the AMA Center, Anguilla's only world-class recording studio. Sip a few rum punches at Sunset Bar for courage, then lay down your track in a pro-level studio built for island legends. Afterward, toast to your triumphs at Leon's while taking in the soulful acoustic sounds of Anguilla's own Omari Banks.

ST. KITTS AND NEVIS

292 Spend a dreamy night in paradise

Savor, soak, and stargaze with the Four Seasons Resort Nevis' Spa Under the Stars experience. Begin with a candlelit dinner for two in a serene tropical setting, then unwind together in a private volcanic stone soaking tub under a canopy of stars. Surrounded by flickering candles and island breezes, this indulgent escape is pure romance.

288 Kitesurfing in Virgin Gorda

ST. KITTS AND NEVIS

293 See the best of St. Kitts by land and sea

Sightsee in stunning St. Kitts aboard the Scenic Railway, a three-hour journey offering sweeping views of lush landscapes and historic sugar plantations. Then switch gears and explore by water—cruise along the coast on a Sea-Doo or a glass-bottomed kayak tour. The perfect blend of adventure and awe, above and below.

ANTIGUA

294 Drift into island time on a glass canoe adventure

There is no better way to explore Antigua's secret coves than on a private glass canoeing experience. Paddle at your own pace across crystal-clear waters, where tropical fish and coral reefs shimmer below. With quiet inlets and hidden beaches all around, you two are free to savor the serene rhythm of this Caribbean paradise—whether you linger in the shallows or venture farther into the blue.

ST. BARTS

296 Live like A-listers on glamorous St. Barts

Charter a superyacht, dance on tables at celeb-loved Nikki Beach, splurge on jeroboams of rosé, and indulge in long, languid lunches at Shellona. Then check into ultra-private Hotel Le Toiny nestled on 42 palm-dotted acres (17 ha), a favorite for weddings and engagements.

ST. BARTS

297 Swim in natural pools then enjoy some cabaret

Just beyond Grand Fond lie St. Barts' *piscines naturelles*: crystalline pools for floating peacefully, sheltered from the surf. After sunset, head to cabaret club Le Ti, where champagne flows, inhibitions fade, and you find yourselves dancing in sultry borrowed costumes.

296 Nikki Beach

BARBUDA

295 Treat your taste buds to a sushi master class at Nobu Barbuda

Set on the pink-sand shores of Princess Diana Beach, Nobu Barbuda offers couples a uniquely intimate culinary escape. Master the art of sushi-making together at the open-air Sushi Bar, complete with sake pairings and take-home handbooks to continue the experience at home. If you are not into sushi, opt for the luxe Japanese barbecue—a beachside feast of grilled lobster, conch, and prime beef, infused with Caribbean flavors.

295 Making sushi at Nobu Barbuda

298 Sea turtles at St. Barts

ST. BARTS

298 Snorkel with sea turtles at blissful Le Sereno before dining at romantic Al Mare

A stay at Le Sereno, the über-chic beachfront retreat on Grand Cul-de-Sac, includes access to a dedicated Turtle Concierge, who educates guests about the endangered sea turtles gliding through the island's lagoon and reef-protected waters. Spot these ancient mariners while snorkeling or kitesurfing, then wrap up your day with a romantic dinner at Al Mare, serenaded by St. Barts' resident crooner, Don Soley.

GUADELOUPE

299 See a kaleidoscope of marine life

Whether via snorkeling, free diving, or drifting aboard a glass-bottomed boat, the Cousteau Reserve is a must for nature lovers looking to feel part of the harmonious wonderland below.

GUADELOUPE

300 Chase waterfalls, then indulge in the island's signature dessert, "torment of love"

Guadeloupe offers lush, untamed environs perfect for couples craving a nature-rich escape. Start your day with a rainforest hike to one of the island's waterfalls, then wind down with a candlelit dinner. Be sure to order *tourment d'amour*—Guadeloupe's signature coconut-filled pastry, meaning "the torment of love"—a sweet, symbolic finale to a day of wild beauty.

DOMINICA

301 Dive deep with gentle giants

Slip into the deep to encounter sperm whales in the world's first marine protected area created for their conservation. Afterward, luxuriate at Coulibri Ridge, a sleek, solar-powered hideaway that offers panoramic views of the island's craggy coast.

CARIBBEAN • **NORTH AND CENTRAL AMERICA**

MARTINIQUE

302 Rise to the challenge of climbing Mount Pelée

Tackle the dramatic slopes of Mount Pelée, Martinique's iconic volcano, which rises 4,583 ft. (1,397 m) above sea level. Summit the verdant, misty peak, then celebrate your ascent with a bottle of bubbly. A round-trip takes three to four hours, depending on your pace and the chosen trail.

302 Mount Pelée, Martinique

ST. LUCIA

303 Rally for romance on the court at St. Lucia's Sugar Beach

Team up—or go head-to-head at Sugar Beach's scenic Racquets Club, where a pro helps perfect your pickleball game against a jaw-dropping backdrop. After your final point, celebrate with crisp champagne, decadent chocolate truffles, and uninterrupted views of the iconic Pitons. This is a love match that blends playful competition with tropical indulgence.

ST. LUCIA

304 Make it all about you two at Caille Blanc

Tucked away in a dreamy corner of St. Lucia, overlooking the majestic Pitons and Soufriere Bay, Caille Blanc Villa offers an intimate escape tailor-designed for two. Enjoy private moments with in-suite couples massages, candlelit dinners just for you, and stunning views from everywhere you turn. This boutique resort redefines romance, offering a secluded haven where you and your partner can unwind and connect without distraction. With this truly personalized experience, love is the only thing on the agenda.

ST. LUCIA

305 Scale new heights at a celebrity-favorite honeymoon hideaway

At Jade Mountain, a celebrity-loved refuge perched above St. Lucia's Pitons, you can secure your own hiking butler. Wander through lush rainforest trails or take on the mighty Gros Piton, at 2,619 ft. (798 m), the island's second-highest peak. Afterward, unwind in your open-air sanctuary—purposefully missing a fourth wall—and take a dip in your private infinity pool, where stargazing, soaking, and even a little skinny-dipping are encouraged.

ST. LUCIA

306 Dance the night away, St. Lucia style

Expect a high-energy night at Gros Islet's legendary Friday night jump-up. The streets pulse with music—and the dancing goes until dawn, which is to be expected when you are sipping on endless rum punch, feeling the energy, and moving to the irresistible rhythms of the Caribbean. Whether you are joining the steamy dance-offs or simply soaking in the vibes, this weekly street party is a must for anyone eager to dive into St. Lucia's lively nightlife scene.

305 Jade Mountain

NORTH AND CENTRAL AMERICA • CARIBBEAN

ST. VINCENT AND THE GRENADINES

307 Channel your inner rock stars on Mustique

A longtime hideout for Mick Jagger and Jon Bon Jovi, Mustique has lured the rich and famous for decades. As the sun sets, head to Basil's Bar, perched above the water, where a live band keeps the party going into the night. With barefoot dancing, salty breezes, and a dash of island glam, this is the Caribbean at its most carefree.

ST. VINCENT AND THE GRENADINES

308 Adopt island time in a postcard-perfect cove

The all-inclusive Sandals resort sits on 50 lush acres (20 ha) and has expansive accommodations that include two-story overwater villas and beachfront suites with private fitness rooms. Between dips in the emerald sea, indulge at sixteen gourmet restaurants. It is the perfect base for soaking up the resort's luxury and the island's untouched beauty.

BARBADOS

309 Explore Hunte's Gardens hand in hand

Wander the winding paths of Hunte's Gardens, a hidden gem tucked in Barbados' lush hills. With towering palms, colorful blooms, and classical music drifting through the air, it's the perfect place to slow down, hold hands, and sneak a kiss—no one's watching but the hummingbirds. Climb the upper steps to Mr. Hunte's house for the best views.

BARBADOS

310 Fly high, sip slow in Barbados

Fuel your adrenaline at an eco-adventure park, where ziplining and treetop obstacle courses slice through the thick Bajan landscape. After the action, wet your whistles with a rum tasting at a historic distillery in the spirit's birthplace.

308 Sandals Resort

CARIBBEAN • **NORTH AND CENTRAL AMERICA**

GRENADA

311 Explore an ever-changing underwater sculpture garden

British artist Jason deCaires Taylor's mesmerizing underwater sculpture garden in Grenada's crystal-clear waters features seventy-five sculptures that include a circle of children holding hands and a man sitting at his desk. Installed in 2006, the pieces are slowly being colonized by marine life and taking on a whole new dimension in the process. At depths of 16–26 ft. (5–8 m), the garden is accessible by scuba diving and snorkeling.

GRENADA

312 Clink, cruise, and canoodle

Three words: Champagne. Lobster. Cruise. Set sail on a breezy catamaran for a day of snorkeling, sipping, and swooning. With fresh-grilled lobster, bottomless bubbly, and island beats setting the mood, this one-of-a-kind experience serves plenty of chances to flirt your way along Grenada's sparkling coast.

GRENADA

313 Indulge in sweet treats at Belmont Estate

Surrender to the aphrodisiac allure of chocolate on a tree-to-bar tour at the historic Belmont Estate. Uncover the secrets of cocoa cultivation, then devour a sumptuous three-course chocolate-themed lunch, where each bite is even sweeter than the last—a perfect treat for twosomes seeking a deliciously rich experience.

TRINIDAD AND TOBAGO

314 Propose amid the magic of Bamboo Cathedral

Slip a very important ring in your pocket and guide your love through the enchanting Bamboo Cathedral, a hidden oasis in Trinidad. As you walk beneath towering bamboo stalks, abundant green arches create a calm, almost otherworldly atmosphere and the soft rustle of leaves and filtered sunlight make this natural wonder the perfect place to pop the question.

314 Bamboo Cathedral, Trinidad

Animal Magic

ARUBA

315 Get up close and personal with wildlife and caves in Aruba

Start with an affectionate encounter at the Donkey Sanctuary, then marvel at the hundreds of exotic butterflies at the Butterfly Farm. But save time for Quadirikiri Cave—a site carved by time and steeped in romance. Legend says two forbidden lovers escaped separate prisons to reunite here, dying in each other's arms as their souls soared through holes in the cave ceiling.

CARIBBEAN • **NORTH AND CENTRAL AMERICA**

316 The Quill, Dutch Antilles

DUTCH ANTILLES

316 Trade crowds for adventure on the unspoiled island of St. Eustatius

Explore vibrant coral reefs and historic shipwrecks on dives through a pristine marine reserve, then hike up the Quill—a dormant volcano in the south of Statia—for all-encompassing views that feel straight out of a movie scene. As the sun begins to dip, settle in for a BYOB picnic surrounded by candy-colored skies and tropical breezes. With Golden Rock Resort as your base, this off-the-radar refuge is your passport to pure Caribbean splendor.

ST. MARTIN

317 Try an anything-goes vacay at a bare-it-all beach in St. Martin

Live it up at Orient Bay, St. Martin's spirited take on Saint-Tropez, where the vibes are carefree, the guavaberry rum flows, and the clothing-optional section makes anything feel possible. Or, for a more mellow scene, head to Mullet Bay's silky sands and calm surf—then linger over a chef-driven, toes-in-the-sand lunch at Kalatua. Hotel wise, La Samanna offers a swanky stay on the French side, while the JW Marriott suits suave couples on the Dutch.

NORTH AND CENTRAL AMERICA • MEXICO

MEXICO
318 Pair holistic wellness with biodynamic wine

In Baja California, achieve balance on a vacation that offers you and your spouse plenty of intoxicating indulgence via private pool villas and estate-grown wine, but also an impressive range of holistic wellness therapies. At Banyan Tree Veya, Valle de Guadalupe, in the heart of Mexico's luscious wine country, you will experience hydrotherapy and shamanic temazcal rituals, and dine on wholesome, sustainably sourced Mexican cuisine.

MEXICO
321 Sunbathe together on deserted beaches

Keep company with each other, and maybe even friendly donkeys, on gloriously empty beaches that line the coast around Ensenada. When you have soaked in enough rays, head inland to Valle de Guadalupe to devour delicious cuisine and fantastic wine by candlelight.

MEXICO
319 Enjoy live music at an otherworldly bar

With a name that sounds coined by naughty neck-biting vampires, Bloodlust is easily Valle de Guadalupe's sexiest wine bar. Its out-of-this-world architecture will make you want to stage a photo shoot, but make sure to enjoy the live music, too.

MEXICO
322 Discover a secret beach for lovers

Get lucky with timing and ask your water taxi captain to steer straight to the photogenic granite Arch of Cabo San Lucas in Baja California for a morning spent sunbathing and swimming at idyllic Lovers Beach, hidden amid dramatic rock formations.

MEXICO
324 Spot shooting stars from your rooftop jacuzzi

Look forward to the sun setting at Cabo San Lucas's most pampering resort, Las Ventanas al Paraiso. Expect cotton-candy skies and the chance to watch for shooting stars through your suite's telescope. End the evening in your private rooftop jacuzzi.

MEXICO
320 Find your bliss in a Pueblo Mágico

Add to your shared history in one of Mexico's exceedingly charming designated Pueblos Mágicos, magic towns. Spend leisure time savoring Baja's artistic surf haven Todos Santos and relaxing at its intimate beach resort Villa Santa Cruz, with seaside sound baths. You will sleep in a plush, tented ocean suite where you can taste mezcal, have sultry hot tub sessions, and make out by your own firepit.

MEXICO
323 Dine in a restaurant clinging to an ancient cliff

Smell the salty sea spray mixing with freshly cooked catch of the day in a moody, low-lit restaurant carved into an ancient cliffside. Start with a three-glass tasting at the Champagne Terrace of Baja's El Farallon before selecting your succulent seafood from a bed of shaved ice, to be expertly prepared by skilled chefs.

322 Arch of Cabo San Lucas, Baja California

NORTH AND CENTRAL AMERICA • MEXICO

MEXICO

325 Go from wine lovers to winemakers

Become winemakers with Grand Velas Los Cabos' Over-the-Top Wine Lovers' Getaway. The package includes spa treatments and indulgent dinners between grapevines, and a private jet to Valle de Guadalupe for vintner-escorted tastings. Before leaving, you will blend your own vintage at D' Poncelis and take home a case.

MEXICO

326 Let a dream watcher customize your stay

Book a romantic escape to Baja's East Cape at Zadún, a Ritz-Carlton Reserve, where you will have a dedicated *tosoani*—"dream watcher" in the Indigenous language Nahuatl—to weave your stay into a real-life fantasy. Think luxury, hacienda-style quarters, intimate breakfasts, agave tastings, and private bonfires.

MEXICO

327 Live amid greenery in a luxury tree house

At One&Only Mandarina, in Nayarit, the eco-designer tree houses nestle high up in the jungle canopy. After a dip in your private infinity pool, go trail riding, take a surf lesson for two from the white-sand beach, or join an immersive culinary workshop in which you will learn how to make traditional Mexican flatbreads or tacos.

MEXICO

328 Release adorable baby sea turtles to sea

Take up temporary residence at Naviva, a Four Seasons Resort, in Punta Mita. Your sumptuous tented accommodation—one of just fifteen on a verdant 48 acres (19.5 ha)—comes with incredible perks. At this playground for adults only, couples cannot go wrong with a snorkel safari, nocturnal forest bathing, or the unmissable newborn sea turtle release on the beach.

MEXICO

329 Become underwater hunters in the Pacific

In Nayarit, slip into the Pacific Ocean to learn a skill that requires great patience and perhaps a little appetite—for the abundant fish swimming around you. Spearmex's spearfishing discovery and guided spearfishing sessions are the surest way to strengthen your underwater skills—and see which one of you snags your future candlelit dinner.

MEXICO

330 Host the celebration of a lifetime at Careyes

Mark a milestone event—engagement, wedding, anniversary—hosting a once-in-a-lifetime party for a group of close friends and family members at Sol De Oriente. This extravagant yellow ocean castle is surrounded by a 360-degree pool at Mexico's 35,000-acre (14,000-ha) protected reserve, Careyes, with 9 mi. (15 km) of flawless beaches.

330 Sol De Oriente Careyes

NORTH AND CENTRAL AMERICA • MEXICO

MEXICO

331 Fly on water with an e-foil surfing class

Learn to fly across water like superheroes and superheroines during a thrilling e-foil surfing class on the spectacular coast that curves along Four Seasons Resort Tamarindo, in Costalegre, Jalisco. Another option: flying in the air in a tandem paratrike—think tricycle meets paraglider. Come down from the shared rush of euphoria gently with a peaceful private yoga and sound-healing session for two, while gazing out at the blue horizon.

MEXICO

332 Celebrate Dia de los Muertos, La Catrina style

The energy and excitement of Dia de los Muertos (Day of the Dead) in the city of San Miguel de Allende is unrivaled. The traditional Mexican holiday takes place annually from October 31–November 2. To get involved in the vibrant action, coordinate with your partner in sultry La Calavera Catrina (Dapper Skeleton) costumes, complete with face paint, and join the unforgettable after-dark parade through the streets.

MEXICO

333 Enjoy art, tradition, and old-world charm

Discover the intriguing inspiration that comes from sleeping in a place saturated with original artwork. The thirty-two-room Hotel Matilda is filled with pieces by contemporary artists, many of them specially commissioned. Walk out onto the cobblestoned lanes of San Miguel de Allende to take in a more traditional, yet equally impactful, side of this romantic and colorful colonial-era hive of Mexican culture.

333 San Miguel de Allende

MEXICO • **NORTH AND CENTRAL AMERICA**

DESTINATION DINING

MEXICO

334 Snag the hottest reservation in the Mexican capital: Rosetta

In Mexico City, dinner at Rosetta, chef Elena Reygadas's acclaimed restaurant in a lush Colonia Roma mansion, is a thoughtful celebration of Mexican ingredients—seasonal, vegetable-forward, deeply rooted in tradition. Book your reservation for two well ahead and start upstairs at Salón Rosetta to enjoy elegant cocktails and house-made spirits in an intimate setting. Return the next morning for the panadería's beloved guava rolls, Mexican pan dulce, and sourdough loaves.

336 Playa Viva

MEXICO

335 Pair Michelin-starred tacos with a luxurious, five-star stay

Justify the ultimate indulgence in Mexico City on an odyssey that places you and your partner at a divine five-star hotel and Michelin-starred taco stand. The Four Seasons Hotel Mexico City is the opulent urban oasis where you cannot help but nuzzle up deep in your king-size bed. But there is a decadent breakfast spread waiting, plus Bosque de Chapultepec park nearby, and whatever excursions the expert concierge can deliver—from hot-air balloon rides over pyramids to graffiti tours and custom-crafted shoemaking. The nonnegotiable element: a feast at circa 1968 El Califa de León, Mexico's sole taco stand to win the coveted Michelin distinction. Order as many tender Gaonera tacos as you can eat, with plenty of pesos to spare.

MEXICO

336 Escape from it all in a manta-ray-shaped tree house in Guerrero

Go literally where no one can reach you at off-grid B Corp–certified Playa Viva resort, southeast of Zihuatanejo. Book a manta-ray-shaped bamboo tree house where you can watch sea turtles digging sandy nests under moonlight from your in-floor hammock.

MEXICO

337 Pair a laid-back cycling tour with a visit to a mezcal distillery

In Oaxaca, set a slow pace on a private bike tour tailored to your shared interests—exploring ancient Zapotec ruins, visiting vibrant artisan studios, or browsing colorful local markets. Continue to a family-owned mezcal distillery to see how your new favorite spirit is made, and say "salud!"

MEXICO • **NORTH AND CENTRAL AMERICA**

339 Celestún Biosphere Reserve

MEXICO

338 Sparkle as you splash and flirt in bioluminescence

Check into a barrel-vaulted suite at the architectural gem boutique hotel Casona Sforza—for adults only—in Puerto Escondido, and savor Pacific Ocean panoramas and the wild beauty of Oaxaca. The latter includes something wonderfully magical: bioluminescent plankton. Head to Laguna de Manialtepec before sundown for a stunning cruise as golden hour deepens into a diamond-flecked lagoon. Leap into the water and send sparkles flying since all your movements leave trails of glowing glitter.

MEXICO

339 Marvel at an immense flamboyance of flamingos

Though it does not have the renown of Cancun or Cabo, the Yucatán Peninsula beach town of Celestún is worth a pilgrimage, especially if you are a couple of birders. Visit the Celestún Biosphere Reserve and its massive saltwater lagoon to watch arguably the most fabulous large bird in existence snack in the shallows. In a flamboyance of up to 2,000, hot-pink flamingos hang out there from fall through winter. Take a boat tour to see the best of them.

MEXICO

340 Reenergize your love on a Soulmates retreat

Strengthen your trust, set new intentions, and reconnect deeply on a four-night Sacred Soulmates retreat guided by a shaman in the Yucatán jungle. The wellness-focused resort Chablé Yucatán plays host to partners seeking evolution in their relationship in a stand-alone casita with its own pool. Stargaze with an astronomer, experience a Mayan ritual to bless your union, take sensual Kundalini yoga together, and embark on a companionship ceremony in the steam-filled temazcal, emerging stronger as a couple.

NORTH AND CENTRAL AMERICA • MEXICO

MEXICO

341 Stay close while scuba diving in a cenote

Crystalline water, limestone tunnels and caverns, mesmerizing marine life, and the occasional shaft of light are the main ingredients of the fantasy world into which you will descend when embarking on a couples scuba dive in a Yucatán cenote. The otherworldly underwater phenomenon that is signature to the area around Tulum is best explored by those with an adventurous streak. Stay close and bring your GoPro to capture the enchantment of it all.

MEXICO

342 Check into Mexico's best spa hotel for a reset

Hide out and let one day flow seamlessly into the next on 50 acres (20 ha) of Riviera Maya beachfront jungle, formerly an Italian duchess's getaway. Hotel Esencia, in Quintana Roo, has Mexico's best spa—and that is saying a lot—so a couples therapy has to be in the cards, following an intimate soak in a tucked-away hot tub. Also check out legendary Mayan ruins at Chichen Itza and Mayapan, and dine on resort-grown fare.

342 Temple of Kukulkan at Mayapan

MEXICO

343 Combine lazy beach days with wildlife quests

On Isla Holbox, tap into your truest desires. The island, which is just 26 mi. (41 km) long and 1¼ mi. (2 km) wide, between the Gulf of Mexico and the Caribbean Sea is a true getaway in the sense there are not even cars. Alternate between lazy, cocktail-addled days in overwater hammocks and energetic quests by boat, bike, or on foot to encounter flamingos, sea turtles, whale sharks, and more.

346 Cenote, Quintana Roo

MEXICO

344 Pair a steam-filled traditional temazcal ritual with sensory couples massage

Join your partner inside the sweaty, steamy environs of an Indigenous *temazcal*, meaning "house of heat." At Quintana Roo's beachfront Rosewood Mayakoba, the resident shaman leads you through an intensely hot ritual that could produce extreme emotions and is bound to cement your bond. Convene again for a long, pampering Eclipse Sun & Moon Journey, during which you will mix a sweet-smelling scrub for your own couples treatment to come.

MEXICO

345 Cruise around the Caribbean's Island of Women

Legend has it that Isla Mujeres, which means Island of Women, was once inhabited only by priestesses and their female entourages, and the tiny paradise still has a certain allure. Board a luxury catamaran to cruise around the isle and soak up its singular spirit. Snorkel up and leap off the side of the boat into lucid sapphire water to explore underwater sculptures by British artist Jason deCaires Taylor.

MEXICO

346 Pair hidden-gem cenotes with lavish couples treatments

Snorkel with stunning visibility on a private tour that promises to leave the well-beaten path of Quintana Roo's famed cenotes and reveal lesser-known sacred sinkholes with delicate, idyllic ecosystems. Then head to Etéreo SANA, an Auberge Spa, for an over-the-top four hours of couples treatments. There's a palo santo ritual, a quartz stone massage, a Mayan clay wrap, a facial, and the finale: sparkling wine and a private jacuzzi.

NORTH AND CENTRAL AMERICA • BELIZE/GUATEMALA

BELIZE

347 Get back to nature at Gaïa Riverlodge

The secluded, sustainable Gaïa Riverlodge lies in a western Belize forest reserve. It promises the most romantic rainforest backdrop with gushing waterfalls and tropical flora and fauna. A booking through Kind Traveler includes a donation to the Cornerstone Foundation.

GUATEMALA

350 Feel enchanted by Guatemala's deep blue crater lake

Navigate Guatemala's dazzling Lake Atitlán and its charming volcano-side villages in a boat from Casa Palopó's dock. The epic boutique hotel is full of character, and opportunities for partners to immerse in all types of Guatemalan culture and cuisine. Between sound healing and authentic tortilla making, take time for a moving shaman blessing that may transform your relationship.

BELIZE

348 Move into a thatched-roof cottage at Turtle Inn

Take up residence at Turtle Inn, on a pristine beach, and meet the locals (mostly wildlife) on two-person kayaks, SUP boards, and beach cruisers. Soak up the sun's rays while sipping Francis Ford Coppola wines from the resort's cellar, too.

350 Lake Atitlán

BELIZE

349 Dive into the depths of the Belize Barrier Reef

Teeming with dolphins, manatees, and five hundred species of fish, Belize Barrier Reef is the largest in the northern hemisphere. Scout out its many wondrous atolls, mangrove forests, cays, and lagoons.

GUATEMALA

351 Paint and play with vibrant color while volunteering

Let the lively colors and heritage patterns of buildings in the small lakeside village of Santa Catarina Palopó boost your mood and shared sense of joy, especially when you get involved in its glow-up. Pintando Santa Catarina Palopó is a years-long nonprofit project helping local families work as a community to design and paint their homes; spread love by volunteering to assist in the effort.

GUATEMALA

352 Re-create *The Notebook*'s rowboat scene in Guatemala

As if the bright Spanish colonial town of Antigua, Guatemala, wasn't romantic enough, lovers can retreat to the sumptuous hacienda Villa Bokéh outside of town and re-create the famous rowboat scene from *The Notebook* for themselves. After the dreamy paddle on the sprawling estate's private lagoon, the fifteen-bedroom hotel's experience inspired by the film concludes in an amorous garden picnic surrounded by green.

353 Rancho Santana

NICARAGUA

353 Shriek and squeal as you sandboard down Nicaraguan dunes

Abundant thrills, available across 2,700 acres (1,000 ha) of rolling hills, postcard-perfect coastline, and dense Emerald Coast jungle, lure active couples who are game for anything. Rancho Santana is that utopia with just seventeen inn rooms and horseback riding, surfing, mountain biking, and sandboarding. For that last one, speed on a modified bodyboard down 100-ft. (30-m)-high Playa Duna then recover at the forest spa.

NICARAGUA

354 Test your skills at a luxurious surf retreat in Popoyo

Hang ten—or simply learn to stand on a board—at Hide and Seek Resort, a cushy Popoyo spot where a couple can dive into the world of surfing together or each do their own thing. There are guided daily surf outings the two of you can join, but also a sauna and ice bath, Pilates, and yoga for spouses with different ideas of fun. Whatever you opt for, be sure to catch a shared horseback ride at sunset.

NICARAGUA

355 Make your love known at an LGBTQIA2S+ centered hotel

In San Juan del Sur, Apogeo Guest House is a beacon of hospitality and safe haven for LGBTQIA2S+ couples, especially queer and trans people of color. Book a stay here for consciously designed guest suites with ocean and mountain views. Experiment in the on-site herb garden and apothecary, lounge around the pool, and find pleasure in sharing delicious cocktails and Nicaraguan food made contemporary and healthy.

356 Ometepe

NICARAGUA

356 Chill out on the island of Ometepe, aka the "Oasis of Peace"

Nicknamed the "Oasis of Peace," this island in the middle of Lake Nicaragua, Central America's largest, is the kind of place you can expect to unwind and do a lot of nothing. Of course, it is impossible to ignore the 5,250-ft. (1,600-m) volcano, Concepción, but that does not mean you have to climb it. Instead, spend lazy days taking gentle walks along the volcano's slopes, with its cloud-shrouded summit above and the shimmering lake below.

Immerse in Nature

COSTA RICA

357 Embark on an enchanted whitewater rafting voyage

Go off the beaten path in Costa Rica to the 52-acre (21-ha) ORIGINS Floral Lodge, where immersion in nature comes in many forms. Adrenaline junkie partners will enjoy streaking past monkeys and tropical birds on a gorgeous whitewater rafting or tubing voyage that ends in a gripping 12-ft. (3 m) waterfall drop. The mystical Earth-centered retreat also specializes in one-of-a-kind experiences that take couples deep into the jungle and to farms and gardens growing produce for imaginative gastronomic meals.

COSTA RICA • **NORTH AND CENTRAL AMERICA**

COSTA RICA

358 Follow coral planting with a tailor-made couples spa treatment

Submerge into Costa Rica's sparkling Culebra Bay for a snorkel outing that is actually far more. With Peninsula Papagayo's Culebra Reef Garden Alliance, get hands-on with coral planting and coral gardening to help restore and propagate the reef. When you resurface, indulge in a luxury spa treatment in a couples suite at nearby Andaz Peninsula Papagayo Resort's ONDA spa.

COSTA RICA

359 Steam things up in a hot mineral river

Ensconced in a rare dwarf forest, Rio Perdido Hotel & Thermal River has a steamy, mile-long (1.6-km) flow of water running beneath thirty-eight secluded bungalows scattered amid the 1,500-acre (607-ha) private reserve. Savor long, languid days spent swimming in the river and maybe slathering on volcanic mud. Later, take things up a notch with canyoning, mountain biking, and rope swings.

COSTA RICA

360 Role-play as Tarzan and Jane in the jungle

The Costa Rican signature canopy zipline was invented in 1979 for the sake of scientific research, but it is now one of the most amusing and stimulating ways for a couple to spend a couple hours in a pristine natural setting, with dozens of courses around the country. Harness up and zoom through the jungle canopy straight into the arms of your partner waiting on a sky-high platform.

COSTA RICA

361 Let ancient wisdom help deepen your bond

Learn to live long and love purely in Punta Islita, a resort town in the Blue Zone of Costa Rica's Nicoya Peninsula. Let the wisdom of local centenarians combine with a focus on well-being to inspire you on your own path of discovery together. At the eco resort, join a new ancestral moon circle, inspired by ancient lunar rhythms, and come out spiritually and emotionally closer than ever.

COSTA RICA

362 Fawn over slow, sweet sloths while helping save them

You may find these slow-moving, cuddly-looking creatures on a guided wildlife walk in Costa Rica's rainforests, but numbers are falling. The surest way for you and your spouse to meet some is by volunteering with an organization working to save and conserve them. Voluntourism could include feeding rescued and rehabilitated sloths, researching and monitoring populations, or helping with community education.

362 Costa Rican sloth

COSTA RICA

363 Book a titillating five-night Sensual Awakening package

There is no hiding your erotic intentions when you and your spouse book the Sensual Awakening package at the Retreat Costa Rica, a holistic wellness resort atop a quartz mountain. Expect heart-opening massage, aero yoga for two, self-love crystal therapy treatments, and a "feel your body" session with your partner.

COSTA RICA

364 Work on your flexibility during a yoga retreat

Get bendier, stronger, and more in tune with your bodies and sexuality in the welcoming boho Blue Zone beach town of Santa Teresa, known for its bountiful surf and yoga scenes. Stretch and *om* side by side in a proper yoga retreat or sidle up to one of many studios with Kundalini and Tantra classes covering breathwork and sacred touch.

COSTA RICA

365 Do good then feel good lying super high in a tree net

Reward yourselves for a day of doing good with an evening just hanging in an SCP Corcovado Wilderness Lodge, 200-ft.-high (60-m) tree net. The good-doing is also part of the fun. Working with marine conservation organization Innoceana, you may get to observe humpback whale migrations or use advanced technology to eavesdrop on their distinctive love songs.

SUPREME WELL-BEING

COSTA RICA

366 Merge wonder and wellness in the Talamanca foothills

Nestle into the plush Talamanca Mountain foothills at an award-winning resort where holistic wellness is the overarching theme. At Hacienda AltaGracia, open-minded couples are spoiled for choice when it comes to sublime experiences and spaces that serve that intention, starting with the divine casitas' coffee plantation panoramas and covetable decor. Your all-inclusive stay features a personal experience designer who will help you balance tender moments with powerful ones, from forest bathing and breakfast on a local family's farm to equine exploits, ficus tree climbing, and über-private candlelit dinners.

368 Nayara Bocas del Toro

PANAMA

367 Pair a Panama Canal cruise with a stroll in historic Casco Viejo

Engineering nerds and history lovers can fulfill a lifelong dream by joining a day cruise through the Panama Canal, a modern wonder. Sailing the 51-mi. (82-km) man-made marvel is unforgettable, especially when paired with intoxicating champagne and, later, a starlit stroll down the UNESCO-listed cobblestones of Casco Viejo with the love of your life.

PANAMA

368 Experience the novelty of the first overwater beach

Go full-on Robinson Crusoe in a bamboo and hardwood tree house 50 ft. (15 m) up in the sky. The tub here fits two for sensual late-night baths and there is a pulley system so you can stay naked through room-service deliveries. At the off-grid private island resort Nayara Bocas del Toro—an all-inclusive for adults only—you will enjoy another architectural wonder, too: the world's first overwater beach.

PANAMA • **NORTH AND CENTRAL AMERICA**

PANAMA

369 Ramble through mangroves and rainforest to an empty beach

Journey together through mangroves to the Indigenous village of Quebrada Sal then continue into virginal rainforest for a hike that rewards you with a gloriously remote, private-feeling stretch of sand. You are likely to have the offbeat beach all to yourselves—save for turtles. It is a habitat for four different species, so you might get lucky and swim beside one.

PANAMA

370 Seek out superbly remote ecotourism possibilities in Panama

Approach your vacation in Panama a bit differently by using the country's grassroots network SOSTUR to seek an intimate stay in an Indigenous destination where it is likely you will be the only two tourists. The ecotourism tool is your guide to the unknown local experiences and cultural gems in the country, all at an approachable cost.

PANAMA

371 Revel in hundreds of stars, both by day and by night

Prepare to be spellbound at first sight of Starfish Cay, one of Panama's famously pristine San Blas Islands (now called Guna Yala after the Indigenous Guna people), a popular place for calm sailing. Join your spouse in counting the rainbows of sea stars gleaming beneath crystal-clear water, then cozy up to take in the glittering night sky, sans light pollution.

371 Starfish Cay

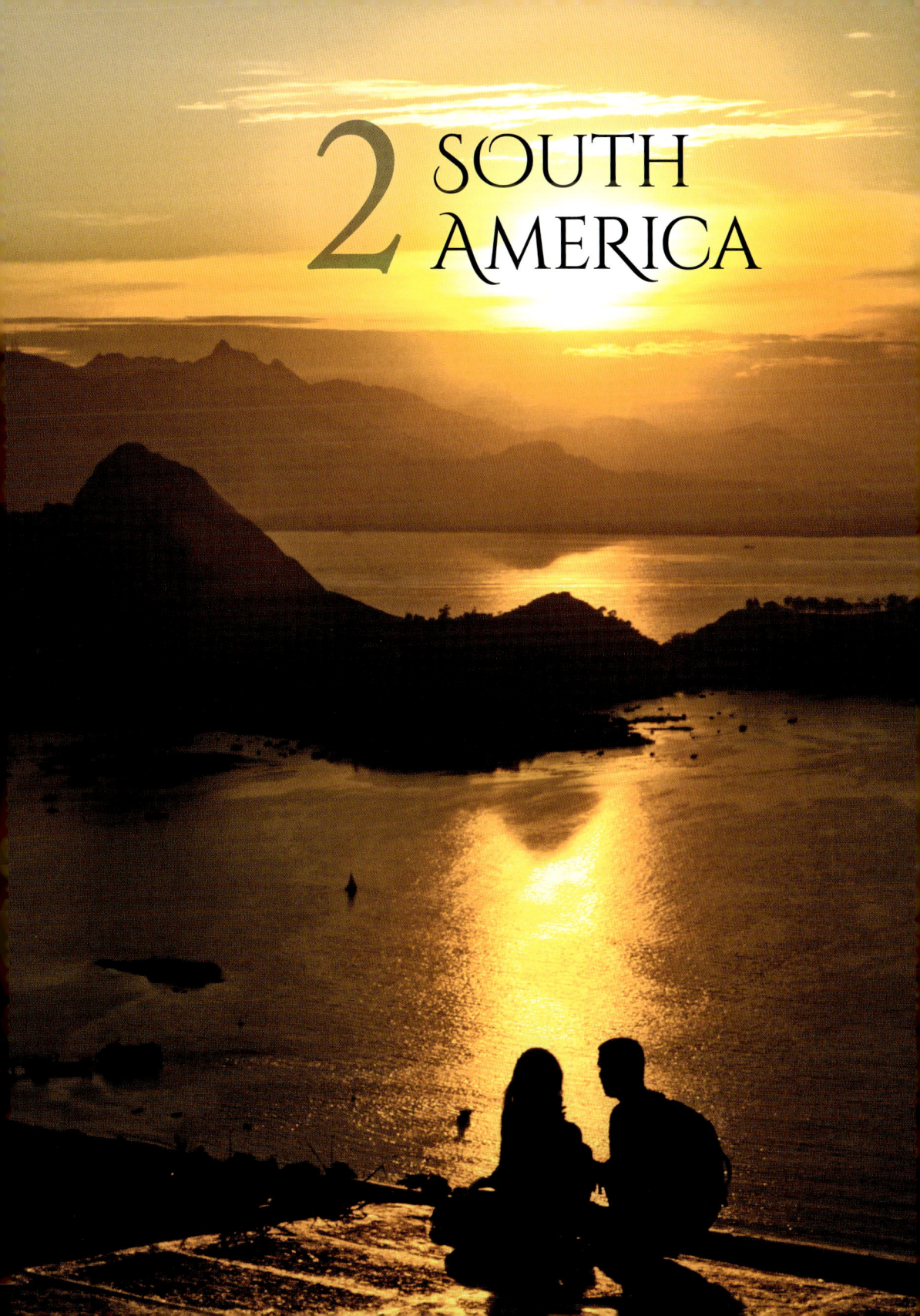

2 SOUTH AMERICA

SOUTH AMERICA • COLOMBIA

COLOMBIA

372 Feel like birds paragliding in Bogotá

You will feel as though you are in a dream, swirling around thermals while soaring like an Andean condor and spotting your partner doing the same during a paragliding exploit in the lush hills of Bogotá. You will each be flying with a guide as you glide weightlessly and peacefully over stunning topography.

COLOMBIA

373 Harvest java with your coffee lover

Couples who bonded over their coffee obsessions will find their dream date outside Bogotá, on a day trip to an intimate family coffee farm. Here, you can actually hand-pick then roast and grind your own beans. What could be more satisfying than toasting to your love using cups filled with the coffee you labored over together?

COLOMBIA

374 Charter a private boat in the Caribbean

Slip into bathing suits that ensure a comprehensive tan for a sultry private boat charter from Cartagena to the Islas del Rosario. Ask your captain to avoid other tourists and take the two of you straight to the most sublime coral reefs for snorkeling and scenic hideaways for sunbathing and diving into the jewel-toned Caribbean.

COLOMBIA

375 Take it slow in Bogotá, then make an emerald ring

Swoon over the beautifully maintained gardens, bursting with blooms, at the top of Monserrate—after a quick, steep funicular ride—before each tossing a coin into Pozo de los Deseos, or "well of wishes." After wandering Bogotá's highest point, focus your efforts on making a precious customized ring together with a brilliant gemstone from one of the region's lowest points, an emerald mine.

COLOMBIA

376 Make memories strolling through Old Town Cartagena

If the energy of Cartagena is stimulating, the vibe of Old Town is infectious. The walled city is full of vivid colonial architecture and plazas in which someone always seems to be playing music or dancing or both. Wind your way through cobblestoned streets, ducking into galleries, the gleaming Gold Museum, grabbing bites from street food vendors and, if you are lucky, encountering a traditional, extravagant *caminata* wedding parade.

375 Monserrate gardens

SOUTH AMERICA • COLOMBIA/SURINAME

COLOMBIA

377 Practice the art of dancing the sensual salsa

Learn how to move together as one during a private salsa lesson in Cartagena. Let all that flirty eye contact and physicality get you riled up for an evening out where a few cocktails should lead to trying your new skills in a hot and sweaty salsa club.

COLOMBIA

378 Board a floating boutique hotel for a river cruise

Be enchanted by Spanish colonial towns, remote Indigenous communities, rare wildlife, and thrumming jungles along Colombia's 1,000-mi. (1,600-km) Magdalena River. One of the most romantic ways to see them all is aboard the sumptuous thirty-room *AmaMagdalena* river cruise ship, replete with special dining experiences under the stars.

SURINAME

379 Find yourselves on an ultra-adventurous helicopter feat

Let your spirit of adventure take you to Suriname and, better yet, to travel into its wild, far-flung reaches. Hire a helicopter to fly you to the top of the granite Voltzberg Dome and pack a picnic to share amid awe-inspiring 360-degree views.

377 Salsa in Cartagena

381 Ecoventura snorkeling trip

SURINAME

380 Seek out a charming, multicultural capital city

Stay at one of the most prestigious locations in Paramaribo, the capital city of under-the-radar Suriname. This tropical riverside metropolis has a collection of wooden Dutch colonial buildings. Use the Royal Torarica hotel as your home base from which to explore the multicultural destination lined with charming canals, and make sure to request the romantic rose petal treatment upon booking.

ECUADOR

381 Get intimate with sea lions and penguins

Arrange a week of close subaquatic encounters with some of the most playful, mysterious, and adorable creatures on the planet. Penguins, sea lions, sea turtles, and harmless but thrilling sharks are all on the agenda during the frequent guided snorkeling trips offered as part of each cruise on Ecoventura's eco-conscious yachts. The underwater antics you will witness are legendary.

ECUADOR

382 Dedicate a week to wildlife conservation

Sign up to be conservation volunteers at a giant tortoise breeding center in the spectacularly biodiverse Galapagos. Activities include feeding the tortoises, carrying out daily head counts, and helping educate visitors to the center. Plus you gain exclusive access to the national park, which is teeming with additional exciting species, including the infamous Darwin's finches.

ECUADOR/PERU • SOUTH AMERICA

EXPLORE, UNWIND, RECONNECT

ECUADOR

383 Tread lightly at land-based eco-lodge Pikaia

Experience all the wild wonders of the Galapagos from the land-based eco-resort Pikaia Lodge. It sits in the midst of a giant tortoise reserve and practices sustainability in ways that might inspire you to take home a few tips. Pair guided explorations that stretch from white sand beaches to grassy expanses—where the ancient tortoises amble around—with exquisite Ecuadorean cuisine. Book a pool suite, where you will have your own cooling oasis in which to plunge when the days get hot or the stars beckon you outside after dark.

ECUADOR

384 Buddy-moon around the Galapagos Islands

Gather a group of your very favorite couples and plan a bucket list buddy-moon—or free-spirited elopement—aboard the 163-ft. (50-m) *Aqua Mare* superyacht. With seven immaculate cabins, it holds sixteen guests and even more crew, including two naturalist guides, ready to cater to your every whim. Think craft cocktails in the roomy jacuzzi, paddleboarding alongside each other, or scuba diving in the wondrous world below the surface.

PERU

385 Follow a kiss in Lima's Parque del Amor with a twelve-course meal

Linger over your own smooch at Lima's famously sensual *El Beso* (*The Kiss*) sculpture by Victor Delfin in the Parque del Amor, as in the "park of love." This landmark in Peru's capital will serve as an amuse bouche for the rest of your evening: a memorable twelve-course Nikkei Experience dinner at Maido, ranked among the World's 50 Best Restaurants and proffering Peruvian ingredients prepared using Japanese techniques.

SOUTH AMERICA • PERU

386 700'000 Heures Impact

PERU

386 Share an unlikely bed high up in a cloud forest

For one of those "is this real life?" types of experiences, look to 700'000 Heures Impact—a holistic regenerative travel operator—and their secluded forest estate in the Cordillera Escalera portion of the Amazon rainforest. During your wild yet ultracomfy stay, head out for a single-night sleepover in the great outdoors, with a twist. A short hike will take you to a candlelit dinner in the cloud forest, then you will share a bed in the most unlikely of places: an open-air observatory tower platform promising a most memorable sunrise.

PERU

387 Browse Peruvian art then experience bliss in Lima

Check in to Country Club Lima Hotel, a historic, 1927 museum-slash-hotel in the Peruvian capital that doubles as a wellness destination. First, get your fill of the venue's collection of majestic paintings, ornate furniture, and Incan artifacts donated by the Pedro de Osma Museum. After decadent treatments such as cocoa body wraps and two-and-a-half-hour couples rituals, the two of you will feel as regal as the portraits.

389 Lake Titicaca

PERU

388 Play bartenders at a cocktail master class

Put the cherry—or in this case, a few dots of Angostura bitters—on top of the perfect day surveying fascinating Cusco (the gateway to Machu Picchu) with a master class at glamorous Palacio del Inka's Rumi Bar. This hotel set in a five-hundred-year-old mansion is the definitive place to play mixologist alongside one of the best, who will teach you to make Peru's quintessential delicious frothy cocktail, the pisco sour.

PERU

389 Reside on the shores of Lake Titicaca

Take things slowly as you see the world's highest navigable lake, Lake Titicaca—12,500 ft. (3,800 m) above sea level—from the serenely romantic home base of Titilaka on its shores. The remote, eighteen-room hotel has everything needed to stay comfortable; think herbal coca tea and a private boat for cruising between the wondrous Uros floating islands. You can borrow a sailboat or kayak for your own explorations, too.

PERU

390 Have a stunning stay in the Sacred Valley

Book a cozy-chic suite at the Sacred Valley's Tambo del Inka resort and immerse yourselves in luxurious amenities—a picturesque swimming pool and a private train station for reaching Machu Picchu among them—as well as Indigenous experiences for two. There are salt mines to see, markets to wander, villages to visit, veggies to harvest from the property's garden, and a shamanic blessing ceremony to top it all off.

391 Machu Picchu

PERU • SOUTH AMERICA

PERU
391 Take a cushy train journey to the ancient Inca ruins of Machu Picchu

Step one to visiting the historic santuary of Machu Picchu, unless you plan to hike the legendary trail for days to reach the ancient citadel: reserve your tickets on the Hiram Bingham, A Belmond Train. Vintage glamour and cushy furnishings make it feel more like a hotel on tracks than any train you have ridden before. Savor culinary and cultural surprises on the super scenic expedition.

PERU
393 Cruise the Amazon in search of pink river dolphins

Step aboard an exclusive Delfin Amazon Cruises ship and traverse the lush Peruvian Amazon rainforest in search of rare pink dolphins leaping around you. There is even an opportunity for you to swim with the dolphins as one of the itinerary activities.

PERU
394 Immerse yourselves in the Amazon canopy

Perched 110 ft. (33.5 m) above the forest floor, Alta Sanctuary's open-walled eco tree house places you at the heart of the jungle canopy. At sunrise, mist drifts through the trees as birds, monkeys, and other wildlife come alive with sound and motion—nature's wake-up call like no other.

PERU
392 Gaze in awe at the dazzling Rainbow Mountain

Peru's Vinicunca, aka *montaña de siete colores*, aka Rainbow Mountain, is one of those things you have to see in person to truly believe. At one time obscured by glacial caps, the layered mineral deposits that create the vivid colors are the work of literally millions of years of tectonic movement and erosion. The mountain is two hours by car from Cusco, and requires a several mile hike, meaning you will very much have earned the rainbow at the end of your journey.

392 Rainbow Mountain

SOUTH AMERICA • PERU/CHILE

PERU
395 Discover the shared wonder of bird-watching

Find out just how intriguing birds can be when you experience them from the most epic environs, at the singular Puqio tented camp in the Colca Canyon. In the high desert destination you will find the space for shared silence as well as birdsong, not to mention incredible flight, thanks to it being a hot spot for splendid Andean condors with their 10-ft. (3-m) wingspans, plus hummingbirds, flamingos, and other wildlife.

CHILE
396 Walk together atop the earthly equivalent of Mars

For lovers of astronomy, there is no more romantic place on the planet to take in the spectacle of space than the Atacama Desert. It is such a unique landscape that it more closely resembles Mars than most other earthly destinations. Feel transported as you enjoy a guided stargazing session under midnight skies at this astronomical research hub. Make wishes on every shooting star you see.

CHILE
397 Become intoxicated with a stay at an exquisite winery hotel

The Viña Vik retreat, Chile's most mesmerizing winery-cum–boutique hotel, sits tucked into the Cachapoal Valley with the Andes mountains beyond. With a futuristic edge to the architecture, there is nowhere else quite like it. Choose between a bungalow with glass walls or a themed suite and enjoy tasting and drinking everything on offer, taking in the artwork, and relaxing in the wine spa.

CHILE
398 Strip down for wild swimming in the Andean foothills

Get back to nature by delving into the virginal landscape of the Andean foothills, specifically the 27,000-acre (66,700-ha) Huerquehue National Park, where crystalline lakes and lagoons are abundant but humans are not. Wildly beautiful hikes weave through the protected mountainous environment where active couples can guide themselves into corners of exceptional beauty to be splashed by gushing waterfalls and go skinny-dipping together in the fresh, clean waters.

CHILE
399 Live it up at Patagonia's coolest luxury lodge

Balance explorations in one of the world's most stupendous landscapes with outstanding food and intimate spa time at Tierra Patagonia, a forty-room design hotel where you will constantly feel awestruck. You will not need to leave your suite, bathtub, or even cozy bathrobes to take in the iconic Torres del Paine panorama. For when you do, book a bespoke tour followed by a pampering body ritual drawing on local traditions.

396 *Stargazing in the Atacama Desert*

SOUTH AMERICA • CHILE

CHILE

400 Prove your love for our planet

Pour your combined love into rebuilding UNESCO Biosphere Reserve trails during a voluntourism stay in Torres del Paine National Park, a popular destination for hiking fanatics thanks to its sublime setting. Several organizations allow volunteers to help repair eroded and damaged trails. During this once-in-a-lifetime trip, take time to discover more about the region's culture and its ongoing program of conservation.

CHILE

401 Make a photojournal at Torres del Paine

Book a guided vehicle tour of Torres del Paine National Park—a journey that promises to deliver a greatest hits of the most postcard-worthy peaks and glaciers of Patagonia. You will see the most famous sights, such as turquoise Nordenskjöld Lake, winding Paine River, the Grey Glacier, and the granite spires of the Torres del Paine themselves. Take selfies at viewpoints with stunning views for a photojournal you'll make back at home

CHILE

402 Book into Earth's southernmost hotel

Experience the extreme adventure of staying in the southernmost hotel on Earth, in the southernmost town in the world, in fact. The property by Silversea—whose ice-class ships are an opulent way to see the White Continent—is in Puerto Williams, the Chilean gateway to Antarctica. Sailing, horse riding, hiking, and ziplining are all options for those with an ambition to get closer to the end of the world.

401 Torres del Paine National Park

CHILE/BRAZIL • SOUTH AMERICA

405 Christ the Redeemer at sunrise

CHILE

403 Revel in seductive isolation on Easter Island

An especially isolated Chilean territory, Easter Island (Rapa Nui), sits in the southeastern Pacific Ocean. Besides sandy beaches and its uncrowdedness, the draw here is the collection of enormous, scattered Moai statues created during the height of the Rapa Nui civilization, roughly 1250 to 1500. Hire a guide to fully appreciate these remarkable volcanic stone monoliths representing ancient humans, some of which reach 60 ft. (18 m) in height.

BRAZIL

404 Dress up for the annual Copa Ball

If dressing up in costume and role-playing different personae is your thing, book a pair of Golden Room tickets and start devising the best couples ensembles for the annual Copa Ball at Copacabana Palace, A Belmond Hotel. The extraordinary party you are signing up for is the most exclusive highlight of Carnival, Brazil's most notorious February festival full of almost endless dancing, samba music, and decadent food and drink.

BRAZIL

405 Enjoy sunrise with Christ the Redeemer

You do not need to be Christian to have a spiritual experience at the nearly century-old art deco statue Christ the Redeemer, which sits on the peak of Corcovado mountain with stupendous panoramas of Rio de Janeiro. The modernist Fairmont Rio de Janeiro Copacabana hotel—in the celebrated beach district—offers guests an exclusive sunrise breakfast experience likely to create an indelible memory.

406 Lençóis Maranhenses National Park

BRAZIL

406 Take sexy, sunny swims in a freshwater lagoon

Discover what may very well be Brazil's most breathtaking landscapes in Lençóis Maranhenses National Park, on the coast in the country's northeast. The park is a vast network of undulating sand dunes, between which—especially from May to September—lie gem-colored freshwater lagoons. But do not expect to experience this natural wonder passively. Pack plenty of swimwear for days spent traversing the stark white sand and swimming in the sexy, serene, sapphire water.

BRAZIL • SOUTH AMERICA

BRAZIL

407 Taste obscure flavors of the Amazon in São Paulo

Take a trek through the untamed Amazon rainforest without leaving your chandelier-lit seats during a divine dinner at São Paulo's Michelin-decorated restaurant D.O.M. Acclaimed chef Alex Atala scours the jungle for small producers to provide virtually unknown ingredients that he whips into surprising, elegant delights. Keep open minds (there may be ants!) as you discover flavors most people will never know.

BRAZIL

408 Feel the rush of the world's largest waterfall system

Book a lovers' getaway at the majestic pink-walled Hotel das Cataratas, A Belmond Hotel, Iguazu Falls, and find yourselves with unlimited access to the largest waterfall system on the planet. The 1950s-style hacienda resort is a plush home away from home for a honeymoon sparkling with caipirinha cocktails and rainforest barbecues. But most thrilling is the opportunity to witness the falls intimately at dawn from a helicopter or boat.

BRAZIL

409 Book Brazil's most romantic hotel, Ponta dos Ganchos

Impeccable environs are just one reason to while away the days in southern Brazil's Emerald Coast, specifically at Ponta dos Ganchos, widely known as the country's most romantic and exclusive resort. Watch the very concept of time disappear as you unwind in your own villa with a private pool, sauna, and whirlpool, and select your outings carefully. Snorkel, practice yoga, and spa by day and dine marvelously by night.

408 Iguazu Falls

SOUTH AMERICA • BRAZIL/BOLIVIA/URUGUAY

BRAZIL

410 Seek wildlife on a nocturnal safari

By vehicle or on foot, venture into the vast Pantanal—over 42 million acres (17 million ha) of tropical wetland—for a nighttime safari. As darkness falls, jaguars, pygmy caimans, and elusive maned wolves are more likely to emerge, their movements revealed with the help of expert guides. Meanwhile, the chorus of frogs, insects, and night birds will make the experience all the more electrifying.

BOLIVIA

411 Stage a couples photo shoot at Uyuni

Ethereal and unbelievable, the world's largest salt flat, Salar de Uyuni, in Bolivia's southwest, is a sight to behold. White clouds and brilliant blue skies reflect on a seemingly infinite stretch of flat, smooth Earth, creating a surreal setting for the most striking of photos. Hire your own photographer in advance—some even specialize in capturing Uyuni proposals—to ensure you get the perfect shot worth framing back home.

BOLIVIA

412 Dine out to drive social change

Reserve ahead for a meal at Gustu, the pioneering restaurant that put Bolivia on the map for those who gladly travel to experience culinary greatness. Awarded the best restaurant in Bolivia, Gustu was conceived by the cofounder of foodie mecca Noma and consistently serves up compelling cuisine at an approachable price. It is also fiercely committed to driving social change.

URUGUAY

413 Spend the night in a tiny, tucked-away wine lodge

In the land of Criollo horses and Tannat vines, Narbona Wine Lodge blends history and rustic luxury on 120 acres (50 ha) of sun-kissed land. Founded in 1909, this working winery boutique hotel offers vineyard views, grape-themed rooms, and lore aplenty. Enjoy farm-fresh meals by candlelight and bottle your own vintage to mark the moment. Every detail—right down to the refurbished cellars—radiates a deep sense of place in Uruguay's wine country.

414 Casapueblo

URUGUAY

414 Get lost in the captivating world of Casapueblo

Ready your cameras to capture keepsake shots of one another amid the fantastic art and architecture of Casapueblo—a seaside museum and hotel perched on Uruguay's Punta Ballena. Created by artist Carlos Páez Vilaró, this whitewashed wonder is part Gaudí, part Santorini, and entirely unique. Wander through its corridors and stay for sunset, when the building glows golden. Whether you are here for the art or the atmosphere, Casapueblo is pure magic on the Uruguayan coast.

URUGUAY

415 Slip into the laid-back groove of a celebrated beach town

Just 12 mi. (19 km) northeast of Punta del Este lies José Ignacio—once a sleepy fishing village, now a haven for surfers and in-the-know travelers. For couples, Bahia Vik tops the list. Tucked among sandy dunes, its stretch of boho-luxe bungalows invites lazy beach days and romantic nights that entail falling asleep to the sound of lapping waves just beyond your window.

URUGUAY

416 Taste your way through award-winning wines and wood-fired fare

Take a pilgrimage to the minuscule town of Garzón for a foodie overnight at Restaurante Garzón, a sanctuary designed for slow living. Enjoy a leisurely lunch fueled by full-bodied reds and chef Francis Mallmann's culinary alchemy before taking a stroll through the vines.

ARGENTINA

417 Befriend the adorable locals of Patagonia Azul

Take a conservation-minded expedition to Patagonia Azul with Journeys With Purpose. Expect sweeping coastal views and the heart-melting experience of being outnumbered by thousands of waddling, chattering Magellanic penguins—the largest colony on Earth. It's a trip that combines the romance of wild beauty, shared wonder, and pure delight in one of Argentina's remotest corners.

417 Patagonia Azul

419 Tango lesson

ARGENTINA

418 Strap on your snow boots for a glacier trek

Discover the beauty of Patagonia with an unforgettable glacier trek in El Calafate. Walk across the shimmering surface of Perito Moreno, one of the world's most iconic and active glaciers. This once-in-a-lifetime adventure offers couples, surrounded by towering ice walls and breathing in crisp alpine air, a chance to connect in nature's grandeur, in one of Argentina's most awe-inspiring regions.

ARGENTINA

419 Tango the night away in Buenos Aires

Learn the passion and elegance of tango in Buenos Aires, the birthplace of the world's most seductive dance. Take a class together to master the intimate steps, or simply sit back and be captivated by a mesmerizing performance of the sultry Rojo Tango at the Faena Hotel. With every embrace and smoldering glance, it is impossible not to feel the magnetic pull of this sensual, time-honored art form.

ARGENTINA

420 Sail into the sunset on the Rio de la Plata

Set sail on a private sunset cruise through the hypnotizing Rio de la Plata delta. As golden light dances on the open water, indulge in a feast of Argentine meats grilled onboard just for you—a must-try *parrilla* experience for two. This is an intimate escape that blends rich local flavor with the magic of a moment shared at sea.

SOUTH AMERICA • ARGENTINA/ANTARCTICA

ARGENTINA

421 Trot through the vines in true gaucho style

Argentine vineyards are best explored on horseback, with real-life gauchos leading the way. Think sweeping landscapes, rich Malbec aromas in the air, and the rhythmic clip-clop of hooves through the vines with the Andes rising in the distance. Whether you are seasoned riders or newbies, this is peak South American fantasy unlocked, especially when you stop for fresh empanadas along the way.

ARGENTINA

422 Indulge in a couples wine-therapy treatment

Treat yourselves to the ultimate couples escape at the Vines Resort and Spa, where vino-therapy meets vineyard views. Unwind with steamy saunas and indulgent spa treatments made from the same grape varieties you will be sipping later. The resort's subterranean spa connects you to the earth—literally—while private spots for yoga, massage, and meditation elevate the zen.

ARGENTINA

423 Meet Argentina's first female winemaker

Start your stay the right way—with a glass of wine and a mini massage—at SB Winemaker's House & Spa Suites, the chic boutique hotel owned by Argentina's first female winemaker. From there, dive into a curated wine experience designed to pamper your palate. With exclusive tastings and vineyard strolls, this is wine country done right.

ARGENTINA

424 Live in the moment in South America's second-largest forest

Explore the Gran Chaco forest on an off-grid, river-based safari and glamping journey through El Impenetrable National Park. Navigate remote waterways by boat on the lookout for wildlife such as jaguars, capybaras, and tapirs, then return to a comfortable, solar-powered tent for evenings under a star-filled sky. Experience the natural beauty of a region that is largely untouched by mass tourism.

ANTARCTICA

425 Dare your partner to do a hand-in-hand polar plunge

Test your mettle alongside your spouse and find out who is more courageous when you pose an ice-cold dare: plunge into the Southern Ocean holding hands. Fulfill the challenge from a Zodiac or a small ship, ensuring you have the proper equipment around to climb out quickly, because the water temperature is significantly more frigid than a typical ice bath.

ANTARCTICA

426 Paddle a tandem kayak past ice caps and seals

Suit up in waterproof gloves, dry suits, and flotation gear for an unforgettable adventure through one of the planet's most surreal environments. In an inflatable tandem kayak, you will glide silently across icy waters flanked by towering glaciers and sculpted icebergs. You might hear the crack of calving ice as you paddle past ice caps, beside seals, and possibly get close to penguins and whales, too.

ANTARCTICA • SOUTH AMERICA

ANTARCTICA

427 See Antarctica through the eyes of polar scientists

Adventure in an all-new way when taking Antarctica by land. Fly in from Cape Town on a cargo plane with Ultima's polar scientists and researchers and embark on jaw-dropping explorations of ice caves after landing on an ice sheet. You will hike iconic mountains, pop in to visit emperor penguin colonies, and go to the South Pole, a place few other humans ever see.

ANTARCTICA

428 Check off your seventh continent on a small ship

Hop aboard one of National Geographic-Lindblad Expeditions' small ships and cruise through Drake Passage for a rugged yet romantic bucket list check of the seventh continent. Take the thrilling voyage with your lover to assure you are not dreaming as you two navigate around blue icebergs, stand on beaches crowded with penguins, and witness whales breaching right before your eyes.

428 National Geographic-Lindblad Expeditions

ICELAND

429 Be wooed by nature's iconic light show from inside a bubble

Experience the wonder of Iceland's northern skies from the comfort of your own transparent bubble at the 5 Million Star Hotel. Nestled in the deeply peaceful countryside near Reykholt, and with minimal light pollution, this unique resort offers a front-row seat to one of nature's most dazzling displays—the aurora borealis. From your bed inside a fully transparent dome, take in 270-degree views of the night sky as ribbons of green, purple, and pink dance across the darkness.

ICELAND

430 Steam up your relationship in an oceanside geothermal lagoon

Pursue bliss alongside your lover in the surreal setting of a 230-ft. (70-m) geothermal lagoon whose infinity edge disappears into the North Atlantic beyond. Just outside Reykjavik, Sky Lagoon's wellness bent makes it a destination to seek balance and warmth, but also protection, best achieved through a lovely sensorial seven-step ritual called Skjól. Don't be saints, however: kiss under the northern lights or enjoy the hot water with Icelandic cocktails at the swim-up, cave-side bar.

430 Sky Lagoon

ICELAND

431 Capture the wonder of blue ice caves

Step into the surreal, cobalt-blue ice caves of southeast Iceland's Vatnajökull glacier. These otherworldly formations—sculpted by centuries of glacial movement and meltwater—glow with an ethereal blue light, creating shimmering tunnels, intricate arches, and crystalline walls that feel almost unreal. Capture the striking patterns and intense hues with photos.

ICELAND

432 Scuba dive between two major tectonic plates

Share in the wonder of a stunning scuba expedition in crystalline glacial meltwater at an important geological site: the Silfra Fissure. This is where the North American and Eurasian tectonic plates meet, but also drift apart. It is possible to explore the fissure with remarkable visibility thanks to the water's natural filtration through underground lava.

ICELAND

433 Go heli-skiing on the Trollaskagi Peninsula

Book a private sea-to-summit heli-skiing experience on Iceland's Trollaskagi Peninsula. The terrain will be tailored to your ability levels, so let loose and fly down the pristine contours. Depending on the time of year, combine your trip to coincide with the northern lights (March to mid-April) or the midnight sun (June) to tick off another bucket list dream.

EUROPE • FAROE ISLANDS

FAROE ISLANDS

434 Tune in for a stimulating drive through a subsea tunnel of Viking art

Rent a car in the untamed Faroe Islands archipelago and tune your radio to the soundtrack created especially for the coolest cruise you could take, through a 6-mi. (10-km) subsea tunnel filled with Viking art. The multisensory journey happens in the Sandoy Tunnel, with nearly 500 ft. (150 m) of water above you, which makes driving through the site-specific art installation a real rush.

FAROE ISLANDS

435 Do go chasing waterfalls—there are plenty of them in the Faroes

Become a pair of waterfall-chasers in an archipelago where the gushing geographic feature is super-abundant. Lush, green, dramatic, and known as the Land of 10,000 Waterfalls, the Faroes are home to so many there is no official count. They aren't for swimming, but for gazing. Enjoy seeking them out with your spouse, knowing that there is always a more beautiful one around the next rugged bend.

435 Saksun, Streymoy, Faroe Islands

NORWAY

436 Kayak and hike in the fjord around an art nouveau nucleus

From the art nouveau hotspot Ålesund, head out into the fjord on a sea kayak for two, where you will make for the island of Hessa, to hike the rugged Sukkertoppen (Sugar Top). This private tour is not for the faint of heart: You will paddle aside large vessels en route to the island for the rocky climb. But the 360-degree panoramas from the summit are well worth the effort.

NORWAY

437 Leap into a chilly swim before an Oslo signature floating sauna

Brave the icy waters of the Oslofjord, where temperatures range from 37–64°F (3–18°C) depending on the season. Then warm up in one of Oslo's famous floating saunas—a local favorite and a unique way to experience contrast therapy. The combination of cold plunge and steamy heat is both energizing and unforgettable, with epic views of the fjord all around.

437 A floating sauna

440 Midnight sun

NORWAY

438 Dine in a place you'll never forget: a floating underwater restaurant in a fjord

Few meals could be considered expedition worthy, but especially for seafood and art aficionados, Iris at Salmon Eye is just that. Newlyweds or intrepid couples can go on seaplane or boat to the floating art installation for an underwater, eighteen-course feast that features foraged, sustainable, and local ingredients spun together exquisitely. For a complete complementarily offbeat itinerary, hire B Corp–certified Up Norway.

NORWAY

439 Cruise past glaciers while immersed in a steaming hot tub

Don swimsuits, which might seem counterintuitive to staying warm in a shivering arctic climate, and immerse yourselves in the generous open-air hot tub atop Hurtigruten's cruise ship. Your most scenic jacuzzi experience ever will likely include towering glaciers, ancient fjords, and snow-crested mountains, and potentially even northern lights dancing across the night sky.

NORWAY

440 Discover the splendor of the midnight sun

Take your pick, dark or light, and head to a country with some of the fiercest extremes. Choose Norway's winter and experience long, quiet nights that offer a rare chance to really slow down, rest, and reset, with cozy cafés and candlelit dinners. Go in the summer and you will be awestruck by the midnight sun and sunsets turning skies pink just before 12 A.M., keeping you energized well into the night.

NORWAY

441 Get cuddly with adorable retired sled dogs while warming up at Café Huskies

Café Huskies is notable not only for being in the northernmost town on Earth (Longyearbyen), but for the cute retired sled dogs who roam freely inside. Intimate, inviting, and vegan-friendly, it is a place that canine-loving couples should visit daily while in town.

438 Salmon Eye

EUROPE • SWEDEN/FINLAND

SWEDEN

442 Keep each other warm in an arctic igloo

Book a stay in the Ice Room at Sweden's one-of-a-kind Icehotel, where everything—from the bedframe to the decor—is crafted from solid blocks of ice. Don't worry, the mattress is thick and covered with sumptuous reindeer hides to help keep the chill at bay. With indoor temperatures hovering around 23°F (–5°C), it's all about bundling up, relaxing, and enjoying a truly unforgettable arctic sleep.

SWEDEN

443 Overnight with your favorite person in a surreal tree house

At Treehotel, near the Arctic Circle in Swedish Lapland, the architecture is the experience. Feel the emerald embrace of the forest canopy during an immersive sojourn in one of the resort's ingenious, one-of-a-kind tree houses. Among the wondrous accommodations are the Bjarke Ingels Group–designed Biosphere clad in 350 birdhouses, Inredningsgruppen's aptly named UFO, and the iconic two-person Mirrorcube by Bolle Tham, and Martin Videgård, with a secret balcony and illusions aplenty. Once you have chosen the ideal tree house for you, make your reservation well in advance to avoid disappointment.

SWEDEN

444 Set sail amid 1,000s of isles in the Baltic Sea

Venture into the Stockholm Archipelago on your very own bright white sailboat, complete with a local captain to weave you slowly through some of its 30,000 islands during a customized six-hour cruise. You'll have a traditional Swedish *fika* coffee and pastry break along the way, plus a fresh, satisfying lunch, and stop wherever you wish to swim or fish.

SWEDEN

445 Explore Stockholm, then soak in a forest pond

Sightsee through photogenic Stockholm's many parks, museums, palaces, and islands by day, then recover after dark in an atmospheric subterranean brick vault with a rich history. The coed sauna and dimly lit Swedish forest pond beneath Hôtel Reisen on Old Town's waterfront are sultry, serene, and full of connection to a storied past—look for the handprint a female builder from the 1690s left behind.

FINLAND

446 Shop for a picnic of Finnish specialties

Get a sense of Helsinki's charm from a morning stroll browsing the city's Market Square. Pick up handcrafted souvenirs to bring home but also some specialties such as reindeer sausage and a couple of trademark *munkki* deep-fried, sugar-coated doughnuts to pack for a blissful picnic. Hop on the ferry to Suomenlinna, a UNESCO World Heritage sea fortress, and find the perfect site to share your feast.

FINLAND

447 Find joy in the world's happiest country

In the world's long-running happiest country, warm your hearts while immersing in Finnish sauna culture at the picturesque seaside sauna Löyly Helsinki. The experience is not just about heating your physical bodies, but about connection and reflection, making it a wonderful thing to do with the person to whom you are closest.

FINLAND • EUROPE

448 Reindeer sleigh ride

FINLAND
448 Cozy up for your own reindeer sleigh ride

Learn all about why reindeer deserve respect, with a private lesson in reindeer husbandry at the farm Tatuka in Finnish Lapland. Then take your pick of two options for a wintry outing: a 1¼ mi. (2 km) sleigh ride in the snow or a 4 mi. (7 km) reindeer safari, during which you will stop for grilled sausages and crepes beside a roaring campfire.

449 Kakslauttanen Arctic Resort

FINLAND

449 Check in for a classic Nordic adventure

For adventuresome couples on the hunt for midnight sun, northern lights, reindeer safaris, and skies with endless stars, there is no better option than Kakslauttanen Arctic Resort. On the fringes of Urho Kekkonen National Park, it's all possible from your incredible dome-shaped glass igloo and in the pristine forest beyond.

452 Alchemist, Copenhagen

DENMARK

450 Hunt for clues and enjoy views atop Copenhagen's greenest hill

Trade a typical date for something unexpected on CopenHill—the capital's energy plant turned urban escape. At the Rooftop bar, buy a map for a playful treasure hunt, uncovering clues about the resort. Along the way, soak up panoramic city views and pick up the pancakes/ice creams/hot chocolate included in the map price, depending on the season.

DENMARK

451 Enter the inner sanctum of global sensation Noma

Sign up for a Black Tomato trip featuring an escapade that is rare and sought after for foodies, a place where few non-chefs have gone before. The highly connected travel operators can get you both behind the scenes to see the innermost workings of the global restaurant sensation Noma in Copenhagen—brag-worthy for sure.

DENMARK

452 Provoke your taste buds on the culinary journey of a lifetime

In Copenhagen, skip lunch before taking a fifty-course, flawlessly choreographed gastronomic trip set in multiple spaces including a planetarium-inspired dome and a play area. At the two Michelin-starred and green-starred Alchemist, all you can expect is to be surprised.

DENMARK

453 Play the ancient game of polo beside an impressive castle

Put yourselves out there trying a sport likely neither of you have ever attempted: polo. The royal, ancient sport is best played out during a private lesson for two at Kokkedal Slot Copenhagen, beside an impressive eighteenth-century castle in North Zealand. There's golf, too.

SCOTLAND

454 Pair a scent butler experience with afternoon tea

Slip into the plush Scone & Crombie Suite at the Balmoral, Edinburgh, and craft a custom fragrance together during a private master class with the hotel's Scent Butler. Afterward, indulge in a modern afternoon tea beneath Palm Court's shimmering glass dome—complete with harp music, palm fronds, and champagne.

SCOTLAND

455 Brew love by the pint in Edinburgh

Cocreate a craft beer inspired by your relationship at Stewart Brewing's Craft Beer Kitchen, where pros guide you and your partner through the whole process. Choose your hops, design a label, bottle the beer when ready, and raise a celebratory toast. Maybe your love is like a rich, complex ale—deepening with time—or a bold IPA, intense, hoppy, and impossible to ignore.

SCOTLAND

456 Test your love on the West Highland Way

This nearly 100-mi. (160-km) trek winds through some of Scotland's most spellbinding landscapes, from misty glens to rugged moors. Along the way, indulge in well-earned luxury at five-star mansions and grand country houses, where crackling fires, gourmet meals, and plush beds offer romantic respite. Standouts like Inverlochy Castle Hotel, Cameron House, and Loch Lomond Luxury Lodges bring a deep sense of place—raw, remote, and undeniably romantic.

SCOTLAND

457 Pay it forward with a purposeful week in the Scottish Highlands

Join conservation charity Trees for Life to help restore the ancient Caledonian Forest—an unforgettable experience of giving back, together. Among other activities, you will plant saplings, spot red squirrels and golden eagles, and end each day in a cozy off-grid lodge or eco-bothy. It is a rewarding escape for couples who want to leave a lasting mark on one of Scotland's wildest, most beautiful corners.

SCOTLAND

458 Call a thirteenth-century Scottish castle home for the night

For a royal-worthy Highland escape, stay in the beautifully refurbished holiday cottage overlooking one of Scotland's medieval masterpieces: Eilean Donan Castle. Perched on its own headland where three sea lochs meet, this luxury romantic hideaway offers uninterrupted views from nearly every window. It is ideal for a cozy retreat—or even a wedding weekend base.

SCOTLAND

459 Head to Fayre Play for a competitive night of fairground fun

Relive the joy of your youth—minus the curfews—on a playful date night at Fayre Play. This grown-up playground pairs delicious bevvies and street food from Scran Daddy with a lively lineup of classic fairground and arcade games. From flirty rounds of ring toss to quirky prizes and neon-lit vibes, it mixes fun, nostalgia, and just the right dose of friendly competition.

458 Overlooking Eilean Donan Castle

SCOTLAND

460 Kick off the evening with a gin master class

Start a night out in Glasgow with a buzz at a cheeky Ginnoisseurs master class, where you will sip your way through Scotland's finest botanicals. Then feast on classics like beer-battered fish and chips at the Corinthian Club, before ending the evening with live tunes and a nightcap at Charlie Parkers.

SCOTLAND

461 Ride first-class on the Jacobite steam train

Settle into vintage carriages for a slow, spectacular journey through Scotland's most cinematic landscapes. Glide past shimmering lochs, pitted peaks, and ancient castles before crossing the iconic Glenfinnan Viaduct—made famous by the Harry Potter movies. There are sweeping views and old-world charm at every turn.

SCOTLAND

462 Enlist the help of a bird to pop the question

Looking for an unforgettable way to propose? Enlist one of Scotland's wisest allies—a white owl. At eight-hundred-year-old Dalhousie Castle, you can arrange for this majestic bird to swoop in and deliver the ring at just the right moment, making for a surprise with fairy-tale flair. Set against the estate's historic backdrop, this is a magical way to begin your next chapter.

461 Glenfinnan Viaduct

ENGLAND

463 Seduce each other in a flirty pole-dancing class

There is nothing like a sultry pole-dancing class to turn up the heat. Explore a new side of your sensuality together at London's Exotique Dance School, an LGBTQIA+-inclusive space that celebrates confidence, connection, and movement. Whether you are total beginners or looking to make it a regular thing—in or out of the bedroom—this is a playful way to bond and maybe even surprise yourselves.

ENGLAND

464 Join a supper club on a 1960s Tube

For couples chasing memory-making date nights, few settings rival the retro charm of a 1960s Victoria Line carriage turned underground dining space. At supperclub.tube, you board a 1960s Victoria Line train for a six-course tasting journey through Latin America—think ceviche, smoky grilled meats, and churros. Candlelit tables add to subterranean allure for an unexpected and undeniably romantic experience.

ENGLAND

465 Sign up for a couples pottery class

Tap into your creative side during a hands-on pottery class at Skandihus, one of London's coolest ceramic studios. Together, you will shape and glaze custom creations—perfect keepsakes to bring home. It is a messy, memorable, and delightfully tactile way to connect and create something lasting.

ENGLAND

466 Swan about in London's highest swimming pool

Start your day with a swim in Shangri-La, the Shard's infinity pool, perched fifty-two floors up, then retreat to your luxurious suite with a bird's-eye view of the City. For the ultimate indulgence, book the Eat, Play, Love package, where you can pick your pleasure: private dinner, relaxing spa treatment, or toast with champagne and strawberries.

ENGLAND

467 Play zookeeper for the day at London Zoo

Take your shared love of animals for a behind-the-scenes zookeeper experience at London Zoo. Care for exotic rainforest creatures, meal prep for meerkats, and get an up-close look at Penguin Beach. Whether you are shadowing real keepers or bonding over animal antics, this immersive adventure is a must for couples who adore wildlife.

ENGLAND

468 Say "I do" under the glass roof of a secret garden

The Barbican Conservatory is one of London's hidden gems—think lush greenery, cascading water features, and a soaring glass roof that floods the space with natural light. With its tranquil ambience and breathtaking design, this tropical haven sets the scene for a swoon-worthy proposal, a stylish wedding, or a dreamy stroll through its living walls.

FOODIE PARADISE

ENGLAND

469 Feast your way through the food stalls at Borough Market

London's Borough Market is a paradise for food lovers, where the scent of sizzling sausage baps mingles with fresh-baked bread and gooey raclette. Graze your way through tempting street eats as you wander from stall to stall, chatting with local vendors and discovering small-batch treasures along the way. Between live cooking demos and gourmet surprises, it is easy to lose track of time in this culinary haven.

ENGLAND • **EUROPE**

EUROPE • ENGLAND

ENGLAND • EUROPE

ENGLAND

470 Get a bubbly buzz with the London Eye's VIP champagne experience

Everything is better with bubbles—especially when paired with panoramic views of London's skyline. Skip the lines and step into your private capsule for the VIP experience, complete with fast-track entry and chilled flutes of Moët & Chandon. Take in iconic landmarks such as Big Ben and Buckingham Palace as you toast to your love-filled relationship high above the city.

ENGLAND

471 Re-create *Shakespeare in Love* at the Globe Theatre

For star-crossed lovers and theater romantics, few places enchant quite like Shakespeare's Globe in London. Step into the world of the seventeenth-century Bard with a premium guided tour that lets you tread the legendary stage and uncover the secrets of the iconic open-air playhouse. Then, linger a little longer over a candlelit three-course dinner at Swan, the on-site restaurant with picturesque views of the Thames.

ENGLAND

472 Have botanical Kew Gardens all to yourselves after hours

Discover a dreamier side of London at Kew Gardens' exclusive evening events, such as Orchids After Hours, where you can sip cocktails and drift through glowing greenhouses and tropical blooms. With the crowds gone and moonlight setting the scene, this rare opportunity to explore Kew by night is nothing short of romantic.

ENGLAND

473 Float like royalty with a Thames River picnic cruise

For centuries, monarchs—including the late Queen Elizabeth II—used the Thames as their royal highway, traveling among palaces like Windsor, Westminster, and Hampton Court. Today, mere mortals can enjoy a more leisurely version of that historic route: a scenic river cruise complete with a picnic lunch and a bottle of wine. If you want to channel Her Majesty in style, swap the wine for her favorite tipple—a classic Dubonnet and gin.

470 The London Eye

EUROPE • ENGLAND

ENGLAND

474 Take your movie night to the max with a Secret Cinema date

Forget the usual popcorn-and-candy routine—London's Secret Cinema transforms movie night into a full-blown adventure, complete with costumes, props, and live performances that make you feel like part of the story. With themed bites and cinematic twists around every corner, this is part screening, part immersive theater, and 100 percent unforgettable for film-loving couples who want to take part in the magic of the movies.

ENGLAND

475 Sleep beneath the stars in Hotel 41's Conservatory Suite

This starry suite has all the bells and whistles for a loved-up stay in the UK capital, including a split-level penthouse floor plan, marble jacuzzi bath, fireplace, and wood-carved bed positioned beneath a glass roof, primed for stargazing. Lounge upstairs by the fire, then retreat to your Savoir king bed, where the night sky sparkles overhead. Want total privacy? Just close the blinds and disappear together from the world above.

ENGLAND

476 Think pink at Sketch's afternoon tea for two

Sketch is easily one of the most photographed spots in London. Its blush-pink velvet Gallery is pure eye candy, making it the ultimate setting for a whimsical afternoon tea that is as stylish as it is delicious. Sip champagne, nibble on dainty pastries, and soak in the art-filled surroundings.

ENGLAND

477 Enjoy a serenade in your hotel suite

When staying in sounds better than going out, let the Royal Philharmonic Orchestra come to you. Book a luxurious suite at London's Milestone Hotel and enjoy a private in-room performance by a solo harpist or string trio playing your favorite songs. For a truly epic night, add candlelight, champagne, and a portrait session with resident artist Shelley Levy.

ENGLAND • EUROPE

479 Greenwich Royal Observatory Planetarium

ENGLAND

478 Attend a (clothed) Sex Club Retreat

Step into the cheekily named Sex Club Retreat, a London-loved workshop focused on intimacy without the pressure. Led by inclusive, kink-aware counselors, you will be guided through creative, nonsexual touch and connection exercises designed to spark curiosity, reignite attraction, and deepen your bond.

ENGLAND

479 Plan a private planetarium date in London

As the birthplace of modern astronomy, Greenwich's Royal Observatory sets the stage for an unforgettable planetarium date. Cozy up under the stars during a private tour of the cosmos—planets, galaxies, and beyond. It's a romantic, out-of-this-world way to connect.

ENGLAND

480 Take to the skies with a helicopter lesson for two

Calling all daredevils: soar to new heights in picturesque Yorkshire, Oxfordshire, or Kent, taking turns at the controls as you glide over stunning landscapes. From the Yorkshire Dales to Blenheim Palace to the White Cliffs of Dover, enjoy a spectacular show at 10,000 ft. (3,000 m).

ENGLAND

481 Visit the Lake District homes of William Wordsworth

Poetry lovers and wordsmiths will treasure Dove Cottage in Grasmere, where Romantic poet William Wordsworth lived with his sister, Dorothy, for eight years. Then explore Rydal Mount near Ambleside, his home for thirty-seven years, and wander the "happy gardens" that inspired his work.

ENGLAND

482 Go on a hot-air balloon expedition over Lake Windermere

Leave the myths of sea creatures far behind as you soar high above England's largest lake, in the aptly named Lake District. With rolling hills beneath and a fiery flame above, a hot-air balloon ride over Lake Windermere offers phenomenal views—and unparalleled Instagram potential. Once back on the ground, celebrate your memorable flight with a champagne toast, included in the ticket price.

ENGLAND

483 Embrace the slow pace of rural life in the Cotswolds

For an escape to the bucolic English countryside, spend the weekend at Thyme in the Cotswolds—an idyllic boutique estate at the heart of a region famed for its rolling hills and honey-hued farmhouses. Wend your way through narrow country lanes on visits to postcard-worthy villages such as Stow-on-the-Wold and Bourton-on-the-Water. Back at the hotel, relax at the Meadow Spa and dine on seasonal farm-to-table fare at the Ox Barn restaurant.

ENGLAND

484 Picnic in Cotswold Wildlife Park and Gardens

Pack a romantic picnic and spend the day wandering the lush grounds of Cotswold Wildlife Park and Gardens. Spot rhinos grazing on the lawn, admire exotic species from arm's length, then bask in the serenity of it all, enjoying an alfresco lunch amid nature's finest.

ENGLAND

485 Become tree house masters in the New Forest

Live the high life in a Treehouse Suite at the storied Chewton Glen Hotel & Spa in Hampshire, where a world of whimsical activities awaits. Spend your days sheep walking or axe throwing, before retreating to your tucked-away treetop haven for a private hot tub session in the middle of the forest.

483 Stow-on-the Wold

487 Halnaker tree tunnel

ENGLAND

486 Buckle up for a refined off-roading adventure in Oxfordshire

For couples who crave adventure with a touch of elegance, Estelle Manor delivers. Head off-road in a heritage Land Rover to explore the estate's ancient woodlands before continuing on foot for a guided walk through the flora and fauna. After kicking up a little countryside dust, retreat to nearby Blenheim Lake for alfresco drinks and snacks on the jetty surrounded by bucolic beauty.

ENGLAND

487 Wander through a fairy-tale tree tunnel in West Sussex

Take a slow, hand-in-hand stroll through the enchanting Halnaker tree tunnel in West Sussex, where a thicket of interlaced branches form an awe-inspiring cathedral canopy. As if that weren't romantic enough—especially for an "I do" moment—the path leads to a scenic hilltop windmill where the setting is flawless for picnicking.

ENGLAND

488 Design your dream wedding rings together

Craft meaningful, one-of-a-kind designs with the Workbench's at-home kit. Hand-carve custom rings, uniquely tailored to your love story, or surprise your partner with a personal symbol of commitment as special as your relationship.

WALES/ENGLAND • EUROPE

WALES

489 Savor a progressive dinner by the sea in Tenby

When in Wales, turn date night into a coastal adventure with a dine-around-town. Start with oysters and rosé at the Fat Seagull, followed by Welsh lamb by candlelight at Plantagenet House. Gelato and sea views at Fecci's to end, perhaps topped off with a surprise proposal.

WALES

490 Reserve a cabin in the Black Mountains

Through Unyoked, book an off-grid, eco-conscious cabin in the Black Mountains, where the wilderness and complete privacy set the mood. Deepen the experience with Come Together, an intimacy course designed by sex and relationship practitioners Normal, to spark connection.

WALES/ENGLAND

491 Ride the rails from London to Wales

Trade London's bustle for Welsh romance aboard the Britannic Explorer, the United Kingdom's first luxury sleeper train by Belmond. Roll past undulating hills and picturesque villages while indulging in a curated culinary journey—think gourmet dinners, fine wines, and breakfast with a view. Plus, the cabins are dreamy, with plush beds and wall coverings reflective of the shoreline and verdant landscape just outside your window.

490 Black Mountains, Wales

EUROPE • NORTHERN IRELAND/REPUBLIC OF IRELAND

NORTHERN IRELAND

492 Pack your clubs for doubles golf

Head to Northern Ireland for a tailored couples golf getaway with Marine & Lawn Hotels' the Grand Tour. Tee off at world-renowned links—such as Royal Portrush in County Antrim—then unwind with spa treatments and bespoke whiskey tastings by night. It doesn't get better than sweeping greens, and golden drams, all wrapped in legendary Irish hospitality.

NORTHERN IRELAND

493 Walk in the steps of giants at sunrise

Wake early to explore the Giant's Causeway on Northern Ireland's Antrim coast. Its dramatic hexagonal basalt columns, formed by ancient volcanic activity, famously doubled as Pyke Castle—seat of House Greyjoy—in *Game of Thrones*. Stay nearby at the Portrush Adelphi for a cozy retreat, and warm up at the Red Sail Room, clad in tartan fabrics.

REPUBLIC OF IRELAND

494 Paint the town rainbow in Dublin

Whisk your partner and your most fabulous outfits to Dublin Pride. This annual event fills the streets with parades, performances, drag brunches, street parties, and pure joy. Dublin's famously warm spirit and inclusive energy make it one of the most heartfelt places in the world to celebrate Pride. Take to the streets, toast to love in all its glorious forms, and dance your hearts out all weekend long.

493 Giant's Causeway

REPUBLIC OF IRELAND • EUROPE

REPUBLIC OF IRELAND

495 Get your rings blessed by St. Valentine

Make your way to Whitefriar Street Church in Dublin, home to the relic of St. Valentine himself. Couples can have their rings blessed at this utterly charming spot—perfect for proposals, anniversaries, or, just because. Later, mosey on over to the Brazen Head, Ireland's oldest pub, for a love-filled lunch of hearty Irish fare and a perfectly poured pint. It's romance with a Celtic twist.

REPUBLIC OF IRELAND

496 Share a kiss at the Blarney Stone

High atop the ancient heights of Blarney Castle, in County Cork, lean into legend and press your lips to the storied limestone, said to bestow the "gift of the gab," the silver-tongued charm of poets and lovers. It is a bit tricky to reach—you will need to lean backward over a sheer drop, safely supported by iron rails—but the daring act is well worth the effort. And once gifted the gab, it is the perfect way to melt those first-date jitters.

REPUBLIC OF IRELAND

497 Get a bird's-eye view of Kerry's rugged coastline

Tingle with thrills (and chills) as you take a helicopter ride over the Ring of Kerry. The best way to witness the dramatic 111-mi. (179-km) driving route is by flying overhead for a unique view of Ireland's rugged coastlines and emerald hills. If you prefer solid ground, scenic trails offer more down-to-earth routes. Either way, visit Skellig Michael, a rocky island crowned with a seventh-century monastery.

REPUBLIC OF IRELAND

498 Picnic together at the Cliffs of Moher in County Clare

Channel your inner Elizabeth and Mr. Darcy with a gourmet picnic on the luxurious Ballyfin Demesne estate, where you can prearrange a Jane Austen–style spread by a grotto, lakeside, or temple. Or, preorder a basket from Brambles Café and dine atop the dramatic Cliffs of Moher, where sheer limestone ledges plunge into crashing Atlantic waves.

REPUBLIC OF IRELAND

499 Trace your love lines at County Clare's Dromoland Castle

Those wishing to explore their ancestral lineage can do so at Dromoland Castle, one of Ireland's most storied landmarks, where a resident genealogist is on hand for a private consultation. Once you have unearthed your roots, venture to ancestral towns, ancient graveyards, or even a family castle, and live like lords and ladies for the day.

REPUBLIC OF IRELAND

500 Take flight in County Mayo, at Ireland's oldest falconry school

Sign up for a proper hawk walk in Ireland, making your pilgrimage to the country's oldest established falconry school, located on the historic grounds of Ashford Castle. Here, you will learn the ancient art of falconry and fly majestic hawks through the woodlands like true nobles.

HISTORIC SLEEPOVER

REPUBLIC OF IRELAND

501 Spend the night in an eight-hundred-year-old castle

Ashford Castle is not just a landmark—it is also one of the finest places to lay your heads—on three-hundred-count Egyptian linen sheets, no less. Indulge in the Jewels & Gin experience, featuring master goldsmith Nigel O'Reilly and a local gin distillery. Or set off on a handcrafted Clinker boat with Frank Costello, the castle's esteemed storyteller and third-generation ghillie, for a lakeside picnic lunch steeped in lore.

REPUBLIC OF IRELAND • **EUROPE**

CHANNEL ISLANDS

502 Stay out late for bioluminescent worms

Wait for low tide to go moon walking with your partner across a dramatic landscape that looks like something from outer space in the Channel Islands' La Rocque Harbour. Pack a blanket, a picnic, and a bottle of wine with the plan to laze about, graze, and sip until well past dark when bioluminescent worms begin to sparkle in the rock pools.

FRANCE

503 Do it for the sweet, amorous photo op

Make sure your *amour* knows exactly how you feel about them by visiting Paris's famous Wall of Love, by artists Frédéric Baron and Claire Kito. The 430-sq.-ft. (40-m^2) wall in Montmartre's Jehan Rictus square is also known as the "I Love You Wall," since the six-hundred-plus enameled lava tiles making it up are emblazoned with "I love you" written in 311 different languages.

FRANCE

504 Climb the Arc de Triomphe at golden hour

Set out for an iconic stroll up Paris's Champs Élysées at golden hour and then climb the 280 steps up to the top of the monumental Arc de Triomphe just before the sun sets. Book your timed tickets ahead to ensure the perfect lighting conditions to savor the city bathed in a warm glow. Stay a little longer to watch the city lights flicker on as the sky begins to darken.

FRANCE

505 Sup, starlit, on an Eiffel Suite terrace

Take in-room dining to the next level with an effervescent dinner under the stars and lights of Paris, with the Eiffel Tower glittering so close you can nearly touch it. This is only possible in the Hôtel Plaza Athénée's singular Eiffel Suite, where your privileged perch makes room service truly unforgettable.

FRANCE

506 Spend a sultry evening at a cabaret

Buy yourselves tickets to one of the most sensual, slinky, and provocative shows there is, at the legendary Crazy Horse Paris cabaret. Let a dancer take you on a private VIP tour behind the scenes of what was once a wine cellar, before the evening's performance begins.

FRANCE

507 Feast on caviar at a hot Parisian spot

Join haute pairs of celebrities and fashion designers at one of Paris's most iconic and decadent eateries, Caviar Kaspia, which first opened its doors in 1927. Pamper yourselves with heaping servings of caviar and caviar-topped everything, of course, during your champagne-soaked meal at the see-and-be-seen landmark that serves up old-world Russian vibes and views of L'église de la Madeleine.

504 Arc de Triomphe after dark

EUROPE • FRANCE

FRANCE

508 Take a blow-out clandestine tour of the Eiffel Tower

In Paris, dedicate a portion of your budget to having a magical, intimate experience at the City of Lights' crown jewel, the Eiffel Tower, on a bespoke tour. Choose what you do and see—perhaps, a champagne toast at the top, a tour of the tower's historic elevator mechanisms, a macaron tasting session, or a professional photo shoot.

FRANCE

509 Stage an artful proposal where life mimics art at Le Musée Rodin

Visit Le Musée Rodin, in Paris, to admire great art together, but also with another goal in mind: an epic proposal. Stroll the garden bursting with roses and through the grand museum until you reach one of the French sculptor's most famed works, *The Kiss*. Take a knee, and ask your big question. Plant someone in the gallery to take a photo of your big kiss. Go on Valentine's Day for the annual Soirée Love celebration of romantic workshops.

508 Eiffel Tower on the City of Lights skyline

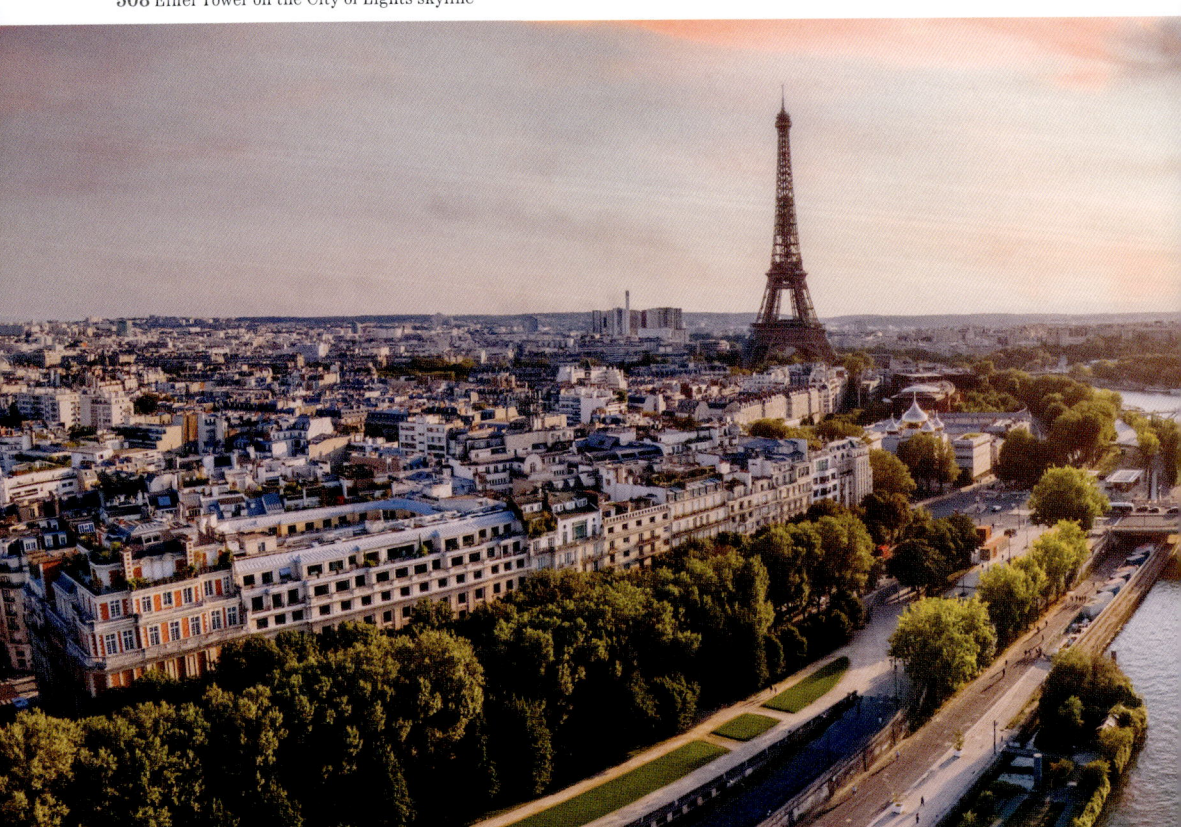

FRANCE · EUROPE

FRANCE

510 Seek out the Temple of Love above a park grotto

Hire a romantic little rowboat, bring a bottle of French wine, and set out to do—and see—something a bit off Paris's beaten path. For an intimate outing that promises to be memorable, paddle your way across Lac Daumesnil in the public park Bois de Vincennes to find the doric-style Temple of Love above a grotto. Share a sweet moment and a toast.

FRANCE

511 Linger longer over storied cocktails at the Ritz Paris

Do as so many greats have done before you and sidle up to Bar Hemingway at the Ritz Paris, a hotel so beloved and glitzy that you may have read about it in such classics as *The Sun Also Rises* or *Tender Is the Night* or seen it in the movie romance *Something's Gotta Give*. Be sure this place becomes engrained in your own shared history with a leisurely evening spent sipping French 75 and Serendipity cocktails.

FRANCE

512 Steal your way into Marie Antoinette's inner sanctum

Book a private VIP tour of the Palace of Versailles that includes a captivating, cheeky peek at Marie Antoinette's innermost sanctum: her personal suite, the Petit Trianon. Go back in time during the storytelling walk through her personal theater and temple of love, then take a stroll in the garden groves, before staying overnight in the luxe hotel on the palace grounds.

EUROPE • FRANCE

517 Eleven Chalet Pelerin

FRANCE

513 Take a private tour of champagne houses

During a stay at hilltop haven Royal Champagne Hotel & Spa, draw on the retreat's offer to organize a private, bubble-filled tour of the sparkling Champagne region. Hop from Taittinger to Dom Pérignon to Veuve Clicquot. Ensure Maison Ruinart, the oldest champagne house, is on the itinerary, and buy a bottle for your next big occasion.

FRANCE

514 Slumber in Burgundy's fine-wine country

Sleep in a property that dates to 1112 and yet is fresh off a five-star reimagining that made Château de la Commaraine, Hotel Spa & Cuverie, a dream of a historic boutique hotel. Sip cocktails in a fourteenth-century tower and go sailing through Burgundy's canals.

FRANCE

515 Experience a Vines for Lovers spa ritual

Treat yourselves to a beautifully hedonistic spa day for two at Les Sources de Caudalie hotel's Vinotherapie spa, amid expansive vineyards in Bordeaux. During the Vines for Lovers ritual you will get side-by-side facials and Fleur de Vigne candle massages before taking an intimate barrel bath together.

FRANCE

516 Live on local products while biking around Île de Ré

Hire two bikes and pedal from oyster shack to oyster shack on the bucolic island off the west coast of France, Île de Ré, happening upon sweet villages, golden beaches, and dunes as the pair of you ride in sync. Stop also to try the local salt and honey for a gastronomic getaway.

FRANCE

517 Go hut-to-hut hiking together in the French Alps

Immerse yourselves in a 360-degree French Alps experience while backcountry hiking to Eleven Chalet Pelerin's private mountain huts through absolutely surreal landscapes. End your days with candlelit alfresco dinners followed by Génépi liqueur.

FRANCE

518 Synchronize your dives into a strikingly turquoise river canyon

Plunge into the most striking-colored fresh water imaginable, ideally synchronizing your dives, cannonballs, or leaps perfectly, at the river canyon Gorges du Verdon. The emerald expanse makes a stunning backdrop for a tranquil outing on a boat so you can motor to the most pristine spots for swimming.

518 Gorges du Verdon

EUROPE • FRANCE/CORSICA/MONACO

FRANCE

519 Be seduced by the power of scent while blending perfume

Fragrance fanatics who find themselves collecting cologne wardrobes will enjoy a perfume garden visit in Grasse, France's legendary perfume capital since the late 1700s. Even better, visit a top fragrance house, where you can put your noses to the test—and to work, blending your own eau de parfum or colognes that pair as perfectly as you two lovebirds. Take home bottles as a scent memory.

FRANCE

520 Combine a passion for art and luxury hotels on the Côte d'Azur

Check into a divine hotel that doubles as an art museum for 24-7 access to world-class paintings and period furniture. At Hotel Le Negresco, in Nice, couples are transported through an almost five-century range across some 6,000 artworks that decorate each room uniquely and provide an endless source of artistic inspiration.

CORSICA

521 Plan a fairy-tale stay on the untamed island of Corsica

On the secluded, idyllic island of Corsica, traipse through wildflower-coated meadows, rolling countryside, and finally, along a white-sand beach on a pair of horses as the sky turns to sorbet. Retire to your own restored sixteenth-century holiday house at the sprawling agritourism concept Domaine de Murtoli for a reflective dinner.

MONACO

522 Dress up and go all in on Place du Casino

Dress in your finest Monaco-ready ensembles and agree on a figure before going all in with your bets on the Place du Casino. Take your winnings and indulge in a glitzy suite and Michelin-starred dinner at the five-star Hôtel de Paris Monte-Carlo, right on the F1 Grand Prix track.

521 Corsica

ITALY

523 Take turns driving a Ferrari F8 Tributo Spider

Spice up your stay at Rome's Hotel Eden by letting them organize the opportunity to take turns driving a fierce and fabulous Ferrari F8 Tributo Spider up Lazio's highest peak. On reaching the very top, slow things down during an epic gourmet picnic for two.

ITALY

524 Get into the spirit of *la dolce vita* in Rome

Revel in *la dolce vita*, meaning "the sweet life," from a deluxe suite outfitted with a dramatic four-poster bed and sumptuous bedding at the intimate boutique hotel J.K. Place Roma. This seductively discreet hotel will woo you with its cocktails and unbeatable location.

522 Hôtel de Paris Monte-Carlo

EUROPE • ITALY

ITALY

525 Take a glam vintage-styled sleeper train

Nothing says *amore* quite like an Italian-made, golden age–inspired train journey through the gleaming countryside. La Dolce Vita Orient Express, a vintage-styled sleeper train, is the definition of glamorous from the opulent train cars and suites to the glossy *ristorante* serving Michelin-level gastronomy. There is also the luxe Italia Rail Espresso Cadore night train, going to the Dolomites, for couples with a less lavish budget.

ITALY

526 Swoon during the Fendi Experience

Fashion-committed couples will enjoy a several-hour Fendi Experience tour, which takes place in the Fendi Roma Palazzo Boutique's gorgeous seventeenth-century building. There, your private guide will give you a lovely Italian fashion history lesson as you ooh and aah over the exquisite collections and architecture. Finish it off with an exclusive by-appointment shopping experience.

ITALY

527 Get messy making your own pasta meal

Join forces with your love and let loose as you work toward a common goal: a perfect bowl of pasta. At Rome with Chef, book a private class for two where you will learn to make your own fettucine from scratch, plus an authentic carbonara sauce with which to top it. The three-hour course includes making tiramisù for dessert and sitting down to enjoy your meal together—naturally, with a glass of wine.

525 View of the Italian countryside from a vintage train

ITALY • EUROPE

528 Spanish Steps, Rome

529 Villa Borghese, Rome

ITALY

528 Share a massive Italian gelato on the iconic Spanish Steps

Role-play as Audrey Hepburn's character in the vintage rom-com *Roman Holiday*—but with the apple of your eye by your side—and order a waffle cone loaded with Italian gelato to split while sitting on the Spanish Steps. The legendary landmark in Rome is a hot spot for lovers whiling away a sunny afternoon with something refreshing and, of course, sharing kisses between gelato licks.

ITALY

529 Pop the question in the fairy-tale environs of Villa Borghese

On a sunny afternoon, decamp to one of Rome's largest public parks, the landscape garden Villa Borghese, for what could be the biggest day of your lives together. With a little pre-trip orchestration, line up a photographer to hide as you pop the big question in fairy-tale environs on land or even in a rowboat. After the "yes!" share a romantic kiss.

EUROPE • ITALY

PRIVATE VIEW

ITALY, VATICAN CITY

530 Admire the radiant Sistine Chapel after hours

Call in the professionals to sprinkle your honeymoon or trip of a lifetime with indelible moments such as a particularly unbelievable one: visiting the Sistine Chapel after hours. The chapel within the pope's residence in Vatican City, whose ceiling is resplendent in Michelangelo's fresco paintings, is always bustling with tourists, but certain operators are able to pull strings to get you in before or after it opens to the public for an intimate viewing. During an exclusive visit, you can expect to be captivated by special moments and even secret spaces you couldn't possibly forget.

ITALY • EUROPE

ITALY

531 Climb in elevation for a Dolomiti eco-retreat

Indulge your adventurous sides at the sustainable yet sumptuous eco-retreat FORESTIS, where you will feast on forest cuisine, learn Celtic wyda yoga, and take winter toboggan runs. Secluded at the top of a mountain, the wildly romantic hideaway is your window to the UNESCO World Heritage Site Dolomites but also luxurious moments of repose, such as couples spa treatments in a room carved into the mountain.

ITALY

532 Find pure indulgence at Lake Como

Check in for a few days at Passalacqua, one of the world's top hotels, set in an eighteenth-century villa, for guided hikes and candlelit rose garden dinners for two. While there, enter atmospheric tunnels on the shores of Lake Como to find lavish indulgences in the form of centuries-old cures and seed-to-skin couples treatments at the hotel's state-of-the-art spa.

221

ITALY

533 Head to the Matterhorn for a quiet Alpine escape

Escape to plush, under-the-radar Cervino at the base of the Matterhorn (Gran Becca to locals) in the traffic-free Italian Alps. The resort is situated perfectly for cozy cable-car rides through the peaks, strolling hand in hand through snow-dusted streets, taking therapeutic Finnish saunas, and sipping hot chocolate by the fire. End each magical day wrapped in blankets, watching the sun dip behind snow-topped mountains.

ITALY

534 Indulge in a relaxing Romantic Escape on Lake Como

Spend a couple lazy days on Lake Como—specifically booking in for a couples' Romantic Escape at lovely lakeside Il Sereno. Pick your own destination for a trip on the hotel's hand-built, wooden Vaporino boat and follow it up with a five-course tasting dinner in the two-Michelin-starred Al Lago restaurant. In between, enjoy in-room breakfasts and a relaxing couples massage.

ITALY

535 Explore medieval towns and Michelin-starred eateries on Lake Garda

Take things slow while navigating the delightful medieval towns, Michelin-starred restaurants, and charming hotels of Lake Garda, a peaceful under-the-radar alternative to Lake Como. Base yourselves in a suite at Lefay Resort & Spa Lago di Garda and spend downtime soaking up the natural paradise.

ITALY

536 Shop in Milan then hit the town for a fancy night out

Head to Milan's Galleria Vittorio Emanuele II, the famed circa 1877 shopping arcade, to select glamorous outfits for a glittery night on the town. There is no better place to don your new looks than the iconic Teatro alla Scala for an enchanting ballet or opera performance.

ITALY

537 Make sweet memories in Verona

Along with your fellow Shakespeare fanatic, make a pilgrimage to fair Verona where you can visit a re-creation of Juliet's balcony. There, pay your respects to the romantic tragedy by leaving your own sentimental love letters. Follow it up with something else supersweet: a gelato-making class for two.

ITALY

538 Visit Franciacorta for a sparkling wine tour

Plan a dreamy harvest season tour of bucolic Franciacorta, the illustrious sparkling wine region within Lombardy's Brescia province. Local operators can arrange a bespoke romantic day or more of being chauffeured through autumnal landscapes to go behind the scenes at wineries such as Ca' del Bosco.

EUROPE • ITALY

ITALY

539 Be enchanted on a sunset gondola ride

It may as well be illegal for a pair of soulmates to visit Venice, considered by many to be the world's most romantic city, and not step into the water-bound chariot of a gondolier in his black-and-white striped shirt. So, do it right and find yourselves seduced as you drift down the canals on a classic gondola at sunset.

ITALY

540 Get your steps in on the steps of Cinque Terre

Take on the iconic stairways and hiking trails that link Cinque Terre's five colorful villages, each perched dramatically on the rugged Ligurian coastline. The steep, winding paths offer breathtaking views of terraced vineyards, olive groves, and the sparkling Mediterranean Sea. As you trek from village to village—climbing and descending through narrow lanes and ancient stone steps—take breaks at coves to cool off with a refreshing swim.

539 Gondola ride, Venice

ITALY • EUROPE

542 View of Florence

ITALY

541 Have a composer write your theme song

Music-loving romantics, head to Grand Universe Lucca with a specific once-in-a-lifetime opportunity in mind: having an Italian composer write a custom song just for you as a couple. You will meet with the musical genius in the hotel's Symphony Lounge and let your personalities shine, then they will go to work, later hand-delivering the bespoke tune's sheet music in a Tuscan leather box.

ITALY

542 Find the romantic corners of Florence

Hire a private guide to reveal to you the most romantic hidden corners of Florence. You will likely stroll through the peaceful Boboli Gardens with their secret groves or visit the charming, winding streets of the city's Oltrarno district, where artisan workshops and intimate cafés abound. Later, take in the city's ancient palazzi and historic churches aboard a sunset cruise along the River Arno.

ITALY

543 Hunt for truffles in pastoral Umbria

Embark on an exciting truffle hunt in the Umbrian countryside, where black truffles are your fragrant prize. Long considered an aphrodisiac, truffles will be a flavorful highlight of a luscious lunch that you will prepare with an Italian chef and then feast upon alongside your partner in life and love—and some intoxicating local wines, of course.

EUROPE • ITALY

ITALY

544 Take a cheeky dip amid Roman ruins

Steal away for an only-in-Italy afternoon spent swimming in a crystalline natural pool around the ancient ruins of a Roman villa, Villa di Pollio Felice. You will have to reach Sorrento's Bagni Regina Giovanna by private boat or on foot, making it all the more special when you two slip into the water to explore.

ITALY

545 Stay at upmarket Monastero Santa Rosa

Book a suite in this beautifully restored seventeenth-century monastery-turned-boutique hotel perched on a cliff on the Amalfi Coast. Enjoy an infinity pool that seems to merge with the Mediterranean, dine at the on-site Michelin-starred restaurant, and unwind in the spa housed within the monastery's original vaulted rooms.

ITALY

546 Savor Italy's traditional aperitivo hour

Engage in the grand Italian tradition of aperitivo hour in one of the most spectacular places for it: Piazza Duomo in Ravello, perched high above the Tyrrhenian Sea. Come 6 P.M., snag a two-top and order Aperol spritzes that match the sunset, toasting to another flawless day on the Amalfi Coast.

545 Monastero Santa Rosa

ITALY • EUROPE

ITALY

547 Steal a kiss at Capri's iconic sea arch

During a stay on Capri, carve out time for a jaunt by boat to the Faraglioni limestone sea stacks. The central stack, known as Stella, features a natural archway carved by centuries of waves. As tradition has it, couples who kiss while drifting beneath the arch are destined for everlasting love. Framed by turquoise water and dramatic cliffs—the adventure is unforgettable.

ITALY

548 Sleep inside an architectural gem

Couples with a soft spot for design can expect to get a buzz from the experience of sleeping in a piece of true architecture by the legend, Le Corbusier. His peach-hued boutique hotel Punta Tragara in Capri could not be more picturesque and full of character, with forty-four uniquely decorated rooms and suites that you will very likely never want to leave.

ITALY

549 Explore the Amalfi Coast in Le Sirenuse's vintage speedboat

Plan ahead and coordinate fabulous retro ensembles with your partner for a throwback exploit in Positano aboard Le Sirenuse's vintage speedboat. Take to the sapphire sea just before sunset with a captain who knows all the secret spots and say *salute* with your glasses of chilled champagne.

549 Positano

550 Trulli

ITALY/MALTA • EUROPE

ITALY

550 Slumber in a romantic little trullo in a Puglian town

Make for the sweet Puglian town of Alberobello, a UNESCO World Heritage Site, and take up temporary residence in a romantic little trullo, a stone hut with a fairy-tale-esque conical limestone roof. Originally shepherd shelters, these huts are now adapted for intimate, luxurious stays. Feel like a true local in an Airbnb trullo or opt for a boutique-hotel-style compound with a swimming pool and spa services.

ITALY

551 Jump in a private hot-air balloon to soar over the incredible caves of Matera

After journeying through the ancient Sassi di Matera and its Paleolithic cave dwellings on foot, be charmed by a fresh perspective of the inconceivable landscape from the air. Make arrangements for a private hot-air balloon flight that will take you both for a serene survey of Basilicata's churches, carved caves, and mazes. Take the trip at sunrise or sunset to see the whole scene drenched in golden light, letting it sear into your memory.

ITALY

552 Dine in a seductive cave restaurant

Follow in the footsteps of generation upon generation of lovers, dating back to the 1700s, and reserve a table at Puglia's Grotta Palazzese, a restaurant built inside a natural cave. The cliffside spot overlooking the Adriatic Sea was first used for parties centuries ago but now as a modern restaurant the experience is a bit different. You can expect tantalizing dishes of pasta and freshly caught seafood accompanied by fine wine.

ITALY

553 Channel James Bond on a helicopter escapade

Take a high-flying adventure that is straight out of James Bond's playbook from your home base at Rome Cavalieri, A Waldorf Astoria Hotel, when you opt for a private helicopter experience touching down on the Pontine Islands in the sublimely blue Tyrrhenian Sea. You will land on Ponza, where a boat awaits with snorkels and towels for secluded exploits while the skipper prepares a memorable lunch featuring fresh seafood and local ingredients.

ITALY

554 Ascend Sicily's Mount Erice before dusk

Take on the 2,464-ft. (750-m) Mount Erice in charming Sicily amid radiant late-afternoon light, opting for a challenging climb in hiking boots or an easy one aboard the funicular. At the top, check out the Castle of Venus, the goddess of love, and take in splendid vistas encompassing the coastline and islands, the region's famous salt pans, and antique windmills. Revel in the medieval beauty before descending, post-sundown, in mystical fog.

MALTA

555 Cross Malta's Grand Harbour in an intimate traditional *dghajsa* boat

When in Malta, climb aboard the local answer to Venice's gondolas, the traditional *dghajsa*, Maltese for "boat." Take the narrow, brightly painted vessel from Valletta across the Grand Harbour and you will be part of a four-hundred-odd-year-old tradition, as the unique seafaring crafts have been used by generations for centuries. Opt for a private tour of the harbor for a more leisurely, but also potentially educational, outing.

MALTA

556 Attend a Valletta festival themed around jazz, film, Carnival, or art

Valletta, the fancifully baroque-styled capital of Malta, is one of the most vibrant and inclusive cities in all of Europe. Joyful celebration is a near constant, so find something you are both passionate about and make a trip out of it, since there are festivals themed around jazz, film, Carnival, art, fireworks, and even one around a marathon.

MALTA/CANARY ISLANDS • EUROPE

556 Celebrations in Valletta

MALTA

557 Douse your day in eye-popping blue

Embrace the sweetest parts of island life on a boat day, saturated in breathtaking shades of blue. In addition to simply cruising, check out the striking Blue Lagoon on Comino Island, with its white-sand seabed and crystal-clear waters, and the beguiling natural spectacle that is the Blue Grotto. This line of sea caverns includes one very appropriate sight dubbed Honeymoon Cave.

MALTA

558 Walk, cycle, kayak, and swim through Gozo

Countless transportation modalities will have you walking, cycling, kayaking, Segway-ing, and swimming your way through Malta's Gozo. The sustainable and lightly touristed island is thought to be the inspiration for Calypso's Isle from Homer's *The Odyssey*. Spend your day visiting the island's stunning beaches, including one with red sand.

CANARY ISLANDS

559 Admire the Milky Way above Tenerife

Lie on your backs, under the midnight summer sky in Teide National Park, a Starlight Tourist Destination and Reserve, where negligible light pollution and a bit of elevation offers you super-clear views of the Milky Way's core. Bring wine and a telescope (or join a guided tour) and keep your eyes peeled for shimmery meteor showers.

CANARY ISLANDS

560 Devour a memorable dinner courtesy of Earth's heat

Tuck into one of the most unique dinners of your lives in Timanfaya National Park on the island of Lanzarote, courtesy of hot, steaming volcanic activity. A table for two at El Diablo Restaurant, set into the side of a volcano, is your ticket to an unforgettable meal of meats and veggies cooked flawlessly over an open grill heated by volcanic rock steaming from Earth's core.

SPAIN

561 Savor a sexy flamenco performance

In Madrid, feel the allure of a sensual, low-lit night watching Spain's national dance, flamenco, at Corral de la Morería. The world's oldest and most storied *tablao* nestles in the historic heart of the city near the Royal Palace and has drawn everyone from royalty to artists to its electrifying performances.

SPAIN

562 Discover sacred sexuality with the art of tantric yoga

Join a couples tantric yoga workshop in Madrid. You will explore a range of techniques to deepen your emotional and energetic connection, including chakra-cleansing rituals, mantra and meditation sessions, and guided partner practices.

SPAIN

563 Be charmed by an indulgent Basque oenophile escape

On the Basque coast, stay at Hotel Iturregi, an Edenic escape overlooking the Cantabrian Sea, for a weekend of tasting, sipping, and supping your way through a region known for its characteristic cuisine and wine. Along the coast at San Sebastián, you will find one of the world's highest concentrations of Michelin-starred restaurants.

GAUDÍ'S CITY

SPAIN

564 Gaze, awestruck, at Gaudí's spectacular work in Barcelona

Make the pilgrimage to Barcelona and marvel at the otherworldly works of famed Catalan architect Antoni Gaudí, from mosaics in Park Güell to the sculpted chimneys of La Casa Milà. Stand awestruck at his masterpiece of Basílica de la Sagrada Família, begun in 1882, and book a private photo session to capture yourselves in the moment and magical light cast by the stained glass within. In summer, time your trip to coincide with a Magical Night at La Casa Batlló, an open-air concert held on the building's serpentine roof.

SPAIN • EUROPE

SPAIN

565 Bond on two wheels in a world-class cycling destination

Make your way to Priorat, Spain, one of the world's most iconic cycling destinations, and a beautiful one at that. At Mas d'en Bruno, commit to an e-bike extravaganza of a vacation on which you also get pampered. There are Roman tubs and double-sided fireplaces in the twenty-four suites, plus the retreat has an outdoor jacuzzi amid vineyards, private wine tastings, and stargazing, too.

SPAIN

566 Lose yourselves in the timeless romance of the Alhambra

Perched above Granada, with the snow-capped Sierra Nevada in the distance, the Alhambra sets the scene for a day of shared enchantment. Wander through Moorish palaces where ornate arches, geometric tile work, and calligraphic inscriptions speak of fine Islamic artistry. Meander through the serene, beautifully planted Generalife gardens, with their cooling water features, and watch the sun set over Granada from one of the scenic viewpoints.

SPAIN

567 Hide away in a Menorcan farmhouse

Sample life at a different pace in a rural respite on the island of Menorca. At Son Blanc Farmhouse Menorca, a divinely designed boutique hotel meets farm stay, there are concerts and dance workshops, pottery sessions and sound therapy. Take things slowly, spending time in the orchard, joining forces in two-person cooking classes, and enjoying unhurried sunset picnics without a soul in sight.

SPAIN

568 Rent a sixteenth-century finca for two

On the island of Majorca, stay in a sixteenth-century finca at Son Bunyola Hotel and Villas. Tucked into a UNESCO World Heritage Site, it allows you ultimate seclusion with wide Mediterranean panoramas and acres of space in which to roam. Spend your days biking through the awe-inspiring Tramuntana Mountains of Majorca, where winding coastal roads lined with ancient olive trees pass through sleepy stone villages.

SPAIN

569 Reserve a suite in a Majorcan fortress

If you were not planning to propose before you got to Cap Rocat, that may change during your stay at the nineteenth-century fortress-turned-boutique hotel—it is that compellingly romantic. Sitting in a 74-acre (30-ha) nature reserve with its own protected beach, the adults-only retreat has suites in the place of cannons, with their own private pools and hammocks, and phones are forbidden at the restaurant and bar.

566 The Alhambra

SPAIN • EUROPE

LGBTQIA+ 24-7

SPAIN

570 Hop between gay bars, music venues, beaches, and shops

Revel in Ibiza's LGBTQIA+ hot spot of Calle de la Virgen, widely celebrated as one of the world's most inclusive and queer-friendly neighborhoods. Do not be afraid to be yourselves and dress the part as you patronize the countless gay bars and clubs plus vibrant music venues including Glitterbox among drag queens and go-go boys, check out fetish shops, and soak up the sun on gorgeous beaches.

SPAIN

571 Indulge in an Ibizan hotel with customized PJs

Save up for the ultimate five-star indulgence in Ibiza to commemorate a major occasion—perhaps a milestone anniversary or birthday—and book the Gran Suite Dalt Vila at Ibiza Gran Hotel. The opulent 1,600-sq.-ft. (150-m²) loft boasts an even larger terrace with your own jacuzzi, infinity pool, and solarium, but it is the Bentley transfers, butler service, and customized couples pajamas that really seal the deal.

573 Rua Nova do Carvalho, Lisbon

SPAIN

572 Food crawl your way through Formentera

Plan a self-directed food crawl on the Spanish island of Formentera, known for its diverse and idiosyncratic cuisine. Sample tapas and seafood signatures as you hop between restaurants, cafés, and *chiringuitos* (beach bars), among them *calamars a la bruta* (fried squid in its own ink) and *bullit de peix* (fish stew with potatoes). Clink glasses of local rosé along the way.

PORTUGAL

573 Be seduced by Lisbon's Pink Street

Embrace the risqué together with a visit to Lisbon's former red light district, Rua Nova do Carvalho, now known playfully as Pink Street and easily recognizable because of its hot-pink lane. The center of the city's nightlife scene makes for dependably fun evenings that might include drinks and dancing or a provocative burlesque show.

PORTUGAL

574 Take a carefree road trip in the Algarve

Resist the urge to plan and simply rent a car and let the road trip reveal itself to you both as you head south from Lisbon. Hugging the breathtaking Atlantic coast of the Algarve you might choose to stop off in Setúbal for fresh seafood by the harbor, explore the whitewashed charm of Évora, or wander the cobbled lanes of Lagos, rich with history and sea views.

EUROPE • PORTUGAL

PORTUGAL

575 Fall head over heels into the fantasy of Sintra's many fairy-tale palaces

Become easily infatuated with the grandeur of Sintra, a sweetly charming town in the forested foothills of the Sintra Mountains northwest of Lisbon, a former royal sanctuary for centuries. Dotting the hills are signs of the destination's bougie pedigree: pastel-hued palaces that to this day create a fairy-tale ambience that cannot be denied. Let yourselves daydream you are part of the stories as you tour through the romantic estates, stroll in lush gardens, and stop for sweet local treats.

PORTUGAL

576 Glide along the Douro River, sipping wine

Cruise the strikingly blue Douro River, through terraced hillsides bursting with grapes, on a private journey aboard a restored vintage *rabelo* boat originally used to transport wine barrels. Enjoy not only incredible environs but also sips of wine en route.

PORTUGAL

577 Take an active tour of Portugal's Douro Valley

Head straight into the heart of Portugal's wine country with a stay at the nineteenth-century manor–turned–Six Senses Douro Valley. There, you will exclusively taste vintage ports straight from the barrel after active thrills such as cycling over undulating hills and wakeboarding or kayaking on the Douro River.

PORTUGAL

578 Paddle into a sea cave in the Algarve

Experience an environment like you have never seen on a beautiful private kayak—or SUP or motorized boat—tour of Benagil Cave, a marine cave formed by twenty million years of erosion. Ready your camera for photos of you two drenched in sunlight pouring in through the fantastic geological site's natural skylight.

PORTUGAL

579 Have a sensual date night in the Azores

Let tense muscles melt into the heat of Furnas Valley's volcanic pools and inhibitions dissipate with them during a sensual date night in the Azores' geothermal hive of activity, which amounts to Europe's highest concentration of hot springs. Soak under a sky full of glittering stars for a private thermal bathing experience after enjoying an atmospheric dinner for two, of *cozido das Furnas* stew, cooked using geothermal heat. By day, visit bubbling calderas, geysers, and mud pools.

PORTUGAL

580 Access a surreal, remote world in the Azores

Seek supernatural wonders, secluded surf breaks, and hidden waterfalls with a hike into Pegasus Lodges' Fajã do Belo, on pristine São Jorge Island. From your cozy volcanic stone villa, you will be enchanted by the ancient lava flow landslides, or *fajãs*, and even swim in their pools.

575 Sintra, Portugal

EUROPE • PORTUGAL/THE NETHERLANDS

PORTUGAL

581 Embrace wicker- and wine-themed traditions in Madeira

Take part in Madeira's distinctive tradition of riding down the steep streets of Funchal in a handcrafted wicker toboggan—an experience found nowhere else in the world. Used as downhill transport in the nineteenth century, the ride has become a cultural attraction. Afterward, attend a guided Madeira wine tasting at seventh-generation Blandy's Wine Lodge.

PORTUGAL

582 Walk Madeira's Vereda da Ponta de São Lourenço trail

Take a walk to what feels like the end of the world—and looks like it, too, with nothing but ocean for hundreds of miles until the African continent. Madeira's Vereda da Ponta de São Lourenço trail is approximately 4½ mi. (7 km) out and back, along a dramatic sliver of land that affords you constant jaw-dropping views as you hike.

PORTUGAL

583 Splash about in natural rock pools in Porto Moniz

In Porto Moniz, on the northwestern tip of Madeira, spend a day at natural volcanic rock pools that fill from the Atlantic Ocean. Pack a picnic and spend the entire hot day wild swimming in the crystal-clear water. For even more stimulation, bring flippers and snorkels to free dive into the sparklingly inviting turquoise world.

THE NETHERLANDS

584 Experiment with being exhibitionists in Amsterdam

Ready to turn up the heat? Slip into spa robes (or don't) and indulge in a coed sauna session at Spa Zuiver, one of Amsterdam's sexiest wellness spots. With steamy rooms built for stolen glimpses, outdoor thermal pools to cool things down, and custom massages for two, it's a thrilling chance to embrace your inner exhibitionists—Dutch-style.

THE NETHERLANDS • EUROPE

Amsterdam City Break

THE NETHERLANDS
585 Tour Amsterdam by tandem bike and boat

Have the quintessential Dutch experience cycling the UNESCO-listed Canal Belt on a bicycle built for two, then hop off to admire masterpieces by Van Gogh, Vermeer, and Rembrandt at the Rijksmuseum. Later, trade wheels for water on a luxury boat with the Pulitzer's private fleet—choose the 1909 teak-and-brass saloon boat *Tourist*, or, in fair weather, *Belle*, an open tender perfect for sun-soaked canal cruising.

EUROPE • THE NETHERLANDS

587 Zaanse Schans windmill

THE NETHERLANDS

586 Stop to smell the tulips in Amsterdam

During the annual Tulip Festival from March through May, more than 800,000 of these beautiful, bell-shaped blooms perfume the entire city. For a fragrant, one-of-a-kind souvenir, visit Amsterdam's famous floating flower market, where colorful bulbs and blossoms spill from canal-side stalls. Couples can easily get wrapped up in the romance of the Dutch tradition.

THE NETHERLANDS

587 Enter a world of wooden houses and windmills

Part of the Netherlands' indelible allure lies in its tulips—and those towering windmills gently turning above open fields. It is truly a sight to witness in person, so head to Zaanse Schans where you will find the most striking examples, plus rows of green wooden houses and handicraft shops selling Dutch pewter, cheese, and Delftware trinkets.

588 Depot Boijmans Van Beuningen, Rotterdam

THE NETHERLANDS

588 Discover Rotterdam's most surprising side

Start your day at Depot Boijmans Van Beuningen—the world's first publicly accessible art depot, in a dazzling mirrored structure housing more than 150,000 works. Then turn up the fun at the Dutch Pinball Museum, where you can flip through decades of vintage and modern machines, including a rare 1853 toupie hollandaise table. Up the stakes with a cheeky challenge: loser buys the next round.

BELGIUM

589 Whip up something sweet in Brussels

Create your own chocolate bar at La Tabletterie, a unique experience offered by La Belgique Gourmande. Located at the company's Rue de la Colline boutique, this interactive station invites you to choose your base—milk, dark, or white—then sprinkle on toppings such as almonds, coconut, caramel, and more, as chocolatiers bring your creation to life. It is a sweet way to connect in the world's chocolate capital.

BELGIUM

590 Visit a historic brewery in Bruges

With its cobbled lanes, medieval spires, and dreamy canals, Bruges drips with old-world beauty—especially at Hotel Heritage, a twenty-two-room boutique stay with an elegant spa. After checking in, head to De Halve Maan, a beloved family-run brewery offering panoramic rooftop views and unfiltered pours of Brugse Zot and Straffe Hendrik—the only place in the world to taste them this fresh.

BELGIUM

591 Savor art and skyline views in Antwerp

Immerse yourselves in Antwerp's stylish, metropolitan culture with a visit to Museum aan de Stroom, home to striking exhibitions and lofty views. Borrow a picnic blanket from the museum and cozy up on the rooftop for a romantic lunch—or opt for a reservation at the scenic top-floor restaurant, where the seasonal tasting menu spotlights Flemish specialties like North Sea shrimp, slow-cooked lamb, and delicate fruit tarts.

BELGIUM

592 Buy some bling in the world's diamond capital

Architectural eye candy, avant-garde fashion houses, and even unexpectedly good pizza are just a few reasons to visit Flanders' largest city—but let's cut straight to the sparkle. Antwerp is the world's diamond capital, home to four glittering *bourses* (trading exchanges) and a dazzling array of storefronts. Whether you are browsing for fun or shopping for the ring, there's no better place to say "yes" to a stone that truly shines.

GERMANY

593 Kink it up at Provocateur Berlin

Book an opulent room at Provocateur, a 1920s burlesque-themed hotel wrapped in velvet and intrigue, and opt for the Made with l'amour package, with bubbly, chocolate-covered fruit, and a flirty time-to-tease set. Hit the minibar for pleasure-centric surprises, and flip the in-room seduction switch for a risqué ceiling show when the mood strikes. Downstairs, La Cave hosts seductive soirées and private events in a sultry space.

GERMANY

594 Sleep in a reimagined 1705 palace in Dresden

Originally built by a king for his mistress, Hotel Taschenbergpalais Kempinski's origin story began as a royal love nest. With timeless elegance and intimate, fairy-tale ambience, you will find no shortage of creature comforts in this opulent baroque palace, which now charms couples with candlelit dinners, lavish suites, and an indoor pool beneath a shimmering starry sky.

594 Hotel Taschenbergpalais Kempinski, Dresden

GERMANY

595 Spend a stimulating day museum hopping in Berlin

Germany's street art legacy is undeniable—Dmitri Vrubel's *Fraternal Kiss*, Birgit Kinder's *Trabant*, and Thierry Noir's *Heads* are just a few of Berlin's iconic facades. Fittingly, the city is home to the world's first museum dedicated to the medium. Start there, then progress to the Schwules Museum, a compelling celebration of LGBTQIA+ history and culture—perfect for shaping meaningful conversation between stops.

GERMANY

596 Get naked at the Baden-Baden baths

Naked bathing culture comes with the territory in Germany, so when in Baden-Baden, embrace being *nackt-nackt*. At the historic Friedrichsbad, couples can soak in seventeen stages of thermal indulgence—ranging from warm-air baths to cold plunges—within a stunning Roman-Irish spa setting. All you need are your birthday suits and each other to appreciate centuries-old wellness traditions and steamy, sensual relaxation.

GERMANY

597 Indulge in mountain magic at Bavaria's most picturesque hideaway

Cradled in a valley framed by snowcapped peaks, Schloss Elmau is the kind of place that feels plucked from a fairy tale. Spend slow, languid days soaking in outdoor thermal pools, sharing a lakeside picnic, or slipping into something silky for dinner at the hotel's Michelin-starred restaurant, where the fresh alpine air is as intoxicating as the wine.

598 Neuschwanstein Castle

GERMANY

598 Follow love's path along Germany's castle-studded Romantic Road

Embark on a scenic journey down Germany's 220-mi. (355-km) Romantic Road, a fairy-tale route that winds through storybook landscapes, passing magnificent palaces, utopian villages, and the iconic Neuschwanstein Castle. Whether you drive or cycle, you will be treated to southern Germany's most enchanting sights along the way, including the beautifully preserved Rothenburg ob der Tauber. With its cobbled streets and half-timbered houses, every stop offers a glimpse into the past—and the chance to make new memories for the future.

GERMANY
599 Stroll on Germany's Martha's Vineyard

Windswept walks along sandy stretches of North Sea beach, horseback rides through villages of traditional thatched-roof Frisian houses, and intimate picnics on the beach. These are but a few of the ultraromantic exploits you can get into on the chic island of Sylt, called the Martha's Vineyard of Germany. Sweep your spouse off their feet with a horse-drawn carriage or sleigh ride on the beach, depending on the season.

599 Sylt

AUSTRIA · EUROPE

AUSTRIA

600 Glide into the magic of Vienna at Christmas

Vienna glows a little brighter come Christmastime, as the city transforms into a snow-dusted dream. Indulge in some festive fun on the ice at the grand Wiener Eistraum in front of City Hall. Then cozy up with warm *glühwein* in mittened hands and explore the city's most iconic markets—the Christkindlmarkt at Rathausplatz, the romantic Spittelberg market, and the artsy Weihnachtsdorf in the MuseumsQuartier—all brimming with vacation charm.

AUSTRIA

601 Swing by a historic Viennese café for cake

Make your sweet-tooth dreams come true by feeding each other bites of the famed chocolate Sachertorte cake where it originated, Hotel Sacher. The rich treat with apricot jam and whipped cream was first made in 1832 for a prince, and savoring it in a historic café with tea is a must. If one slice simply isn't enough, take a Sachertorte baking class, too.

600 Wiener Eistraum, Vienna

AUSTRIA/SWITZERLAND • **EUROPE**

AUSTRIA

602 Meander through sparkling chambers

Step through the mouth of a moss-covered giant into the glittering dreamscape of Swarovski Kristallwelten, a museum in Wattens dedicated to the iconic jeweler's artistry. Don your sparkliest outfits and wander through multifaceted domes and ruby-red halls, past a piano man suspended midair above crystal keys. Every corner reveals a surreal spectacle; a dazzling celebration of creativity you will both remember forever.

AUSTRIA

603 Go for an Alpine forage together

Rosewood Schloss Fuschl sits like a mythical castle mirrored in the glassy waters of Lake Fuschl. This fifteenth-century gem blends historic charm with modern luxury, offering year-round wellness and Alpine serenity. For a one-of-a-kind experience, join the resort's herbalist on a guided foraging walk, then craft your own salves and tinctures using wild seeds and flowers gathered from the surrounding forest.

AUSTRIA

604 Live the glamorous life in Lech

If powdery runs and lavish après-ski lunches appeal to you, hit the slopes in Lech, one of Austria's most scintillating mountain escapes. Whether you are carving fresh tracks or popping bubbly fireside, Lech delivers high-end luxury at every turn—with high-profile visitors, chic chalets, and world-class skiing. Throw horse-drawn sleigh rides and candlelit dinners into the mix, and you have got the ultimate Alpine romance.

SWITZERLAND

605 Have a sexy spa rendezvous at midnight

In Zurich, treat yourselves to a sultry late-night spa rendezvous with the Meet Me at Midnight package, where the two of you will have the Dolder Grand's vast spa all to yourselves from 10:30 P.M. to 12:30 A.M. Indulge in scantily clad experiences in the sauna, the "snow paradise" room, the sand baths, and more, warming up for romance thanks to candlelight, rose petals, champagne, and patisserie.

SWITZERLAND

606 Fly to a glacier for ooey, gooey raclette

Make Bürgenstock Hotel & Alpine Spa your home away from home, and book an only-in-Switzerland, ooey, gooey Swiss cheese raclette prepared by a personal chef atop the Alps. The champagne-accompanied package for two comes once you land from an exhilarating private helicopter flight above the peaked landscape. Return to your sumptuous Lake Lucerne digs to continue the epic coziness.

SWITZERLAND

607 Luxuriate in powdery runs and gourmet meals

Delight in the decadence of a place that appeals to both your sporty and culinary interests, Andermatt. The destination is known for its long, powdery runs across two ski mountains, but also for its multiple Michelin-starred restaurants. Dedicate your days to racing around on the snow-blanketed world-class slopes, and your après hours to chasing down momentous meals at high-end boîtes.

602 Swarovski Kristallwelten

609 Tour du Mont Blanc

SWITZERLAND

608 Opt for elegant debauchery in Vals

Find euphoria on a shamelessly hedonistic day in Vals, starting with a Louis Roederer Cristal toast at the top of a remote glacier you will have reached by private helicopter. 7132 Hotel Vals' Once in a Lifetime package also includes the Kengo Kuma–designed penthouse, an eight-course dinner at the two-Michelin-starred restaurant, and private thermal baths.

SWITZERLAND

609 Tackle the Tour du Mont Blanc

Be dazzled by astounding Alpine panoramas as you tackle the 106-mi. (170-km) Tour du Mont Blanc, which takes you through Switzerland, Italy, and France. Traipse between sweet mountain hamlets, verdant meadows, fresh lakes, and up to an 8,478-ft. (2,584-m) peak, breaking in the most paradisiacal spots to sample local wine, cheese, and chocolate.

SWITZERLAND

610 Let adrenaline flow on a speedy bobsleigh

Tuck into a bobsleigh together, one in front of the other, for the most intense seventy-five seconds of your life, hurling down the St. Moritz-Celerina Olympic Bobrun track at some 84 mph. (135 kph) an hour. For couples seeking high-speed thrills, this vintage ice track—the oldest in the world—promises the most electrifying rush.

SWITZERLAND

611 Ski, skate, and watch snow polo in St. Moritz

Take your newlywed—or longtime wed—partner to one of the most beloved winter wonderlands in Europe, St. Moritz, where you will ski and ice-skate, ride the scenic Glacier Express, and even try kite skiing. The most exciting thing to experience may be the destination's famed high goal polo tournament, which is played on a field of ice that coats a frozen lake.

SWITZERLAND

612 Ride an invigorating cable car up to Europe's highest station

Step aboard a panoramic cable car in Zermatt for the stimulating ride up to the highest mountain station in Europe, at Matterhorn Glacier Paradise. The journey is the destination on this unbelievable ride, which reaches 12,740 ft. (3,883 m). At the top, step onto a viewing platform with 360-degree views across France, Switzerland, and Italy, and featuring fourteen glaciers and thirty-eight peaks.

EUROPE • ESTONIA/LITHUANIA

ESTONIA

613 Visit the surreal environs of Soomaa

Spend a delightful day paddling on a romantic canoe trip in the surreal environs of Soomaa National Park, Estonia's hidden gem of a Ramsar-protected wetland environment whose name means "land of bogs." Swamps may not sound all that romantic, but this one is stunning. After your exploration, heat up in a healing Võro smoke sauna, an ancient UNESCO-listed spiritual tradition.

LITHUANIA

614 Choose Lithuania's castle-strewn Vilnius

Feel medieval vibes in the Lithuanian capital, where three ornate, storied Gothic castles add to a landscape of baroque and neoclassical architecture. Tour the Old Town's cobbled streets and historic squares as pedestrians first. Then gain a different perspective on board a private hot-air balloon ride, looking down over the towers, stone walls, and sapphire lakes from above.

613 Soomaa National Park, Estonia

LATVIA/POLAND • **EUROPE**

614 Vilnius, Lithuania

LATVIA

615 Explore Latvia's attractive capital, Riga

Travel to Latvia's meticulously preserved ancient capital, Riga, for both its charm and its culture. Expect to be beguiled and fascinated by the UNESCO-listed Old Town on an art nouveau architecture walking tour that winds through cobbled streets past pastel-colored buildings. Follow it with a meal that features Latvian honey and the national botanical-filled liquor, black balsam.

POLAND

616 Experience a one-of-a-kind Polish meal

Enjoy the romance of a spontaneous late-night supper or an early morning indulgence at Ćma, one of Warsaw's most distinctive restaurants. Open twenty-four hours a day and helmed by celebrated Polish chef, Mateusz Gessler, this intimate spot is the place to experience a true taste of Poland. Break homemade bread together, sip artisanal cocktails, and enjoy beautifully presented plates designed to be shared and prepared right in front of you.

POLAND

617 Sleep in a nineteenth-century palace in Warsaw

Make lasting memories on a cultivated lovers' escape in Warsaw when you book a suite at Raffles Europejski for not only its prime location on the edge of Old Town, but the chance to nuzzle up with your babe in a nineteenth-century palace. From its inception, the palace was an artistic hub, and that is still true as a five-star hotel giving aesthetes front-row access to the best collection of contemporary Polish artwork around.

POLAND

618 Voyage to the medieval "City of Lovers"

Take an odyssey to the medieval "City of Lovers," Chelmno, where you will feel as though you have stepped back in time through ancient Gothic structures. The city houses a relic of St. Valentine that bestowed its reputation as Poland's love capital. Desire is most definitely in the air, and when touring around the sights, steal a kiss at the top of the bell tower.

POLAND

619 Inspire each other to make art

Make your way to a small eastern Poland town, Kazimierz Dolny, known as an art colony full of galleries selling folk and fine art plus artists who flock there to paint. Find your own sources of inspiration while exploring castle ruins, picturesque streets, and creative enclaves, then join an open-air painting workshop where you will each create a special memento to take home.

POLAND

620 See Krakow by horse and by boat

Discover the most bewitching parts of Krakow by taking a two-pronged approach to the city. First, hire a horse-drawn carriage with a tour guide driver who will take you on an idyllic trot around to the best landmarks and historical sites. Then turn up the flirtation on a sunset boat cruise for two on the Vistula River. Either one of these activities is proposal perfect.

CZECH REPUBLIC

621 Stroll through a castle under stars

Take a nighttime private walking tour of the glamorously intricate Prague Castle, a vast complex built in the ninth century that once housed kings of Bohemia and Roman emperors. By avoiding the daytime crowds clamoring to see crown jewels and more, you and your partner can pretend it's the site of your very own fairy tale.

CZECH REPUBLIC/SLOVAKIA/SLOVENIA • **EUROPE**

621 Prague Castle

CZECH REPUBLIC

622 Leave a mark of your love on a wall in Prague

When in Prague, sign up for an experience that would normally feel reckless: spray painting your own creation on a wall of graffiti. Andaz Prague's Spray Can Symphony workshop allows the artistically inclined to leave an evocative symbol of their love in one of the city's free-to-spray zones, but only after learning can control and advanced skills from a famed graffiti artist.

SLOVAKIA

623 Climb willingly aboard a UFO . . . tower

For couples who geek out on alien conspiracy theories, there is nothing cooler than the iconic symbol of Bratislava, an observation deck shaped like a UFO. A vestige of the Soviet era, the tower hovers more than 300 ft. (90 m) above the Danube River, and promises impressive views over Austria and Hungary.

SLOVAKIA

624 Learn how to say "cheers" in Slovak

Practice your *Na zdravie!* ("to your health") before and during a spell at Bratislava's mysterious Mirror Cocktail Bar, named one of the world's best bars. Say it again and again as you toast fantastic multisensory cocktails that tell stories about Central Europe. Opt for a concoction that doubles as art, served in bespoke glassware, or one from the Nature menu, dispensed inside a botanical arrangement.

SLOVENIA

625 Spend a weekend in the City of Love

Slovenia's capital, Ljubljana, is widely known as the City of Love—literally, its name translates as "the beloved." Spend a dreamy weekend meandering through scenes that look like they could be from a Disney movie, and ride a funicular up to the castle for a decadent dinner. The next day, glide on water in a traditional, wooden *pletna* boat, manned by a standing rower.

SLOVENIA

626 Retreat to a Slovenian lakeside villa

Surround yourselves with pristine natural beauty courtesy of the rugged Julian Alps and Slovenia's Lake Bohinj, when checking into the quietly luxurious boutique hotel Vila Muhr, at the water's edge. Formerly a monarch's hunting lodge, the place has quite an aura about it, one that only fosters intimacy, especially in the timber-wrapped suites.

EUROPE • SLOVENIA/ROMANIA

SLOVENIA

627 Set off for a ten-day gastronomic caper

Tour through Slovenia with a local chef leading you in a tour de force of culinary innovation. On your ten-day gastronomic caper with Black Tomato, expect to sample farm-to-table dishes made using locally sourced ingredients, interspersed with a wide range of exploits that include wine-tasting, cheese making, and truffle hunting. You'll also enjoy VIP experiences at chef Janez Bratovž's restaurant.

SLOVENIA

628 Hit vineyards on a Slovenian wine safari

Whet your appetites for world-class wine and excitement by climbing into a Jeep for an immersive wine safari in bucolic Goriška Brda. The Slovenian wine region bordering Italy is low-key yet bursting with delectable treats that are not only of the wine sort. Taste, snack, learn production secrets, and sip. With panoramic views and plenty of pours, it's an intoxicating joyride in every sense—minus the pretension.

ROMANIA

629 Roam through virginal mountain forests seeking brown bears

Seek brown bears in the dense, virginal forests of Romania's Carpathian Mountains. With an intimate Exodus Adventure Travels trip, a local guide will walk you through the bears' native habitats by day. Then, with a forester, you can attend a bear-watching evening at Europe's largest brown bear sanctuary. Along with plenty of hiking, visit remote, charming villages, too.

629 Carpathian Mountains, Romania

ROMANIA · EUROPE

MOUNTAIN RETREAT

ROMANIA

630 Discover the luxurious side of Transylvania near Dracula's castle

Whether it is vampires that have you curious about Romania, or the country's idyllic, untouched landscapes, you will find both in Transylvania. The first order of business should be checking into a deluxe room at MATCA. The sixteen-room, two-villa hotel elegantly blends Transylvanian style with contemporary comforts through cozy-chic fireplaces, airy wood-clad interiors, and privileged views from both the swimming pool and hyperlocally sourced restaurant of the Bucegi Mountains. Styled after a traditional farmhouse with its own bee colony, there is plenty of time for tenderness and pampering—there's a spa, too!—but also countless opportunities to explore. Don't miss a visit to Bran Castle, which inspired Bram Stoker's Count Dracula.

631 Szechényi Thermal Bath

HUNGARY

631 Feel tension melt away in Budapest

Enter Budapest's Széchenyi Thermal Bath with all the stresses of life held in your shoulders, and exit with a newfound sense of relaxation, having been seduced and soothed by the mineral-rich healing powers of one of Europe's largest bath complexes.

HUNGARY

632 Admire roses on Margaret Island

Immerse yourselves in the sweet-scented loveliness of Margaret River's historical rose garden, which dates to the early nineteenth century. After your stroll, settle into a candlelit dinner on a Danube River riverboat, amid twinkling surroundings and live music.

HUNGARY

633 Overnight in a castle built for love

Curled up inside a castle, inspire your lover to make a gesture as grand as Baron Zsigmond Schossberger when he built the place out of love for his wife. The fairy-tale, circa 1883, neoclassical and neobaroque wonder is now a hotel named BOTANIQ Castle of Tura, with a spa and fine dining.

HUNGARY/SERBIA • EUROPE

637 Most Ljubavi (Bridge of Love), Vrnjačka Banja

HUNGARY

634 Reserve a gorgeous moving hotel room

Along with just fifty others, embrace slow travel along the glorious rural route of the sleeper Golden Eagle Danube Express train in one of its few glamorous en suite sleeping cabins. On your leisurely tour, drink in the incredible beauty of Hungary along the famed Danube River and pass landscapes at their most vibrant in the fall. Divine, romantic dinners embed edible memories, too.

HUNGARY

635 Witness a singular light phenomenon on Hungary's Lake Balaton

On the lovely shores of Lake Balaton in Hungary's wine region, share a bottle while admiring the surreal light phenomenon that creates a golden bridge as the sun rises and sets each day, and a silvered one when the moon reflects on the still water.

SERBIA

636 Bike and boat your way through Belgrade

Commit to some light exercise in the name of a very good cause: wine tasting. In the ancient city of Belgrade, take to the road on a wine-tasting bicycle tour where you will sip as you cycle. Later, completely relax on a magic-hour joyride on the Danube River, taking in city sights that include Kalemegdan Fortress, Great War Island, and Branko's Bridge.

SERBIA

637 Leave a symbol of your everlasting devotion

Devoted couples can engage in the age-old tradition of eternal romantics in Vrnjačka Banja at the original love lock bridge, the very first so-called Bridge of Love. In the Serbian destination, lock your hearts together in an unbreakable symbol of your everlasting affection before indulging in couples spa treatments in the place known for its healing mineral springs.

639 Plitvice Lakes National Park

CROATIA

638 Pick olives in a world-famous olive oil region

Plan a fall tour of Croatia to coincide with the bountiful harvest in one of the world's very best olive oil regions. In Istria, pick olives from a coastal grove, learning all about the ancient tradition as you go. Savor the fruits of your labor over a seductive dinner on an Edenic, family-run farm.

CROATIA

639 Soak up the beauty of Plitvice Lakes

Savor the incandescent beauty of Croatia's Plitvice Lakes National Park. Take to the water for a peaceful paddle on stand-up boards or in a kayak, where you will float into the dreamlike turquoise of the Mrežnica River. Afterward, back on land, hike along boardwalks to a secluded picnic spot overlooking waterfalls or rapids.

CROATIA

640 Go island-hopping in the Adriatic Sea

Charter a catamaran or sailboat for two in Croatia's Marina Baotić, just outside Split, and set sail on the shimmering Adriatic. As you hop from island to island, be sure not to miss Brač's charming village Bol, Biševo's mesmerizing Blue Cave, medieval Korčula, and Hvar's famed Fortica fortress.

CROATIA

641 Pedal around the Dalmation Coast

Rent bikes to pedal your way through, and zigzag across, the Dalmatian Coast. Winding roads will lead you to charming fishing villages and past glittering Adriatic beaches. Cycle the stone streets of Split or head south to Dubrovnik to explore its fortified city walls with sea vistas.

CROATIA

642 Glow through a SUP tour at sunset

Bask in the most radiant golden hour you have ever seen, on a pair of stand-up paddleboards during a guided sunset tour of the Dalmatian Coast. The inconceivably beautiful scene is only made better by snorkeling and clinking glasses of local wine.

CROATIA

643 Let boutique hotels guide your travels

Take a different approach to planning your Croatian honeymoon or anniversary trip: let exceptional boutique hotels be your guides. In a country with many intimate stays, crafted to celebrate the local culture, select your destinations by first seeking out incomparable hotels where ultra-personalized experiences are par for the course.

CROATIA

644 Sleep in a monastery on Lopud Island

Dial back through the centuries amid the sumptuous environs of a fortified fifteenth-century monastery that has been meticulously restored to create an exclusive-use villa. An art museum as much as it is a luxury hotel, Lopud 1483 has an arresting collection that combines medieval tapestries with Renaissance pieces and contemporary works.

MONTENEGRO

645 Embrace the Mediterranean lifestyle

Nestle into the surroundings of hidden-gem Tivat, on Montenegro's glam Bay of Kotor, for a taste of the good life, Mediterranean style. Devour an unforgettable meal—or several—of succulent, just-caught seafood and Montenegrin wine. Round out your evening with a long, slow stroll along the Tivat waterfront promenade.

645 Bay of Kotor, Montenegro

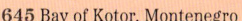

EUROPE • MONTENEGRO/KOSOVO/BULGARIA/GEORGIA

MONTENEGRO

646 Escape to a luscious seaside resort

Check into the opulent seaside resort One&Only Portonovi, tucked between medieval villages and lush Black Mountains on a submerged river valley called a *ria*. The UNESCO-designated fjord-like setting is an aquatic playground and wellness haven for couples who seek shared bliss.

KOSOVO

647 Witness the sun setting behind snow-covered peaks

Select a fine bottle of Kosovar wine as a reward for climbing 1,722 ft. (525 m) above sea level where the remains of Prizren Fortress, first built by the Byzantines, overlooks Kosovo's cultural capital, Prizren. Take in the sun setting behind snow-covered mountains as you toast to your intrepid travels.

BULGARIA

648 Enjoy an amorous dinner atop a seawall

Step onto a water taxi in Bulgaria's ancient seaside city of Nessebar, bound for Sunny Beach. There, in the vibrant resort town, you could play paintball or ride go-karts for a lighthearted afternoon date before dedicating your evening to a sultrier liaison: a romantic dinner of fish straight from the Black Sea, atop the St. Vlas seawall, timed to the setting sun.

GEORGIA

649 Stay in a landmark of Tbilisi's creative cool

Spend a few days at the bold, devastatingly cool Stamba Hotel. Set in a repurposed Soviet-era publishing house, the design blends industrial with vintage glamour, pairing exposed concrete and original printing presses with lush, velvet-upholstered furnishings. Enjoy your beguiling room with its gold-clad bathtub for two-person soaks, but your exploits must also include a dip in the glass-bottomed swimming pool that is five stories up.

GEORGIA

650 Sip, soak, and swing in the Caucasus

Sign up for a private tasting session with a Georgian sommelier in the ancient wine-growing region Kakheti, before retreating to Lopota Lake Resort & Spa for a detoxifying Slavic bath ritual for two. You will be in a natural fantasyland surrounded by the Caucasus Mountains and crystal-clear water, but even more fun is to be had in the form of the property's acoustically excellent Jazz Club.

GEORGIA

651 Climb to an iconic church in the mountains

Built in the fourteenth century, the iconic, cross-cupola Gergeti Trinity Church sits 7,120 ft. (2,170 m) above sea level. It is one of Georgia's most famous landmarks, and the first stage of the epic climb of Mount Kazbek, the country's third tallest peak. Amid breathtaking views, hike up the glacier-covered mountain, led by a guide, recounting legendary tales of Prometheus (credited for crafting humanity from clay) as you go.

651 Gergeti Trinity Church, Georgia

ALBANIA

652 Discover the Adriatic's hidden heart

Set sail on a Variety Cruises yacht for a lesser-traveled discovery of the Adriatic Sea that encompasses Albania as well as Croatia. As the able captain tours you around the offbeat region you will fall in love with rich folklore, historic cobbled streets, and decadent flavors.

GREECE

653 Acropolis-gaze while rooftop dining

Spend an evening gazing across at the ancient Greek landmark, the Acropolis of Athens. At the glam, sixteen-room boutique hotel Villa Brown Ermou, you will find alluring couples spa treatments that set the tone for a candlelit dinner on the romantic rooftop with citadel views.

GREECE

654 Steal away to a glitzy Athenian Riviera resort

Embody the glitz and glam of 1960s Athens at the site of a former A-list beach club that is now home to the heavenly resort, One&Only Aesthesis. It is a flawless honeymoon choice, with round-the-clock butler service for your every whim plus a restaurant with three Michelin stars.

GREECE

655 Make a day of sightseeing in Athens

Pick up some new knowledge of Greek gods and goddesses on a mythology-themed walking tour of ancient Athens, with the iconic Parthenon at the forefront. Start early to beat the crowds and heat before embracing on a National Gardens stroll and finishing up with wine tasting in quaint Plaka.

GREECE

656 Find new ways to explore Greek cuisine

Via helicopter, pop over to Sifnos and Naxos with Michelin-starred Pelagos chef Luca Piscazzi to immerse yourselves in their gastronomic heritage, feed each other local nibbles, and cook alongside grandmas. Back at the Four Seasons Astir Palace Hotel Athens, feast on a tasting menu influenced by your escapade.

GREECE

657 Cliff jump on the island of Milos

Clasp your beloved's hand tightly before leaping off the top of a cliff together at a beach that looks like moonstone. The fantastic lunar-like landscape bleeding into aquamarine heaven is found on the northern coast of Milos, a quintessential Greek island that is alluringly very lightly touristed.

657 Lunar-like landscape, Milos

GREECE

658 Relax on Myrtos Beach, Kefalonia

Blend a bit of history with a whole lot of relaxation on the island of Kefalonia, when you strike out with your dearest for a fifteenth-century castle visit and romantic stroll around Assos before plopping down on the arresting white sand and pebbles of Myrtos, one of Greece's most dramatic beaches.

GREECE • EUROPE

658 Myrtos Beach, Kefalonia

GREECE

659 Charter a chic private catamaran

Embark on an extremely luxurious outing together, aboard a private catamaran, cruising the Saronic Gulf with a crew catering to only you two. Choose an afternoon sailing for a dose of hot Greek sun in which to bathe, before the sky begins to fill with vivid sunset shades.

GREECE

660 Master two Greek traditions on Chios

On the off-the-beaten-path isle of Chios, take a Greek dancing class led by local instructors and learn simple traditional dances. In the village of Pityos, your cultural saturation will continue with another local skill-bestowing class: making *hilopites*, a type of hand-rolled pasta. Say, *kali orexi*! as you dig in.

GREECE

661 Spend a slow day or two on chichi Hydra

Wander the artsy enclave of Hydra, a car-free protected island just two hours from Athens, where the chicest Greeks weekend. Browse the boutique galleries, slide into the island's diamond-like water from rocks, and later dance until you drop at a beach bar, fueled by colorful craft cocktails.

EUROPE • GREECE

SOULFUL SIMPLICITY

GREECE

662 Feel blown away by the magic of a cave pool suite on Mykonos

Take your passion to a primal place in a cave suite at Cavo Tagoo, a one-of-a-kind hotel built into a cliffside with a 120-ft. (35-m) aquarium bar, a spa, and—accommodation a lovestruck couple must book—a Cave Pool Suite that is even more magical than it sounds.

GREECE

663 Sail to secluded skinny-dipping spots on Mykonos' quiet side

Hole up in a raw, chic, and totally covetable sea-facing suite or villa at the Wild Hotel, a Cycladic gem on Mykonos' quieter side. From there, embark on a sailing voyage through jewel-hued water to secluded skinny-dipping spots away from the crowds of party people.

GREECE

664 Live in your swimsuit in a superior swimming pool

Head to Cali Mykonos on the eponymous uninhibited island, where you will get to play all day in an incredible 426-ft.-long (130-m) swimming pool, whose graceful infinity edge bleeds into the cyan Aegean Sea. Break away for a secluded jaunt to the golden sands of Kalafati Beach below.

GREECE • EUROPE

GREECE

665 Cuddle up in a driftwood tepee at Antiparos' seductive the Rooster

For couples who travel to experience something authentic and unexpected, Antiparos' charismatic resort the Rooster is the promised land, a spellbinding retreat from travel tropes done in an astoundingly modest way. With homey touches, breezy outdoor showers, a private pool, and captivating views, you will feel ensconced in the vacation home you wish you had. Tote a packed picnic basket to the beach, harvest your lunch from the organic garden, try a Grecian fire ceremony, and lounge in a driftwood tepee by the Aegean.

666 Ios, Greece

GREECE

666 Be reminded of love everywhere you look at Calilo Ios

Feel romanced by an Ios resort where messages of love and hearts are hidden, and emblazoned, all around as part of the creative owners' mission to playfully uplift their guests and inspire them to feel deeper. In the art-filled sanctuary, reserve a singular suite with your own grotto-like water passage and cave pool where love—making, sharing, and growing it—will certainly be top of your mind.

269

GREECE

667 Explore five-thousand-year-old Akrotiri's streets and painted houses

On the beloved island of Santorini, step back in time on an exploration—guided or not—of five-thousand-year-old Akrotiri, the time capsule–like prehistoric buried city that was uncovered in the 1960s. After checking out the beautifully preserved streets and painted houses, find a flawless little beach on which to sprawl side by side, letting the sound of the surf take you to cloud nine.

667 Santorini

GREECE/CYPRUS • EUROPE

GREECE

668 Enjoy breakfast with endless champagne

Check into Santorini's Grace Hotel, Auberge Resorts Collection, for its volcanic caldera views, minimalist rooms, or oasis-like pools, but especially for its extravagant champagne-drenched breakfast. Awaken eager each day to taste your way through an exquisite five-course breakfast with said indulgently free-flowing champagne. The menu changes daily, but you can expect it to feature Greek yogurt with honey and pistachios, a range of egg dishes, fresh-baked pastries, and local specialties.

GREECE

669 Scoot around the island of Naxos

Pack your international driver's licenses before hitting the island of Naxos, where you will rent a scooter on which to explore the island. Use your cute two-wheeler to zip within walking distance of the ancient sites that include the Temple of Apollo, which dates back to the sixth century BCE and thirteenth-century Naxos castle, before uncovering culinary joys and pretty mountain towns such as Filoti and Halki.

GREECE

670 Eat just-caught lobster on Sifnos

Slumber inside a windmill or at a sizzling boutique hotel on the island of Sifnos for a foodie escape featuring a bounty of locally fished and grown ingredients. Dine at typical tavernas and fish bars, try local Sifnian traditions, and spend full evenings tasting fancy gastronomy on clifftops. At least once, feast on freshly caught lobsters served with spaghetti on the jetty.

CYPRUS

671 Patronize Cyprus's only luxe boutique hotel

Take your mutual infatuation to the UNESCO-recognized village of Lefkara for a sweet, slow few days at the Agora. With its name meaning "a place to gather," the resort fosters a sense of connection in many ways, including with complimentary bikes ready to be taken out on bucolic cycling routes perhaps to local wineries or a traditional lace-maker's workshop. For a soulful tryst, there is nothing more sublime.

671 Lefkara, Cyprus

TURKEY

672 Sleep in a sumptuous Ottoman imperial palace

Check into your splendid suite in the 1870s Ottoman imperial palace that is now Çırağan Palace Kempinski Istanbul, and open your eyes to the beautiful Bosphorus Strait every morning, feeling like royalty. You will not need to go anywhere to soak up the luxury of the city's grande dame. Toast delicate glasses of champagne under crystal chandeliers, visit the spa together, and float in the riverside outdoor pool. When it comes to exploring, the hotel sits in one of Istanbul's most vibrant and scenic districts between Ortaköy and Beşiktaş.

TURKEY

673 Dine on two continents in the same day—same country, too

Enjoy the novelty of dining on two continents in the same day—in the very same country. Istanbul is the only city split between Europe and Asia, so you can start with breakfast on the western side of the Bosphorus, cross the strait by boat for a waterfront lunch in Asia, and then return for a divine dinner back in Europe.

673 Dining in Europe, Istanbul

TURKEY • EUROPE

TURKEY

674 Get scrubbed and steamy in a sixteenth-century hammam

Strip down together to experience one of the oldest bathing rituals in existence: the Turkish bath. Inside the grand domed chamber of Suleymaniye Hammam—which was built for a sultan in 1557, designed by prolific sixteenth-century architect Mimar Sinan—you will discover the "bath" actually takes place on marble slabs. After getting doused in water, frothy bubbles, and scrubbed thoroughly, you will emerge with baby-soft skin.

TURKEY

675 Skim along Bodrum's crystalline water on a private yacht

Complement your Bodrum beach resort getaway with a seductive way to experience the jet-set lifestyle: a yacht trip. Arrange to have the motorboat all to yourselves, don your skimpy swimwear, and request a hidden gems itinerary for the day trip, which should take you to quiet bays where you can leap off the boat holding hands and plunge into the sapphire Aegean Sea—snorkels optional.

675 Bodrum

TURKEY • EUROPE

676 Cappadocia by hot-air balloon

TURKEY

676 Take in a surreal sunrise from a hot-air balloon basket for two over Cappadocia

Feel the sensation of floating through a fairy tale when you fly in a hot-air balloon for two above the surreal land of Cappadocia. As the rising sun paints the sky in pastels and your balloon sails into the dreamscape, there is no better way to see this surreal landscape scattered with hoodoos and other striking geological formations.

TURKEY

677 Frolic through fairy chimneys and sleep in a cave (hotel!)

It is hard to imagine a landscape more enchanting than Cappadocia, where perhaps the world's most iconic topography is thanks to millions of years of lava erosion many millions of years ago. Explore the legendary fairy chimneys, peek inside ancient rock houses, and explore underground cities, all while staying in your own beguiling cave—with its own private pool—at Cappadocia's über-romantic Argos resort.

677 Cappadocia

4
AFRICA AND THE MIDDLE EAST

AFRICA AND THE MIDDLE EAST • JORDAN

679 Candlelight at Petra

JORDAN
678 Let the good times flow at the Dead Sea

In the lowest point on Earth, opt for a resort that makes you both feel high. With its ancient Hanging Gardens of Babylon–style architecture, Kempinski Hotel Ishtar Dead Sea does just that, thanks in part to its nine glamorous swimming pools and one of the largest spas in the Middle East. Pampering treatments for two are a must.

JORDAN
679 Be transported in the candlelit magic of Petra

At Petra, the singular Rose City in southern Jordan with ancient rock-cut architecture, 1,500 flickering candles and a canopy of twinkling stars is the setting for the most romantic of nights. Explore the Treasury and more under the warm glow of the thrice-weekly night show.

JORDAN
680 Snuggle under the stars in otherworldly Wadi Rum

Spend a mystical and majestic night beneath a blanket of constellations in the storied, UNESCO-designated Wadi Rum, an immeasurable desert landscape that speaks to lovers of rare archaeology, history, and nature. Bedouin-style camping at one of many camps can be pretty plush, so there is no need to give up your creature comforts while hiking, riding 4x4s, and stargazing atop the red-tinged sand that glows radiantly at sunrise and sunset.

JORDAN/SAUDI ARABIA • **AFRICA AND THE MIDDLE EAST**

JORDAN

681 Float impossibly buoyantly together in the Dead Sea

Contrary to its name, you will feel incredibly alive in the Dead Sea. It is hard to even swim here, the water is so dense and salty—nearly ten times more than the ocean. Rich in minerals such as magnesium, calcium, and potassium, the mud and water have been prized for their therapeutic properties since biblical times. Lie back, close your eyes, and just levitate, letting tranquility wash over you in Jordan's most ancient and ephemeral spa.

SAUDI ARABIA

682 Gallop on fine Arabian horses along a Red Sea beach

On a pair of beautiful Arabian horses, take a private scenic ride along a long, sandy beach fringing the Red Sea, which is actually a lustrous turquoise hue. Take your guided, trot-filled tour in late afternoon, and bring a Polaroid camera, so you can catch instant shots of each other splashing hooves in the water as the sun sets in a full blaze.

680 Glamping in Wadi Rum Desert

683 Our Habitas AlULa, Saudi Arabia

SAUDI ARABIA

683 Surrender to spectacular scenery

Book a stay at Our Habitas AlULa and prepare for seduction of a new kind. The soulfully luxurious and sustainable desert resort is built into a canyon embraced by fantastic sandstone mountains. The retreat draws inspiration from nomadic Arab tribes and opens the door to guests exploring a living museum of ancient architectural wonders.

SAUDI ARABIA

684 Explore Indigenous trading culture while deepening your bond

Dive into the illustrious Nabataean trading culture at the desert oasis of Six Senses Southern Dunes, The Red Sea. There, grow closer as you discover the deep traditional roots and significance of the ancient and vibrant Bedouin art of sadu weaving, a UNESCO-listed intangible cultural asset.

BAHRAIN

685 Savor a day on Bahrain's Pearling Path

Follow Bahrain's Pearling Path, a 2-mi. (3.5-km) trail through historic Muharraq. It tells the story of the island's pearling legacy—a trade that shaped its economy and culture for 2,000 years. Along the way, visit a traditional jeweler and pick a pearlescent treasure to save for your thirtieth wedding anniversary.

BAHRAIN

686 Visit a vanishing island off the mainland

Witness the ephemeral beauty of a sandy island that disappears with every high-tide rush of emerald saltwater, and live in the moment with the sun kissing your skin on the evanescent paradise. Get there by private boat from Bahrain and bring a picnic to nibble before the water starts to rise again.

QATAR

687 Romance your love at an exquisite hotel

Book a room at the ultraluxe Rosewood Doha, whose two towers draw inspiration from the thriving coral reef just beyond in the Arabian Gulf. It makes for a joy-filled vacation studded with boat trips to beaches and snorkeling spots, not to mention eight impeccable culinary options.

QATAR

688 Witness a centuries-old tradition with a modern twist

Delight in the novelty of watching a captivating tradition in the Qatari desert as you take a joyride with your partner, alongside the country's famous camel race. Instead of human jockeys, however, you will see the animals ridden by brightly clothed robot jockeys.

UNITED ARAB EMIRATES

689 Channel Aladdin during a magic carpet dinner

Go native on a camel or opt for the exhilarating contemporary custom of dune bashing in a vehicle with partially deflated tires en route to a fairy-tale dinner on a magic carpet—just like Aladdin—in the Abu Dhabi desert.

UNITED ARAB EMIRATES

690 Bask in the amorous ambience of an eco sanctuary

Settle into an ornate overwater bungalow in an unlikely location: an eco sanctuary in the United Arab Emirates, specifically Ras Al Khaimah. Anantara Mina Ras Al Khaimah Resort's ultra-private accommodations amid mangroves and a pristine beach are a first for the region.

689 Dune bashing in the Abu Dhabi desert

691 Dubai Miracle Garden

UNITED ARAB EMIRATES

691 Pair a bloom-filled morning with a sky-high dinner

Be the first to enter the Dubai Miracle Garden in the morning for a euphoric amble through the world's largest flower garden, with more than fifty million blooms styled into gorgeous displays, including a series of heart-shaped arches. Later, take your Dubai affair to new heights when you find yourselves hanging from a crane at 160 ft. (50 m) for a heart-thumping gourmet Dinner in the Sky.

UNITED ARAB EMIRATES

692 Check into a vertical resort in a Dubai skyscraper

Consider a vacation up in the clouds at the vertical resort One&Only One Za'abeel, where your sumptuous room will look out to the world's tallest building, the Burj Khalifa. By day, you will splash around and soak up the rays from the Emirates' longest rooftop infinity pool—in a record-breaking 328-ft.-high (100-m) cantilevered structure. Choose from eleven restaurants when it comes to dining.

UNITED ARAB EMIRATES

693 Fall head over heels all over again in a seven-star hotel

Let your butler wow you with romantic arrangements when you reserve a princely suite at the extravagant seven-star Jumeirah Burj Al Arab hotel, easily Dubai's most recognizable icon with the graceful sail shape. Revel in the feeling of hovering over the Persian Gulf from the beach club, live it up in the spa having twosome treatments, and dine at the Michelin-starred Al Muntaha all the way up on the twenty-seventh floor.

OMAN/MOROCCO • **AFRICA AND THE MIDDLE EAST**

OMAN

694 Go formal for a refined evening out

Pack your finest formalwear to enjoy a glamorous night out in Muscat. First, take in a romantic ballet or opera inside the contemporary Omani-styled Royal Opera House Muscat, with an interior fit for royalty. Afterward, retire to the bougie beachfront Mandarin Oriental, Muscat, where you can dine on a special post-theater feast and then toast each other over nightcaps in the hotel's glittering lounge.

OMAN

695 Strike out on a scuba-diving mission

Dedicate your next vacation to learning a new skill together: scuba diving. You can study up before flying to Oman, but the country's 1,800-mi. (2,900-km) coastline provides plentiful conditions for beginners' first hop into the sublime saltwater world. The warm, calm Arabian Sea is a fascinating place to test out your abilities and potentially spot a whale or dolphin.

MOROCCO

696 Trek the Atlas Mountains then chill in a posh fortress

Let the pristine air of the Atlas Mountains intoxicate you as you trek through the storied range studded with quaint villages and astounding panoramas. Those vistas will follow you to the posh pool at Kasbah Tamadot, a resplendent refuge styled after a citadel with delightfully vibrant bedrooms and splendid Berber tents with private plunge pools.

696 Kasbah Tamadot

MOROCCO • **AFRICA AND THE MIDDLE EAST**

BLUE HUES AND MOUNTAIN VIEWS

MOROCCO

697 Roam in amazement through the magical Blue City

Get lost, intentionally, as you roam through pure enchantment in the form of Morocco's most brilliantly hued destination, Chefchaouen. For half a millennium, the charmingly mazelike town stepping down foothills of the Rif Mountains has been overwhelmingly blue, an appealing mosaic of cyan, indigo, azure, and cornflower shades. The photo ops are infinite, so keep your camera or phone battery charged as you explore, enraptured by the intimate arches and corners in which to pose.

AFRICA AND THE MIDDLE EAST • MOROCCO

MOROCCO

698 Feel the warmth of gracious hospitality

For the most genuine overnight in Fès, take a room in the winding medieval medina at the grand Karawan Riad, very private and traditional in the sense that each of the seven suites is like a miniature palace, endowed with spectacular details and lavish furnishings. Book a guided tour of the medina to discover its cultural and historical sights—palaces, mosques, and souks among them.

MOROCCO

699 Visit a famed souk and retreat to an oasis

Tastes, smells, textures, and astonishing sights—think snake charmers!—will have you both marveling during a slow wander around Marrakech's famous souk. Follow the bustle of the market with an escape to the oasis-like riad Villa des Orangers for a serene afternoon on sunbeds that slips easily into a night dining on Mediterranean-Moroccan decadence surrounded by twinkling fairy lights.

MOROCCO

700 Stroll an iconic botanical garden

Art aficionado couples and horticulturists cannot pass up the opportunity to take a morning walk through magical Jardin Majorelle, the botanical garden created by French artist Jacques Majorelle over forty years, starting more than a century ago. So much love went into building the dream desertscape of cacti, succulents, bougainvillea, and palm trees, each selected for their sculptural silhouettes.

MOROCCO

701 Binge on luxury at the sumptuous La Mamounia

Indulge in a two-story suite at one of the world's best hotels, La Mamounia, in the heart of Marrakech. From the moment you are given a signature orange leather card holder—to keep—with your room key, you will be cared for like family. Royal family, that is. Savor mornings in your robes with room service on the terrace in the lap of luxury.

MOROCCO

702 Chauffeur your lover in a quad bike escapade

Steal away for an off-road quad bike escapade outside Essaouira, with you driving your spouse on the exhilarating journey over dunes and windswept beaches. Later, calm things down during a private couples Moroccan hammam treatment, which will involve exorbitant amounts of steam and special black soap, plus scrubbing until your skin feels like silk.

MOROCCO

703 Ride a party wave in Imsouane's Magic Bay

Sign up for camp—surf camp, that is—and learn how to longboard on Imsouane's incredibly perfect break dubbed Magic Bay, where the right-handed wave breaks flawlessly, offering consistent curls that are friendly for beginners. Reserve a private room, but be ready to make new friends during long days in the water and delicious shared Moroccan meals.

700 Jardin Majorelle

AFRICA AND THE MIDDLE EAST • MOROCCO/SENEGAL

MOROCCO

704 Journey into the Sahara desert for a starlit overnight

Take a swaying camel ride deep into the Sahara desert, between sweeping sculptural dunes and mind-blowing orange sandscapes, to discover a secluded Berber tent for two tucked into the otherworldly scene. Trudge up to a peak for sundown, then sample bread baked in the hot sand with your starry, candlelit dinner.

SENEGAL

705 Be awed by the pinkest lake in the world

Share a moment of awe at the rare beauty of the world's pinkest lake, Senegal's Lake Retba, just outside Dakar, aka Lac Rose. Its water can present as shocking pink, especially in the dry season from November to May. Time your visit right to admire it from a boat, on a Jeep dune tour, and a side-by-side float in the syrupy, super-salty water.

SENEGAL

706 Discover the joys of birding in Senegal

Develop your newest hobby as a couple, birding, in the so-called Gateway to Africa, where there are more than 650 avian species flitting about. The joyful pursuit of electrifying and beguiling birds is quite gripping, as you will find out on one of many small-boat birding safaris such as those on offer in Djoudj National Bird Sanctuary.

704 Sahara desert camping

CAPE VERDE/GUINEA-BISSAU/SIERRA LEONE • **AFRICA AND THE MIDDLE EAST**

CAPE VERDE

707 Play out your luxury yacht fantasies

Brush up on your *bom dia* before stepping aboard Relais & Châteaux's *Le Ponant* ship holding just thirty-two guests and as many staff to guide and pamper you through the Portuguese-speaking Cape Verde archipelago. The immersive, weeklong sailing adventure reveals brightly colored towns, white-sand beaches, and cerulean waters.

GUINEA-BISSAU

708 Island hop across a little-traveled archipelago

Venture to the Bijagós Islands in the Atlantic Ocean, and island hop your way across an archipelago where time has stood still. Eco exploits aplenty—saltwater hippos, traditional mask dances, mangrove kayaking—await adventurous couples for whom luxury is not important, only reverence for a place unexplored.

SIERRA LEONE

709 Adopt an orphaned chimpanzee together

Wildlife-adoring duos will find additional objects of affection in Sierra Leone at Tacugama Chimpanzee Sanctuary, which works to rehabilitate orphaned chimps. Occupy an eco tree house in the luscious forest reserve with waterfalls and, after visiting the entertaining primates, choose one to adopt. They stay put, but your support will go on.

707 Cape Verde

LIBERIA

710 Visit a place none of your friends have been to

Embrace eco-tourism in Liberia, for a getaway that can be all about authentic experiences for you and your significant other. Base yourself somewhere like Libassa Ecolodge, in an oceanfront tropical forest, and day trip to rainforests, waterfalls, and habitats for adorable native pygmy hippos.

COTE D'IVOIRE

711 Take your chocolate lust to the next level

Get your fill of the most delectable aphrodisiac, chocolate, in the country that produces one-tenth of the world's supply. Take your fellow chocaholic to the Côte d'Ivoire and satisfy those cravings once and for all, visiting cocoa plantations and chocolate factories to witness every step of the process. Visit the bustling markets in Abidjan or pick up locally made bars and truffles to bring the experience home.

710 Libassa Ecolodge, Liberia

AFRICA AND THE MIDDLE EAST • GHANA/BENIN/SÃO TOMÉ & PRÍNCIPE

712 Gold Coast, Ghana

GHANA

712 Laze on caramel-colored beaches

Lovestruck sun-worshipping partners seeking easygoing relaxation and tropical vibes with a cool culture will find happiness in Ghana, where half the country's coastline is sandy beach dusted with caramel-toned sand. Along the Gold Coast, you will find coconut trees dancing in the breeze, infinity pools for when the Atlantic Ocean is too rough, and freshly caught lobster to eat under moonlight.

BENIN

713 Cruise around a Venice-like lake village

Hire a private boat for a romantic spin around the Technicolor lake village of Ganvié, nicknamed the Venice of Africa since it exists entirely overwater, with houses on stilts built of bamboo and teak. Learn all about the fascinating Tofinu people who built this village, and stop for a picturesque lunch at a floating restaurant, too.

SÃO TOMÉ & PRÍNCIPE

714 Explore the African Galapagos together

Embark on a paradisiacal adventure in São Tomé and Príncipe, known as the African Galapagos for its ecological diversity and many endemic species. A customized Stanley Safaris itinerary ensures you will get intimate with the local marine life and culture as you snorkel off secluded perfect beaches and take luscious chocolate and coffee tours.

TUNISIA/EGYPT/CHAD/ETHIOPIA • **AFRICA AND THE MIDDLE EAST**

TUNISIA

715 Make lasting memories on a beach with flamingos and camels

Opt for a different kind of beach day on Djerba, one featuring fantastically pink flamingos—winter is prime time—and fancifully dressed camels. Hire a pair for an odd yet amazing vantage point of the surreal turquoise lagoon water and conclude your memorable day unwinding at Dar Dhiafa guesthouse.

TUNISIA

716 Get swept away by the luscious flavors of Tunisia

Take a delectable culinary tour on the stunning coastal island of Djerba, with a local guiding you to secret spots to taste and witness its Jewish-meets-Islamic flavors and riches. Stay another day and sign up for a culinary workshop so the two of you can re-create your favorite dishes together for years to come.

EGYPT

717 Summit Mount Sinai for an absolutely unforgettable sunrise

Experience the hushed awe that is the most spectacular sunrise you will ever see, at the top of Mount Sinai, a sacred site for three major religions. The only question is how to get there. Active couples can choose to trek on foot, starting before dawn in the dark and climbing, at one point, 3,750 steep steps. Go on camels for less of a burn.

EGYPT

718 Admire ancient pyramids on a Nile cruise

Cruise past ancient Egyptian pyramids along the Nile River aboard an intimate purpose-built Viking River Cruises ship with Scandi aesthetics. Along the way, stop off to visit royal tombs, spice markets, and ruins, and enjoy traditional *felucca* sailing outings that will send you back in time.

CHAD

719 Sign up for an inspiring safari

Zakouma National Park is one of Central Africa's greatest conservation success stories. Once heavily impacted by poaching, it has seen a remarkable revival and is now home to thriving populations of elephants, lions, giraffes, and hundreds of bird species. Adventuring couples will find Zakouma's regeneration efforts deeply inspiring.

ETHIOPIA

720 Take part in an Ethiopian coffee ceremony for two

Gain appreciation of Ethiopian flavors and culture in the capital of Addis Ababa during a traditional coffee ceremony for two. It is an elaborate core ritual that introduces partners to local values. Follow it with a cooking class or street art walking tour to enrich your visceral memories.

AFRICA AND THE MIDDLE EAST • ETHIOPIA/REPUBLIC OF THE CONGO

ETHIOPIA

721 Survey rock-hewn churches and highlands on horseback

In a country with literally millions of horses, sign up for an amazing equestrian escapade of Lalibela, Ethiopia's ancient town known for rock-cut churches from the twelfth and thirteenth centuries. During your tour, take in the mysterious monoliths and admire the sweeping mountain highlands as you clink glasses of ancient honey wine called *tej*.

ETHIOPIA

722 Rough it to reach the wildest environment on Earth

Strike out with a guide for a place that is one of the driest, lowest, and hottest on the planet. The Danakil Depression's active volcanoes, lava lakes, and fantasy of rainbow-colored acidic hot springs will absolutely blow your minds. Prepare for extremes: heat, harsh weather, and basic makeshift camping. But also nature's wildest wonders.

ETHIOPIA

723 Disconnect from modern life at a serene lakeside forest spa

Retreat to Kuriftu Resort & Spa Bishoftu, a waterfront venue on unspoiled Lake Bishoftu some forty-five minutes' drive from Ethiopia's capital of Addis Ababa. Prepare to disconnect from the outside world at this forest spa setting, swimming pools, sauna, and all, finding bliss and harmony beside your soulmate during rituals inspired by the wisdom of nature.

721 Rock-hewn church, Lalibela

REPUBLIC OF THE CONGO

724 Go way off the beaten path with Extraordinary Journeys

Embark on an off-grid expedition into one of Africa's oldest protected places, Odzala-Kokoua National Park. With several major rivers streaking through the remote biodiverse tropical forest, you will use boats and your own feet to track impressive western lowland gorillas plus forest elephants and a host of other entertaining animals. Extraordinary Journeys will custom-build your entire itinerary, including art gallery visits in the capital of Brazzaville.

722 Danakil Depression

AFRICA AND THE MIDDLE EAST • UGANDA

725 Volcanoes Safaris' Kibale Lodge

UGANDA

725 Live in rustic luxury in western Uganda

At Volcanoes Safaris' Kibale Lodge, stay in a chic handcrafted banda overlooking the Rwenzori Mountains, home to lush, tropical rainforest and bamboo woodlands. When you're not tracking chimpanzees, baboons, and monkeys in Kibale Forest National Park, make good use of the services of your personal butler and indulge in the lodge's complimentary spa treatments.

UGANDA

726 Take a Nile safari that makes a difference

Enjoy a romantic wildlife safari on the gleaming Nile River—quite literally, Lemala Wildwaters Lodge sits on a private rocky island amid the flow—with the knowledge that your stay has a positive impact on young Maasai girls and the environment. Take a moment or two during your stay to learn about the local projects to which Lemala is committed.

UGANDA

727 Have a fairy-tale forest stay

Bwindi Impenetrable Forest National Park is famous for being home to nearly half the world's endangered mountain gorillas. Make Gorilla Forest Lodge your elegant base camp for trekking and meeting the Indigenous Batwa guardians. Other options on the resort itinerary include a walk through dense forest and bamboo groves and a birding walk, looking for rare species.

UGANDA/KENYA • AFRICA AND THE MIDDLE EAST

729 Afternoon tea at Giraffe Manor

UGANDA

728 Weave grass baskets and learn to cook

After your remarkable gorilla trek in Bwindi Impenetrable Forest National Park, spend the remainder of your day with your better half connecting with local group Ride 4 a Woman. The ladies at this inspiring NGO will teach you to weave grass baskets to take home or how to cook traditional Bakiga tribal dishes.

KENYA

729 Take tea with a giraffe or two

Wake up to find an extraordinary creature spying on you through the bedroom window, then grab them some food. At Giraffe Manor, a circa 1932 wonderland for Rothschild giraffes and humans who love them, you will not only get to feed the tallest terrestrial animal on Earth, but get close over breakfast and afternoon tea, too.

KENYA

730 Be hypnotized by the Singing Wells ritual

Witness the singular and beautiful cultural tradition of the Maasai and Samburu people known as the Singing Wells. Ensure your private itinerary customized by &Beyond includes this striking early morning ritual practiced by cattle-herding warriors who sing haunting rhythms while digging wells for their herds.

731 Nay Palad Bird Nest

KENYA

731 Sleep in a giant—superluxe—bird's nest, surrounded by wild animals

Only in Kenya, specifically in Segera Retreat's 50,000-acre (20,000-ha) private reserve in the savanna grasslands of the Mount Kenya foothills, can you stay in a life-size bird's nest with wildlife such as lions, cheetahs, and way more all around you. Nay Palad Bird Nest is the deluxe, open-air accommodation encircled by a massive wreath of branches woven by the community for a nocturnal experience you will never forget.

KENYA

732 Take inspiration from a royal engagement for a cozy cabin stay

If it is good enough for a certain king in waiting, it will wow your future fiancé. Rutundu Log Cabins, on a lake's edge in the remote Lewa Conservancy, was the site of a royal engagement, and is the charmingly down-to-earth hideaway where you will cook dinner together, with a fire roaring. Consider popping the question yourself on a memorable hike up the slopes of Mount Kenya the next day.

KENYA

733 Soar high above the herd in a hot-air balloon

Channel Meryl Streep and Robert Redford from *Out of Africa* on the most cinematic safari imaginable, at iconic camp Angama Mara, which means "suspended in midair" in Swahili. It floats above the Great Rift Valley, giving couples iconic panoramas and wildlife encounters. Take it to the next level with a hot-air balloon safari flight before sipping cocktails beside a marvelous herd.

KENYA

734 Giddy up for a surreal horseback safari

Make your safari in Chyulu Hills, with Mount Kilimanjaro as your backdrop, even more of a bucket list dream by starting the morning on a pair of gorgeous horses. At ol Donyo Lodge, ride beside your life partner across grassy plains to find cheetahs, giraffes, and other game—guided, of course—as you journey to a steaming-hot private breakfast set up beneath an acacia tree.

KENYA

735 Explore Lamu on land and by sea

Lamu, an island off Kenya's Indian Ocean coastline, holds untold magic on land and at sea. First, explore Lamu Old Town on foot. East Africa's oldest Swahili settlement, a UNESCO World Heritage Site, will romance you with its narrow streets and striking architecture. Later, hop on a traditional wooden dhow for a sparkling sunset cruise or to a dolphin hot spot for swimming.

AFRICA AND THE MIDDLE EAST • KENYA/RWANDA

KENYA

736 Dine inside an 180,000-year-old coral grotto

Dine on delicacies from the sea with fine wine surrounded by stalactites at Ali Barbour's Cave Restaurant in Diani Beach. Part of a much larger cave system, and 30 ft. (10 m) below ground, the cave has a natural skylight that lets in the stars.

RWANDA

737 Savor garden-to-table cuisine in the Virunga Mountains

Appreciate the craftsmanship and homegrown Rwandan cuisine at Singita Kwitonda Lodge, where suites with decadent bedding, heated plunge pools, massage tables, and bathtubs with a view make a sweet base for epic gorilla treks.

737 Singita Kwitonda Lodge

RWANDA/TANZANIA • **AFRICA AND THE MIDDLE EAST**

RWANDA

738 Hit the lake for idyllic wildlife experiences on water

Choose a classic safari experience in a tent that is way beyond glam—think rose-colored bed nets—in Akagera National Park's Magashi Camp, set in the loveliest of settings on the shore of Lake Rwanyakazinga. Head out by boat for gorgeous game viewing.

RWANDA

739 Book a retreat with swinging treetop bridges and monkeys galore

Marry eco-retreat with five-star luxuries and active amazement at One&Only Nyungwe House, set in a lush forest among wild mountains filled with cheeky monkeys and chimpanzees. With its own working tea plantation and swinging treetop bridges, the place is a lover's playground.

TANZANIA

740 Discover deepened cultural connections

Add a new dimension to a safari organized by Micato Safaris with a heli-cultural angle. You will be able to connect deeply with African cultures and take in special, rarely witnessed traditions on a trip full of flight-seeing excursions across Tanzania via helicopter. Consider making a secluded visit to the Pokot tribespeople or meeting fishermen from the Luo tribe on Lake Victoria, making unique memories to last a lifetime.

TANZANIA

741 Get up close and personal with dolphins

Volunteer with African Impact's dolphin conservation project in Zanzibar. Taking part in the research program, you will make daily boat trips to help track the intelligent, fun-loving creatures' behaviors and movements. You will also have an opportunity to swim with the dolphins. In Jambiani, the cluster of villages in which you will be based, you can take boat cruises, learn to kitesurf, and dine together at local family homes.

TANZANIA

742 Have an adults-only vacation in Zanzibar

Go for seclusion, privacy, and the utter treat of having your own butler, plus private plunge pool, at the adults-only resort Kilindi Zanzibar. At the 50-acre (20-ha) boutique resort (which pretty much defines the concept of paradise) you will be able to wind all the way down from the rugged safari—or daily grind—that preceded this beachfront escape, and spend one-on-one time together, like on sunset dhow cruises.

AFRICA AND THE MIDDLE EAST • TANZANIA/ZAMBIA

TANZANIA

743 Stay in the abundant Ngorongoro Crater

Vacation or honeymoon in one of the most extraordinary natural wonders on Earth—the Ngorongoro Crater. Formed over two million years ago, this vast volcanic caldera spans 100 sq. mi. (260 km²) and is almost 2,000 ft. (600 m) deep. Tens of thousands of animals—lions, elephants, rhinos, zebras, and more—roam its fertile grasslands. At Ngorongoro Lodge Melía Collection, you will find yourself immersed in this ancient ecosystem, where every view is framed by staggering beauty.

TANZANIA

744 Follow the famous Great Migration

Secure front-row seats to the once-in-a-lifetime event of the Serengeti's Great Migration by reserving a Roving Bushtops tent. Your accommodation moves according to migration patterns and a host of other conditions to deliver you the most exceptional game viewing possible. Go during the Great Migration, typically between July and October and witness the largest movement of land mammals on Earth—more than a million wildebeest and hundreds of thousands of zebras and gazelles.

ZAMBIA

745 Dare to swim at the edge of Devil's Pool

Take the ultimate infinity pool swim at the edge of the world: Devil's Pool. The natural rock pool is sandwiched between the thundering water streams of Victoria Falls—the world's largest waterfall—at a height of 345 ft. (105 m). With mist rising around you, creating magical rainbows in the light, the experience of peering over the edge, with the Zambezi River plunging into the gorge below, is unrivaled. Plan your trip for the dry season when water levels are low enough to make it safe.

743 Ngorongoro Crater, Tanzania

745 Devil's Pool at Victoria Falls, Zambia

ZAMBIA/MALAWI/NAMIBIA • **AFRICA AND THE MIDDLE EAST**

ZAMBIA

746 Escape to an intimate bush hideaway

In North Luangwa National Park, experience slow living at Takwela Camp, an intimate, off-grid retreat with just four chalets and stunning views of the wilderness. Settle in to a simple life, with meals crafted over wood fires using homegrown and locally sourced ingredients. Breakfast, lunch, and dinner are all served in the open air, surrounded by the sights and sounds of the bush.

MALAWI

747 Spend time on the water at Lake Malawi

Soak up the rays in the tiny country known as "The Warm Heart of Africa" during crystalline swims in its dazzling Lake Malawi. The water is so clean it supports more than eight hundred species of cichlid fish, which are the most radiantly colored freshwater fish alive. Prepare to spend ample time on snorkeling excursions or dives, drying off for tandem kayaking jaunts timed perfectly with the sunset.

MALAWI

748 Get a jolt at a Mzuzu coffee farm

Take a scenic private day trip to Mzuzu's verdant arabica coffee farm for a fascinating walk through of the operations that produce delicately sweet, floral coffee. Enjoy getting to interact with local farmers and embark on a coffee cupping session that might reveal new favorite flavor profiles or techniques to improve your ritualistic morning brew.

NAMIBIA

749 Become shipwrecked on the Skeleton Coast

Rent your own miniature, shipwreck-styled cabin, complete with porthole windows and a fur-throw-topped daybed from which to gaze out at the rough and tumble waves breaking on an infinite stretch of beach known as the Skeleton Coast. At the deluxe and intimate Shipwreck Lodge, couples are immersed in the unbelievable, ever-changing environment of contrasts via quiet drives to seek desert-adapted elephants and exciting surf fishing in the swell.

NAMIBIA

750 Venture out on a wild rhino chase

At Hoanib Valley Camp, which supports Save the Rhino Trust, you will need to rouse yourselves before dawn for black rhinoceros trekking. Exploring the untamed desert and jagged mountains surrounding the camp, you will need to be persistent. At times, the venture can feel like an impossible chase in pursuit of this elusive and coy species—with zebras, hyenas, giraffes, and more along the way—but stick with it for a euphoric reward.

NAMIBIA

751 Climb up Big Daddy dune and moon walk down the other side

Big Daddy dune is an awe-inspiring 1,000-ft.-plus (300-m) tall. As you climb to its pinnacle, the vivid red sand nearly swallows your feet with every step. At the top, you will be rewarded with views over Deadvlei, a clay pan dotted with the sculptural remnants of six-hundred-year-old acacia trees. Best of all, however, is your descent, which will see you whooping as you slide or moon walk down the dune's steep, sandy side.

AFRICA AND THE MIDDLE EAST • NAMIBIA

DARK-SKY WATCHING

NAMIBIA

752 Slumber outside in an International Dark Sky Reserve

Sleep under literally all the stars, in Africa's first designated International Dark Sky Reserve, on a plush bed and with nothing separating you from the cosmos. This dream romance scenario is reality at Kwessi Dunes in the vast Namib desert, where staff will make up your chalet's private outdoor second bed whenever you desire. As indelible as your nights will be, it is safe to expect days to match, since the camp experience includes drives and drinks in stupendous settings plus swimming while watching oryx and zebra drink.

NAMIBIA/BOTSWANA • **AFRICA AND THE MIDDLE EAST**

NAMIBIA

753 Feel like the only two people on Earth

Traverse deserted roads across the second least densely populated country on the planet, feeling, at times, like the only two people in existence. To have this wild and secluded adventure, rent a 4x4 vehicle with a rooftop tent and plot out a route that takes you to campsites in a variety of unique ecosystems, from mind-blowing deserts and lush wetlands to mountain escarpments and bushveld.

BOTSWANA

754 Sip afternoon tea with elephants

Journey to Abu Camp in the Okavango Delta, where a memory of rescued elephants await to deliver you and your spouse beautifully touching, maybe even tear-jerking, interactions. You will rest up for each exciting day in a dream of a tented safari suite and, one night, an open-air starbed, before feeding, taking walks, and, yes, even tea with the gentle giants.

753 Traversing Namibia

BOTSWANA

755 Spend the night in an emblematic baobab

If staying in rare and uncommon places is your thing, reserve a night in an accommodation that is completely unlike any other in the world. Xigera Safari Lodge's Baobab Treehouse is a twisted steel sculpture in the form of the iconic tree that you can actually sleep inside or on top of, in an open-air bed more than 30 ft. (9 m) above the wildlife-thronged Okavango Delta floor, beneath the southern stars.

AFRICA AND THE MIDDLE EAST • BOTSWANA/ZIMBABWE/MOZAMBIQUE

BOTSWANA

756 Take a wellness-focused break in the bush

Experience all the magical ways wilderness and wellness go hand in hand at Atzaró Okavango Camp, where you'll do yoga side by side and swim in the pool all while gazing out at the radiant Okavango Delta. After game drives led by female guides you'll wind down with holistic pampering spa treatments in the Wellness Sanctuary.

ZIMBABWE

757 Experience a rarity in Kafue National Park

Fuel a joint passion for wildlife on an unparalleled island affair in the middle of Zimbabwe at Wilderness Shumba Camp. The desirable lodge is only open five months each year, making it all the rarer to see the flying lions leaping over floodplain channels as they hunt.

ZIMBABWE

758 Raise a glass to your encounters with elephants

Experience the awesome privilege of getting close to herds of elephants and other wildlife at Somalisa Camp, known as a haven for the largest safari animals. Watch masses of elephants drink, bathe, and play as you eat your breakfast, drink your evening cocktails, and dine on multicourse dinners.

MOZAMBIQUE

759 Watch artists work in charming Maputo

Get to know the soul of Maputo through a personalized art safari. Your guide will take you to hidden-gem galleries in the port city and into artists' studios to watch them at work. Mozambique's capital city has clusters of Portuguese colonial architecture and a Havana, Cuba, vibe. Be sure to swing by the romantic, historic CFM Maputo Railway Station with its bronze dome.

MOZAMBIQUE

760 Seek iridescent shells on an orange beach

Delight in an impeccable sunbathing setup on a vivid orange-sand beach at Santorini Mozambique, where you will have your own palapa for shade, beanbags for cuddling, two loungers for tanning, plus a cooler full of Mozambican beers, wine, and other beverages on ice. Fly a kite if you are feeling playful, or spend time combing for exquisite treasures to take home, on sand covered in iridescent, shapely shells.

MOZAMBIQUE

761 Explore breathtaking Benguerra Island

Engage in captivating marine research fieldwork in the cyan megafauna-rich waters around transcendent Benguerra Island with the Bazaruto Center for Scientific Studies as part of your bucket list interlude at Kisawa Sanctuary. The 740-acre (300-ha) eco oasis has a special room for couples sound baths. Still, you might find it hard to leave your stunning residence with Indian Ocean–view pool, record player, and curvaceous bathtub for two.

OLD-TIME CHARM BY RAIL

ZIMBABWE

762 Choose slow travel on the glam Rovos Rail

Opt for quality and quantity aboard the glamorous Rovos Rail, with its vintage wood-paneled coaches. You will be spending close, meaningful time together and have plenty of it during this extraordinarily attractive train journey from Victoria Falls through Zimbabwe to Pretoria or Cape Town in South Africa. Take a Royal Suite for the plushest accommodation and pack evening attire for enchanting dinners that feel like they belong to a bygone time.

AFRICA AND THE MIDDLE EAST • ESWATINI/SOUTH AFRICA

ESWATINI

763 Combine wildlife with culture in teeny Eswatini

Equine adoring couples will find happiness in the teeny landlocked country of Eswatini, where a horseback safari will quietly deliver you both much closer to wildlife—think zebras, warthogs, and wildebeests—than the alternative Land Rover. A multiday itinerary will take you across breathtaking landscapes and introduce you to local culture. Have a blast attempting traditional Swazi dancing—but do not try the awe-inspiring singing—at a cultural village.

SOUTH AFRICA

764 Explore Cape Town from a plush landing pad in the V&A Waterfront

Use Cape Grace as your ticket to the buzzy V&A Waterfront and beyond in vibrant Cape Town. Your cushy room comes with an exceptional view of water or mountains. Explore the sights on a champagne cruise, a nature-immersive walk at Kirstenbosch National Botanical Garden, and a sunset spin up the Table Mountain Aerial Cableway. Complete your day with a hyperlocal dinner and luscious South African wine at the hotel's Heirloom restaurant.

SOUTH AFRICA

765 Hover high over Cape Town in water, and then at Lion's Head

Breathe in the intoxicating panorama of Cape Town from a striped pool float high atop the Silo Hotel, an urban sanctuary for lovestruck pairs of aesthetes. From the wondrous boutique hotel's eleven-story rooftop pool you will spot Lion's Head, the distinctive peak that will be your most unforgettable hike yet. Begin climbing in the late afternoon with a bottle of wine to share at the top as the sun dips into the ocean and the moon rises.

765 Lion's Head, Cape Town

SOUTH AFRICA • **AFRICA AND THE MIDDLE EAST**

766 Boulders Beach

SOUTH AFRICA

766 Swim with soulmate pairs of African penguins

Penguins famously mate for life, and the adorable species of African penguin is no different. Book a deluxe ocean-facing suite with a generous private terrace at Tintswalo Boulders for the very best access to the black-and-white birds, who nest right outside your door on Boulders Beach. Slip into the water yourselves, GoPro in hand. You might find yourselves gliding just feet from a curious penguin or two darting playfully past.

SOUTH AFRICA

767 Try out life as an 1800s farming couple

Sample a long-gone alternate reality: as an 1800s farming couple in the winelands of South Africa. At the bucolic working farm Soetmelksvlei, which operates like an interactive living museum, you can undergo a pastoral immersion full of charming tasks such as churning butter, blacksmithing, quilting, and tending to sweet animals. Take time to connect with your partner, enjoying the slow pace.

SOUTH AFRICA

768 Bask in South Africa's version of utopia: Babylonstoren

Luxuriate in the utopia that is Babylonstoren, a centuries-old Cape Dutch farm with such botanical diversity that nearly everything you will consume on-site was grown there. That includes the boutique estate's world-class wine, which you can taste on an intimate cellar tour. Book a serene Fynbos Cottage for privacy, and dive together into the idyllic swimming pool after a glass of wine at the help-yourself bar.

SOUTH AFRICA

769 Wake up to parading peacocks and glorious light

Let the first thing you see in the morning be peacocks parading around outside your door at La Residence, fanned-out feathers blazing. Then notice the unparalleled luminosity of your environment in Franschhoek. The decadent, vibrantly decorated boutique hotel has romantic spots aplenty for couples to relax in awe of their surroundings. A bespoke helicopter wine tour is also an option, full of guided wine farm experiences and views.

SOUTH AFRICA

770 Spot wildlife on a solar-powered aerial safari

In the halcyon "Forgotten Mountains," step aboard a solar-powered cable car for the world's only zero-carbon aerial safari, and follow your guide's gaze to view exciting African wildlife from above. The singular experience is a hallmark of Few & Far Luvhondo, where you will have destination cocktails, swim in waterfalls, snuggle on a mountainside star bed, and soak in your private plunge pool amid an unreal panorama.

769 La Residence

AFRICA AND THE MIDDLE EAST • SOUTH AFRICA/MADAGASCAR

776 Avenue of the Baobabs

SOUTH AFRICA

771 Go on a 007-esque culinary journey in the Kalahari Desert

Sign up for the ultimate destination dining experience. Jump into a Land Rover for the adventurous drive to a divinely mysterious meal that is anything but ordinary. The gastronomic exploit that is dining at Klein JAN is worthy of James Bond, with edible surprises, multiple locations, and a journey beneath the Kalahari Desert's surface incorporated into your endlessly pleasurable lunch or dinner.

SOUTH AFRICA

772 Make friends with a mob of meerkats at Tswalu

Fly to South Africa's largest private reserve—more than 460 sq. mi. (1,200 km^2) of extreme desert beauty—for a truly mind-blowing life experience. Together, as Loapi guests in a stand-alone tented safari home, you will venture out, guided, to track a cheetah or get intimate with habituated meerkats. Savor ranger coffee (with hot chocolate and Amarula cream liqueur) by a watering hole, before returning to brunch prepared by your private chef.

SOUTH AFRICA

773 Dine at Cape Town's gourmet go-to restaurant

Pop a welcome amuse bouche then take a seat across from your partner at a classic white tablecloth-draped two-top and await the bombshells that will come. (A prix fixe meal at La Colombe always includes many.) The Constantia restaurant in wine country is regularly ranked one of the best in the world, and the exquisitely created epicurean expedition you will embark on together lives up to its reputation.

SOUTH AFRICA

774 Take a safari to support antipoaching

In a stay that aids antipoaching efforts, remarkable rendezvous with leopards, lions, and rhinos are par for the course at Singita Ebony Lodge, a dream-come-true safari escape in the abundant Sabi Sand Game Reserve. Newlyweds and life partners occupy a sumptuous suite above the Sand River—with watercolor sets for when inspiration strikes, and gin and tonic fixings at your private bar—where, from your private pool, you will likely spot elephants frolicking in the river.

SOUTH AFRICA

775 Take your time driving the Garden Route

Wonder at the phenomenal landscapes through which you will drive along South Africa's 186-mi.-long (300-km) Garden Route. Hugging the coast from Mossel Bay to Storms River, verdant forests, whale-studded beaches, and massive cliffs are among its diverse features. Take things slowly over the course of a week, cuddling up at idyllic retreats or tree houses along the way, and savoring bountiful blissful picnics provided by the Wilderness Picnic Co.

MADAGASCAR

776 Take in the fairy-tale scene at dawn on Madagascar's Avenue of the Baobabs

Be romanced by the wondrous mysticism of western Madagascar's Avenue of the Baobabs, an 850-ft. (260-m) stretch of dirt road lined with some twenty endemic, broad-trunked Grandidier's baobabs (*Adansonia grandidieri*) rising to the heavens like tree giants. Plan a passionate proposal or a special walk at dawn down the path, looking for the pair that are known locally as the "baobabs in love."

777 Tsingy de Bemaraha National Park

MADAGASCAR

777 Discover the eighth continent's limestone wonder

There is a lot about Madagascar, the so-called eighth continent, that is otherworldly. Its remoteness, mega biodiversity, and high number of endemic animals make it a wondrous world well worth exploring. You can do just that from one of Namoroka Tsingy Camp's low-impact, solar-powered tents in perhaps the wildest environment of all: *tsingy*. The name derives from the Malagasy word for "walking on tiptoes," which gives you a clue to how carefully to wander through the incredible landscape of razor-sharp limestone pinnacles.

MADAGASCAR

778 Seek out the cutest lemurs in Madagascar

Steal away to the spectacular untamed island nation of Madagascar on a mission to find the fluffiest, funniest, cutest lemurs around—say, crowned lemurs or dancing sifakas. There are more than one hundred lemur species, most of them threatened or critically endangered, making each one you are lucky enough to witness extra special.

MADAGASCAR

779 Experience euphoria while helicopter hopping in paradise

Move in to your own fantasy of a secluded private island villa at Miavana by Time + Tide. The Nosy Ankao resort, off Madagascar's northeast coast, defines perfection for seekers of flawless white beaches, diamond-clear water, and they-thought-of-everything amenities. The aquamarine-hued helicopter is the only way in or out; it will take you anywhere—to a mountain plateau, *tsingy*, or lemur-studded forest—to pop champagne and toast to your grand adventure.

MAURITIUS

780 Chase waterfalls together in a tropical paradise

Follow the sound of rushing water as you trail through the verdant forests of Mauritius on the lookout for some of its many waterfalls. You will find dramatic falls like Chamarel Waterfall, the island's tallest, and serene Alexandra Falls, nestled in the Black River Gorges National Park. Some of the remoter spots are best reached with a local guide—Eau Bleue and Tamarind Falls both offer pools perfect for a cooling swim.

779 Miavana by Time + Tide

783 Four Seasons Resort Mauritius at Anahita

MAURITIUS

781 Engage in water sports at Île aux Cerfs

On the wild offshore island of Île aux Cerfs, hire a glass-bottomed boat for a private outing that just may take your breath away. The large lagoon you will be exploring is brilliant turquoise, with strikingly clear water for excellent snorkeling. Plan to spend your vacation in swimwear, because after the boat trip, parasailing, and waterskiing, you will want to plop on the picturesque beach.

MAURITIUS

782 Escape to a tropical golf playground

Vibrant Shangri-La Le Touessrok is a tropical playground with five sandy beaches plus its own private island for the most intimate liaisons. For sandy rendezvous of a different sort there is access to two eighteen-hole championship golf courses—one designed by Ernie Els, the other by Bernhard Langer—complete with shimmery lagoon views.

MAURITIUS

783 Drift with dolphins, snorkel with seahorses

At Four Seasons Resort Mauritius at Anahita, dive into the great ultramarine surrounding the island with an ocean conservation manager to snorkel among delicate seahorses in their mangrove habitat. The captivating and endangered little creatures are not the only wonder you will witness there: Book a cruise to watch frisky dolphins leap about.

SEYCHELLES

784 Pair island padel and surf-simulator sessions with five-star luxuries

Embrace the laid-back island lifestyle at Cheval Blanc Seychelles, a world-class resort where luxury meets adventure. Settle into a breezy Creole-style villa, complete with a private 41-ft. (12.5-m) infinity pool and sweeping views of the Indian Ocean. Fill your days with friendly games of doubles padel and learn to surf on the resort's wave simulator. Relive the day's highlights over beautiful meals in one of the resort's exceptional dining settings.

SEYCHELLES

785 Charter a yacht for an epic adventure sailing the Seychelles

If you are experienced seafarers, pick a glossy bareboat yacht charter for a sailing adventure on the open Indian Ocean. The island republic of some 115 islands is a wishlist vacation for those who can expertly sail between islands, to vanilla plantations, over coral reefs, and to find legendary giant tortoises. Novices, hire a skipper to navigate and teach you the ropes.

SEYCHELLES

786 Take a nature-immersive yoga hike in the jungle

Make memories trying something you could never do at home, such as setting out on a guided nature-immersed Vibhava yoga hike through the lively jungles of Sainte Anne Marine National Park. This luscious mindful practice, along with sunset Creole dinners, is only possible at Club Med Seychelles, a sustainable 50-acre (20-ha) retreat with scuba diving and a spa.

AFRICA AND THE MIDDLE EAST • SEYCHELLES

SEYCHELLES

787 Stage your own sexy photo shoot on Anse Source d'Argent

Make it your mission to pose for photos on the powdered sugar sand at one of the world's most famous—and most photographed—beaches, Anse Source d'Argent. It will take a ferry and a walk, but the recognizable granite boulders and seductively shallow emerald water are worth it. Take your own sultry photos for perpetuity.

SEYCHELLES

788 Experience stealth architecture up close

Decamp to the granite island of Félicité in a protected national park with the intention of relaxing deeply and reconnecting with your honey. At eco-sensitive Six Senses Zil Pasyon you will find yourselves perched on rock above the vivid Indian Ocean, in deluxe villa accommodations that qualify as modern-meets–nature integrated stealth architecture. Ask your Guest Experiences Maker to organize island hops, Creole language class, and turtle swimming quests.

787 Anse Source d'Argent

790 Piton des Neiges, Réunion

SEYCHELLES

789 Get away from it all with giant tortoises

Truly escape on a giant tortoise conservation island–cum-resort, where one of seven pristine beaches has a "Beach Occupied" sign for when the two of you want to be completely alone. There are just sixteen villas at Fregate Island, making it an enchanting place to combine seclusion—there are almost endless places to have a secret dinner, including a mountaintop—and a dash of doing good via outings like turtle tagging and sea coral cultivation.

RÉUNION

790 Explore Africa's safest LGBTQIA+ destination

Train in the days leading up to your vacation on stunning Réunion Island and start strong, taking a full day to climb the challenging shield volcano Piton des Neiges—the Indian Ocean's highest point at 10,000 ft. (3,000 m). Whether or not you summit and savor the mind-boggling 360-degree panorama from the top, treat yourselves to days lazing on the black or white sand beaches in Africa's safest country for LGBTQIA+ couples.

5 ASIA

KAZAKHSTAN

791 Go for the gold on a sporty winter's day

Plan a frozen day of excitement in Kazakhstan. Start on the snowy slopes of Shymbulak in Ile-Alatau National Park, central Asia's premier mountain resort. Here, you can rent not only the skis or snowboards, but also warm clothes for keeping you toasty. Next, attempt pairs figure skating at Medeu, the world's highest ice-skating rink at 5,548 ft. (1,691 m) above sea level. Finally, take the Kok Tobe Hill Gondola Cableway up above the town of Almaty at sunset for a view of the city amid snowcapped peaks.

KYRGYZSTAN

792 Take a daring journey on horseback

Between jagged, rocky peaks and glaciers, alpine meadows, red rock canyons, and crater lakes, the Kyrgyzstan scenery is unimaginable—until you journey through it slowly and hyper present on the backs of two horses, camping remotely in a yurt at night. Get local travel agency I'm Nomad to craft and lead you on a tailor-made tour that might also involve traveling by motorcycle, bicycle, and on foot.

792 Kyrgyzstan on horseback

KYRGYZSTAN/UZBEKISTAN/MONGOLIA • ASIA

KYRGYZSTAN

793 Visit the lunar landscape of a salty lake

Chief among Kyrgyzstan's outrageously beautiful scenes is Issyk-Kul Lake, with its lunar-like dried riverbeds, deep, salty water that is an intense blue color, and 5,272-ft. (1,606-m) elevation with a backdrop of snowcapped mountains. Several companies offer lakeside camping in yurts, where you can spend your days floating side by side in the striking lake, sunning on its beaches, and admiring the ever-changing light.

UZBEKISTAN

794 Embrace a most romantic gesture

Embark on a private guided tour for two through Uzbekistan's fascinating history, and make sure to include the Silk Road city—and one of the oldest cities in the world—Samarkand, where the architecture and intricate tile work is mesmerizing. Visit a masterpiece that doubles as a major romantic gesture: Bibi-Khanym mosque, which a fourteenth-century ruler's wife commissioned as a gift for her beloved husband.

MONGOLIA

795 When in Mongolia, go dune sledging

If adrenaline rushes drive you on vacation, head to Mongolia's vast Gobi Desert, where the wind has carved Khongor's deep-orange sand into dunes of almost 1,000 ft. (300 m) in height. They are perfect for dune sledging, an experience not that unlike sledding on snow. See for yourself and hear the deep, resonant hum of the shifting sands as you go—a sound that has earned the dunes the moniker "Singing Dunes."

MONGOLIA

796 Stay at a desert wilderness retreat

Embark on a multi-night wilderness journey in the middle of the Gobi Desert at Mongolian-owned luxury escape Three Camel Lodge. The country's best eco retreat is imbued with nomadic traditions, flavors, and furnishings sure to captivate culture-curious couples. Ride two-humped camels and get playful with native Mongolian Bankhar puppies, which the sustainable lodge breeds to protect the environment and local communities.

796 Three Camel Lodge

325

ASIA • CHINA

CHINA
797 Stroll beneath crimson autumn foliage

Plan your trip to Beijing for the fall, so you can take a long, winding walk under the dramatic autumn foliage of Fragrant Hills Park (Xiangshan Park), admired for its many maple trees that turn striking shades of red. The ancient former imperial garden sprawling over 465 acres (188 ha) has paths zigzagging over its hills and cute cable cars for couples to view the vibrancy from above the treetops.

CHINA
798 Sip champagne on the Great Wall

Hire a travel coordinator to weave an epic two-person picnic worthy of the world's longest man-made structure: the Great Wall of China, a UNESCO World Heritage Site. Make it a surprise for your partner, who will have no idea there's a wildly romantic table with champagne on ice around the next bend in the seemingly infinite fortification. Dining on Michelin-quality cuisine atop the Great Wall makes for a fab proposal, too.

CHINA
799 Appreciate aesthetics in ancient-meets-contemporary Shanghai

Design a vacation around Shanghai's aesthetic beauty. In the city where ancient architecture melds with contemporary, and culture reigns, reserve tickets to a show at the glamorous New Bund 31 Performing Arts Center, which is as lovely inside as it is out. Afterward, retire to the Artyzen New Bund 31 Shanghai hotel, a green oasis inspired by classical Chinese gardens and with stunning views of the metropolis.

797 Cable cars, Fragrant Hills Park (Xiangshan Park)

ASIA • CHINA

800 Ultraviolet by Paul Pairet

CHINA

800 Treat your senses to a sonic, high-tech dinner in a windowless bunker in Shanghai

Seek out a secretive steel bunker for an outrageously avant-garde meal where you will join just eight other people for a twenty-course menu that stimulates every sense you have. The gastronomic joyride at Ultraviolet by Paul Pairet pairs projection on screens and synchronized special effects with food unlike any you have seen or tasted before. Book well in advance for the pleasure of sharing a rapturous evening of eating, drinking, and feeling.

CHINA

801 Snuggle a giant panda in Chengdu

Head to Chengdu, the world's panda capital, to try out your cuddling skills on an iconic, giant, black-and-white bear. At the Chengdu Research Base of Giant Panda Breeding, you can engage in volunteer programs to help educate others about conservation of the much-loved, fluffy mammals, and maybe even help make panda cakes or prepare their bamboo meals.

CHINA

802 Time travel at the stylish Hylla Vintage Hotel

Retro obsessives will enjoy a restorative break oozing of old-school charm at Hylla Vintage Hotel, in Lijiang, a time capsule set between a cozy Scandi hygge haven and flawlessly curated mid-century-modern-filled villa. It's nostalgia all the way.

CHINA

803 Explore Hong Kong's vibrant bar scene

One of Earth's most intoxicating cities for nightlife, Hong Kong offers everything from moody candlelit speakeasies and sleek rooftop lounges with glittering skyline views to intimate craft cocktail parlors tucked behind velvet curtains.

CHINA

804 Treat yourselves to a Michelin-starred day

In Hong Kong, foodie fanatics on their honeymoon or a culinary mission can go for a traditional lunch of roast goose at a single-starred establishment for around $40, before indulging in an exquisite three-starred French milestone dinner at Caprice.

CHINA • ASIA

JUNK BOAT CRUISE

CHINA

805 Marvel at the rainbow-hued Symphony of Lights

In Hong Kong, take your gaze off the psychedelic rainbow lights of Victoria Harbour's nightly Symphony of Lights show momentarily to clink glasses with a "cin-cin" aboard a lively junk boat cruise. If you prefer something a bit more intimate, opt for a private luxury yacht to cruise around in the harbor before overnighting at the stylishly elegant the Upper House, high above the city.

ASIA • NEPAL/INDIA

NEPAL

806 Try a dose of romantic Nepalese life

Experience a charming taste of the Nepalese way of life on a five-day journey with Pavilions Hotels that takes you on offbeat exploits through bucolic villages, farms, paddy fields, and a Buddhist monastery. Your incredibly peaceful interlude includes yoga, bird-watching, and a culinary experience at the not-for-profit FAB Hospitality School, plus plush accommodations, of course.

NEPAL

807 Take an enchanted jungle honeymoon safari

Whisk your partner away for a jungle safari in Nepal's humming Chitwan National Park. The über-biodiverse UNESCO site is astonishingly beautiful, with the Himalayas as its backdrop. Enlist Nomadic Expeditions to create a fantasy caper packed with rare encounters such as with Bengal tigers, giant butterflies, exotic birds, one-horned rhinos, and whatever else Mother Nature has in store.

INDIA

808 Role-play as Indian royalty in Mumbai

Encounter a memorably royal welcome at the Oberoi, Mumbai, perfectly positioned on the coastal Marine Drive. Even the hotel's signature scent is designed to seduce guests into feeling like VIPs. In your ocean-view residence, let a butler look after you nearly 24-7, lining up chauffeured spice trail experiences and private candlelit dinners. They can keep the champagne flowing, too.

INDIA

809 Engage in snow leopard conservation

Make off for the former Buddhist kingdom of Ladakh with a mission to partake in a worthy cause: snow leopard conservation. The B Corp conservation travel specialist Journeys With Purpose will pair big cat lovers with veteran expedition guides for a once-in-a-lifetime undertaking—tracking the so-called ghost of the mountain on foot or in 4x4 vehicles. It is impossible not to be changed by this magnificent, memory-making experience.

INDIA

810 Get drenched in the rainbow on Holi

Timing is everything if you wish to be saturated in every color of the rainbow during India's most vivid holiday, Holi. The joyous Hindu event, whose date changes based on the lunar calendar, is known as the Festival of Colors, Love, Equality, and Spring, making it a beautiful tradition that surpasses religious beliefs. In Mathura or Vrindavan, Uttar Pradesh, prepare to get messy as you and your fellow revelers take on all the Technicolor hues.

INDIA

811 Take a moonlit tour of the Taj Mahal

Choose absolutely the best conditions for admiring one of the most famous monuments on Earth built for love—the Taj Mahal, in Agra. Reserve two of the limited, timed slots for a full-moon night viewing of the white marble mausoleum, and manifest a clear night. You will have thirty minutes to take in the glorious piece of architecture built by a seventeenth-century emperor as an eternal passionate testament to his late wife.

811 Waiting for nightfall at the Taj Mahal

INDIA

812 Stay in a fictional queen's palace at Raffles Jaipur

Spend a night in India's famed Pink City at its most decadent hotel, Raffles Jaipur. Inside, this place is over-the-top ornate and dripping in gilded murals, marble, and inlay, including your room, with a generous balcony bathtub. Your gracious butler takes care of everything, even escorting you to dinner or the Writers Bar for libations.

INDIA

813 Pair a tiger safari with a private yoga session atop battlements

Road trip to Rajasthan in a chauffeured vehicle to sleep in a fourteenth-century fort that is now a palatial resort for peaceful well-being, and strike out on a tiger safari in Ranthambore National Park. A naturalist will guide you on the exciting search for rare Bengals, and maybe even leopards and sloth bears, before returning to Six Senses Fort Barwara for an extraordinary yoga class atop the parapet.

INDIA • ASIA

813 Six Senses Fort Barwara

INDIA

815 Stay in a luxury wildlife resort

Journey to the Oberoi Vindhyavilas Wildlife Resort to take a romantic safari inspired by royal caravans of yore in Bandhavgarh National Park, just minutes away. Take a daytime safari looking for black panthers, leopards, and rare white tigers, then return to the resort for the Oberoi Experience, a two-hour spa session featuring therapies tailored to your needs.

INDIA

816 Glide through Kerala's backwaters

Cruise around the sublimely scenic backwaters of Kerala in the city of Alleppey for a honeymoon aboard a luxurious houseboat, the perfect place to fall in love all over again with plenty of intimate time away from crowds. Request candlelit dinners and floral decorations to make it extra sweet.

INDIA

814 Palace hop around lake-filled Udaipur

In Udaipur, enlist the services of a personal guide to tour you around the many glittering ancient palaces that sit on banks of peaceful lakes. As you take in the exquisite, sprawling retreats, fantasize about what it was like to be the *maharaja* and *maharani* living in them. Then get closer to that daydream by checking into a suite at Taj Lake Palace.

ASIA • SRI LANKA

819 Uga Chena Huts

SRI LANKA
817 Go on a gemstone- and jewelry-buying spree

From mesmerizing moonstones to brilliant blue sapphires, rubies, and chrysoberyl cat's eyes, Sri Lanka is the sustainable, ethically mined source of untold gemstones, and it is a wonderful place to purchase them, too. Take your love on a gem- or jewelry-buying spree in Ratnapura or Kandy, two top destinations on an island with a long history of mining sparkly stunners. You might feel moved to pop the question right there!

SRI LANKA
818 Share meaningful moments in Galle

Take a romantic vacation to Galle on the southwest coast of Sri Lanka. Stroll barefoot together on golden beaches, surf the waves, make sunset visits to Galle Fort, and learn to cook spicy Sri Lankan food. Add a meaningful layer to your escape via GoEco, spending time with local women as you help them learn English. The shared, heartwarming exchange will stay with you both for years to come.

SRI LANKA
819 Rent a luxurious and intimate thatched cabin

Exclusivity and seclusion are two of the main goals at Uga Chena Huts, an all-inclusive hotel just five minutes from Yala National Park, where private safari drives often deliver you to leopard sightings. The sumptuous vernacular huts with their low-slung roofs are a newlywed dream with your own private pool built into the wooden deck. Then there are the secret happy hour drives, exciting bush walks, and starlit dinners.

SRI LANKA • ASIA

SRI LANKA

820 Embody peace in the Central Highlands of Sri Lanka

Experience the embodiment of peace as you take long, loving nature walks through perfectly manicured rolling tea fields and verdant mountains in the UNESCO-designated Central Highlands of Sri Lanka. Reserve one of Ceylon Tea Trails' historic colonial bungalows around Castlereagh Lake for a laid-back escape that fills your cups with quality time.

SRI LANKA

821 Retreat for a next-level Ayurvedic wellness reset

Rebalance, detoxify, recover, or de-stress as your partner goes on their own journey to well-being at Santani Wellness Kandy, a divine resort in a luscious valley where the architecture is as quiet as can be to let the comprehensive Ayurvedic offerings shine. You will savor gourmet, hyper-personalized food, treatments, and sessions, plus unspoiled wilderness outings for two.

820 Central Highlands, Sri Lanka

ASIA • MALDIVES

MALDIVES

822 Book a table for the most romantic dinner of your lives

Up the romance at One&Only Reethi Rah, where you will wine and dine at eight unique restaurants and five bars, but also privately, too. Be seduced into thinking you are the only people on the island over a personalized menu atop an elevated sunset perch at Reethi Ah-Li (meaning "beautiful light"), taste through seven courses in a tree house, or savor a moonlit dinner together on a secluded sandbank.

MALDIVES

823 Follow an active day with a meal eaten blindfolded

After jumping into a biologist-guided snorkeling expedition in the turquoise lagoon, riding barrels in the surf, taking a seaweed bath for two, and swaying in your hammock above the Indian Ocean at Gili Lankanfushi, choose a grand finale that teases your taste buds. The team will organize dinner at a secret, sandy spot where a private chef cooks you four courses to eat blindfolded, electrifying all your senses.

MALDIVES

824 Submerge in a two-person submarine

Surprise your partner with an adventure neither of you have taken before: a submarine voyage. At Patina Maldives, you will submerge in a two-person sub dubbed *Ocean Pearl* for a fantastic under-the-sea experience 100 ft. (30 m) below the surface. Not only does the trip involve an excess of awe and wonder at the reality of sitting, dry, in the ocean, but also data collection and documentation that aid the resort's conservation research efforts.

MALDIVES

825 Spot tropical fish and stingrays during your massage

Keep your eyes open for part of a lavish twosome treatment in Anantara Dhigu Maldives Resort's couples spa bungalow and you will be able to play "I spy" with your spouse as you are gently rubbed and kneaded into a state of bliss. Glass portals to the ocean below your massage beds mean creatures such as puffer fish, reef sharks, and stingrays regularly swim by.

MALDIVES

826 Check yourselves into the Maldives' first floating villa

At Soneva Secret in the Maldives, indulge in the singular floating accommodation, the Castaway, and have it moved around the island at your whim to catch sunrise or sunset. In whichever secluded spot you find, you can slip down a curvy waterslide, straight into the lagoon. Come bedtime, simply press a button to reveal the twinkling night sky above you.

MALDIVES

827 Scuba dive with a marine biologist

Scuba-diving soulmates should make their way to Velaa Private Island, a secluded Noonu Atoll getaway that specializes in meaningful moments. The resort runs an ambitious coral restoration project in which you can scuba dive alongside a marine biologist to witness all the progress made and adopt your own fragment, allowing you to stay connected to the island forever via biannual updates.

MALDIVES • ASIA

831 SKY Observatory

MALDIVES

828 Leap into the ocean from your bungalow

JOALI Maldives' idyllic overwater bungalows with gracious infinity-edge pools are the quintessential island dream. Revel in the novelty of being able to jump directly from your deck into the jewel-like water and swim beneath your partner hanging out in the suspended hammock net.

MALDIVES

831 Gaze at the night sky and learn about the universe while drinking cosmos-themed cocktails

Order a couple Pisces, Aquarius, or Full Moon cocktails at Anantara Kihavah Maldives Villas' sparkling SKY bar before heading upstairs for an appointment with the cosmos. At the resort, a knowledgeable storytelling Sky Guru will take you on a private trip in the Maldives' first overwater observatory—complete with a powerful research-grade telescope—where you will gaze at faraway galaxies, planets, and other celestial wonders.

MALDIVES

829 Learn the art of champagne sabering

Learn the precise and dramatic art of champagne sabering. The Napoleon-era act is a nightly ritual at the St. Regis Maldives Vommuli. To try it yourselves, head to InterContinental Maldives Maamunagau Resort, where the sommelier at Sunset Bar will show you the ropes and let you practice with the saber over the golden-hour seascape.

MALDIVES

830 Discover a sense of shared well-being

Connect with your partner on deeper levels, both physically and emotionally, during a shared multiday well-being discovery journey on an island that is just like heaven. At JOALI BEING your spectacular villa is just the beginning. Emerge to be pampered side by side with reflexology, massages, facials, and cryotherapy treatments, plus whatever else sparks your fancy—from movement classes to sensory walks.

ASIA • MALDIVES/BHUTAN

833 The Muraka, Conrad Maldives Rangali Island

MALDIVES

832 Snorkel together with manta rays

Find yourselves filled with wonder as you snorkel through a ballet of massive manta rays whose wingspans are wider than the two of you put together. Experience this singular marvel en masse at Hanifaru Bay.

MALDIVES

833 Sleep surrounded by fish in an underwater villa

Sleep with the fishes, quite literally, in a deluxe bedroom suite 16 ft. (5 m) below the surface of the luminous Indian Ocean. Each morning, you will wake up to find a rainbow of sea life all around you. Book Conrad Maldives Rangali Island's the Muraka three-bedroom, two-level residence for this distinctive and rare pleasure.

MALDIVES

834 Watch the marine life as you dine under the sea

Jump onto a speedboat that will whisk you out over waves to a staircase surrounded by water. You will then descend 20 ft. (6 m) to Subsix, Niyama Private Islands Maldives' subaquatic dining room for a champagne breakfast or multicourse Nikkei lunch under dangling capiz shells, with sea turtles and even sharks visiting as you dine.

BHUTAN

835 Take a hot river stone bath before a body scrub

The belief in Bhutan is that happiness comes from good health, so try out the country's age-old hot river stone bath ritual, called *dotsho*, in which stones rich in riverbed minerals are heated and added to bathwater for purification. Follow it up at Six Senses Spa Thimphu with a couples Bhutanese Herbal Body Scrub you craft yourselves using Himalayan salt.

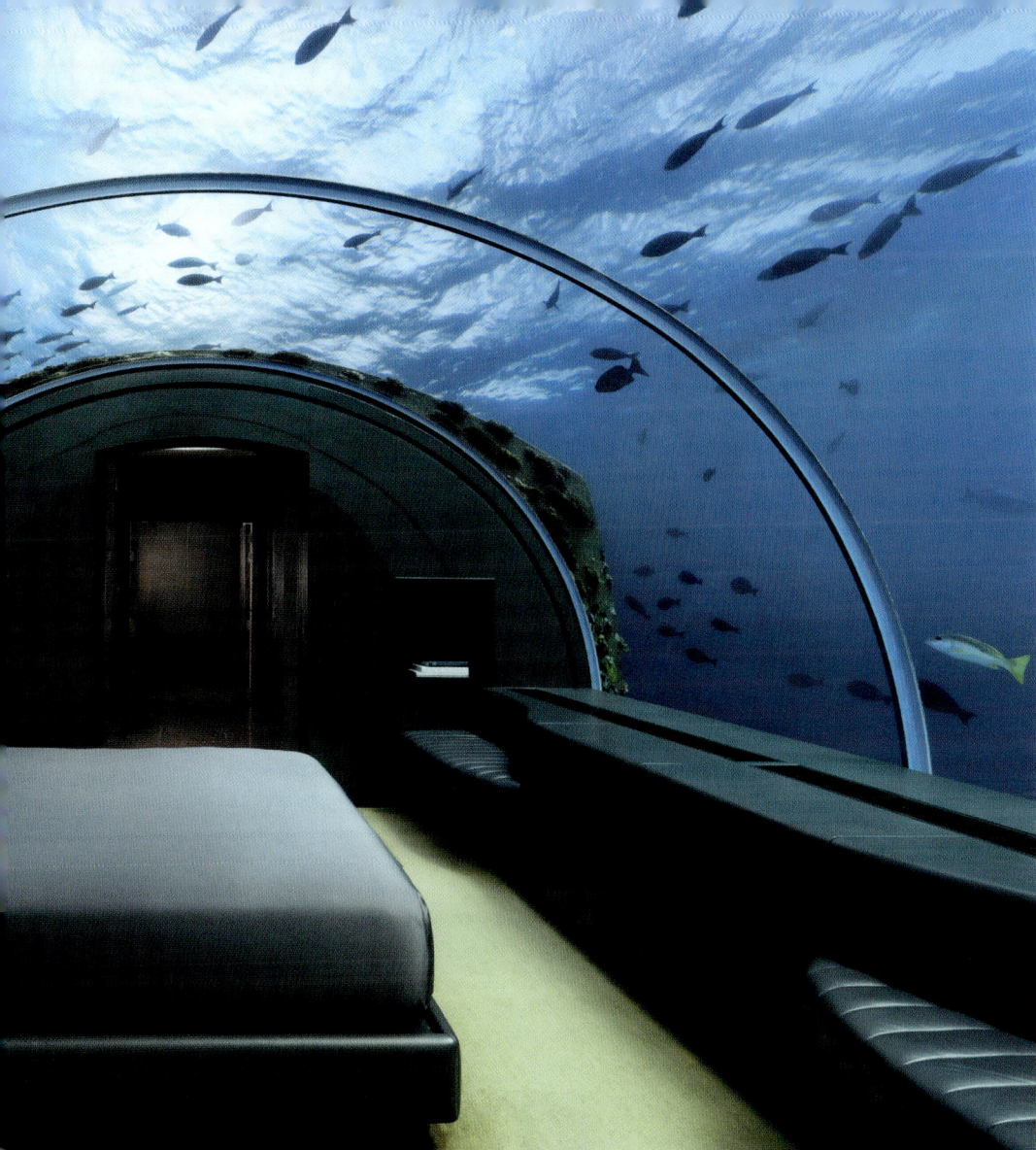

BHUTAN

836 Play a funny game of "spot the phallus"

Travel to a place where phalli are a symbol of good luck. With your partner, turn it into a game, spotting colorful penises painted on walls, hung from rooftop eaves, and disguised as scarecrows in fields.

BHUTAN

837 Read the stars in a country where happiness is prized

Feel your smiles growing bigger as you explore Bhutan, a tiny kingdom where Gross Domestic Happiness is prioritized over GDP. Together, share the joy of discovering Bhutanese astrology with a reading under the stars to learn more about your relationship or the perfect day to wed.

BHUTAN

838 Journey five hours on foot to the iconic Tiger's Nest

Take a hike that will leave you spellbound. Climb five hours with a guide to the iconic Tiger's Nest monastery, built in the 1640s on a cliffside, some 9,800 ft. (3,000 m) above the Paro valley. You will feel euphoria over your accomplishment and the colorful prayer flags flying at the top.

BANGLADESH

839 Take a tea pilgrimage to Bangladesh

Follow your mutual love of tea to an off-the-beaten-path destination, Bangladesh, specifically Sreemangal, a destination locally known as "the land of two leaves and a bud." Elysian landscapes and abundant tea gardens conjure a hushed, tranquil environment where couples can leave hustle and bustle behind and focus solely on each other. Beyond the requisite tasting of the region's famous seven-layer tea and taking tea garden and bicycle tours, pairs of nature fanatics will not want to miss a waterfall trek.

838 Tiger's Nest monastery

840 Bagan by hot-air balloon

MYANMAR

840 Hop into a hot-air balloon before sunrise to marvel at Bagan's ancient pagodas in mystical light

The only thing better than admiring Bagan's 2,000-plus ancient Buddhist pagodas and temples (some in romantic ruins) in transcendent sunrise light is doing so from a hot-air balloon. So, get up at the crack of dawn to do just that.

MYANMAR

841 Lounge around on ethereal Inle Lake

In a small boat, traverse this dreamy, floating water world, aka the "Venice of the East." Here, quaint villages, artisan workshops, markets, restaurants, and even hotels all float or perch atop stilts.

LAOS

842 Take part in a lovely Buddhist tradition

Feel good by doing good when you wake before dawn to give alms to orange-robed Buddhist monks outside your Luang Prabang hotel, Amantaka. The contemplative ritual will enhance your chic stay.

ASIA • LAOS/THAILAND

845 Longtail boat, Capella Bangkok

LAOS

843 Get intimate with gentle giants in Laos

In the "Land of One Million Elephants," learn to be elephant whisperers—or at least tune into the silent wisdom of the great gray giants. MandaLao Elephant Conservation, a non-riding sanctuary outside Luang Prabang, welcomes couples for emerald treks alongside incredibly intelligent creatures rescued from logging camps and tourist attractions. Connect further as you prepare and feed them healthy treats, then spread word of your ethical encounter.

LAOS

844 Plan an immersive stay in northern Laos

In a beautiful setting above a lush valley, Rosewood Luang Prabang offers a singular base for exploring northern Laos. Reserve the most glamorous hilltop tent on stilts imaginable, festooned with vibrant Lao hill tribe artifacts and designs. A waterfall flows through the resort, but it is worth leaving for a stroll to the swimmable jade-colored Kuang Si Falls and to visit cute moon and sun bears at the nearby Tat Kuang Si wildlife sanctuary.

THAILAND

845 Enjoy a low-key stay in Bangkok

At the sublime hotel Capella Bangkok, lounge on the outdoor daybed of your riverfront room, savoring your privileged view of the Chao Phraya River and its parade of interesting vessels. When you have relaxed enough, hop onto the hotel's private longtail boat for your own laid-back explorations by water and then land, on an iconic tuk-tuk. Returning to your hotel, embark on an intimate couples meditation session with a monk.

THAILAND • **ASIA**

THAILAND

846 Indulge in a twenty-course tasting menu at a Michelin-starred restaurant

In Bangkok, eat through twenty scintillating courses of progressive Thai-Chinese cuisine, picking up cultural tidbits as you go, at Michelin-starred Potong. Follow your meal with a nightcap at the seductive speakeasy Opium Bar upstairs. Pour nightcap round two while snuggled on a leather sofa beside the fully complimentary bar inside your dreamy suite at Aman Nai Lert Bangkok.

THAILAND

847 Learn to cook Thai food by the river in Bangkok

Take a thrilling tuk-tuk ride with your love to a Thai market to pick up fresh ingredients for your private riverside cooking class back at the Siam in a charming antique teak house. There, learn delicious dishes you can re-create collaboratively at home.

THAILAND

848 Strike a pose with your love on top of the world

Shuffle out onto the 1,017-ft.-high (310-m) glass tray of Bangkok's Mahanakhon Skywalk for an awe-inspiring—and heart-thumping—photo op that proves you are both brave. The seventy-eighth-story platform is the highest in Thailand, and should make you feel on top of the world.

847 Tuk-tuk ride through Bangkok

ASIA • THAILAND

THAILAND

849 Shimmy into PJs for a most intense spa experience

For the most authentic Thai spa experience, you will not need to strip down to nothing. Instead, you will change into loose-fitting pajamas and lie down on a big mattress on the floor. The shared, potentially intense, experience of a genuine Thai massage—a bodywork session involving acupressure and lots of deep stretching—can be found in any major city in Thailand.

THAILAND

850 Live it up in a top LGBTQIA+ destination

Bangkok is the capital of one of the world's most incredible LGBTQIA+ destinations. Couples will find a city that is wonderfully inclusive and welcoming for couples of all sexualities and gender identities. Carouse with your life partner, from floating markets to glittering temples under the hot sun to the pulsating nightlife scene after dark in Silom, a street full of bars and shows of all styles.

LIVING AMONG GENTLE GIANTS

THAILAND

851 Curl up with your lover inside a clear bubble and wake to elephants outside

Spend a wondrous night in a Jungle Bubble at Anantara Golden Triangle Elephant Camp & Resort, Chiang Rai, where you will sleep inside a giant transparent (and air-conditioned) bubble, gazing up at twinkling stars. As magical as that sounds, the best part comes when you wake enveloped in the glowing light of morning to rescued elephants grazing and strolling just outside. The gorgeous animals go about their business as you two marvel at them from bed or your own elevated deck for a privileged, super-private perspective. Add another immersive experience to your stay with a joyride in a pair of Royal Enfield Classic 500 sidecars.

ASIA • THAILAND

THAILAND

852 Be serenaded during dinner in Chiang Rai

Share an intimate white-tablecloth dinner in an awe-inspiring destination: the elephant field at Four Seasons Tented Camp Golden Triangle. The bucket-list evening is made even more memorable by live musicians playing just for the two of you.

THAILAND

853 Plant mangroves before a mud scrub

Dedicate your days to conservation efforts such as planting mangrove trees via International Volunteer HQ. Spend nights spicing things up at the Standard, Hua Hin, either by the pool or at the spa's Mud Lounge, painting each other with infused mud scrubs.

THAILAND/VIETNAM • ASIA

THAILAND

854 Savor a vacation in a throwback safari tent

Book a vacation where peace is assured—no kids are allowed at Twinpalms Bangtao Phuket Tented Resort—on the island of Phuket, where the vibe is twentieth-century safari expedition in a tropical jungle. There is a shimmering turquoise lagoon for seductive swims, but many of the glamorous canvas tents have their own plunge pools, too, just beside the white sand beach and Andaman Sea. Book an appointment at the Spa Tent for a famous Thai massage.

THAILAND

855 Fuel the flames of passion on a go-kart race

Take your date on an outing that will spark your passion and competitive streaks. Phuket's go-kart tracks, indoor, outdoor, and through jungle landscapes, are a fun, speedy way to get frisky.

THAILAND

856 Sample tasty invasive species

Dine at Jaras, on Phuket's Kamala Beach, where 100 percent of the ingredients are sourced from local villagers and farmers, but with a twist. Each of the nine courses on this tasting menu features invasive plants and animals—water mimosa and black shin tilapia among them. As you eat, you can feel good that your delicious meal, a partnership with World Wildlife Fund Thailand, is helping to save local ecosystems.

THAILAND

857 Have a playful pillow fight and candlelit bath

Reserve a beachside villa for an indulgent getaway with your spouse and a third party: the biggest bed you have ever seen. At Krabi's spectacular Phulay Bay, a Ritz-Carlton Reserve, the double-king-size bed—plus your two candlelit pool-like bathtubs, one indoor and one outside— act as an invitation to play and sleep. Before doing either, have dinner surrounded by two thousand candles.

THAILAND

858 Relish a treetop breakfast for two

In Trat, embark on a verdant breakfast adventure at Soneva Kiri, where you will dine in a hanging bamboo tree pod. It will be raised high into the emerald jungle foliage so you can swing gently and gaze out at the ocean while sampling gourmet treats served by a ziplining waiter who flies through the trees with your food.

VIETNAM

859 Savor wagyu you'll never forget in Hanoi

It is not the obvious meal choice in Vietnam's charming city of Hanoi, but sitting shoulder to shoulder beside your partner at Capella Hanoi's serene teppanyaki grill Hibana by Koki is a splurge you will never forget. The Michelin-starred boîte has just fourteen seats and a many-course tasting menu of rich, nuanced plates featuring delicacies from Japan and starring exquisite Kyori beef, a wagyu with exceptional marbling, tenderness, and flavor.

854 Twinpalms Bangtao Phuket Tented Resort

VIETNAM

860 Sail through Bai Tu Long Bay's karst islands

Skip iconic yet tourist-thronged Ha Long Bay in favor of a sailing voyage on a traditional junk through Bai Tu Long Bay, where towering karst limestone islands sculpted over millions of years emerge from the emerald green waters. The boat, dubbed *L'Amour Junk*, is a handcrafted wooden vessel with a single cabin. Book a multiday cruise around the UNESCO-protected seascape, seeking out secluded little beaches and incredible limestone formations as you go.

VIETNAM

861 Watch the water turn gold in Hue

Drift down Hue's elegantly named Perfume River on an even more elegant craft: the 55-ft. (17-m) hardwood cruise boat *Nam Xuan*, with lipstick-red trim. From Azerai La Residence's private vessel you will take in the ancient locale's dragon boats on golden water, mountain vistas, and historical sites while on a sunset cocktail cruise for two, complete with artisanal drinks, canapés, and a visit to the iconic circa 1601 Thien Mu Pagoda.

860 *L'Amour Junk*, Bai Tu Long Bay

VIETNAM

862 Explore an unseen side of Vietnam by river

Discover the historic temples, small villages, and craftspeople of Vietnam—and even into Cambodia and Laos—as you slide across the surface of the Mekong River in a five-star boutique river-cruise vessel with Heritage Line. Romance is a by-product of the experiences you will have along the way, since there is a certain undeniable charm to exploring Southeast Asian cultures by water.

VIETNAM

863 Plan an activity-packed day in Hoi An

Paddle a traditional round basket boat off a golden beach in picturesque Hoi An, then ride water buffalos bareback before diving into an immersive Vietnamese cooking class. After devouring the tantalizingly bright, fragrant feast you prepared in concert, unwind in a cloud of bubbles in the two-person bathtub just behind your bed at Four Seasons Resort the Nam Hai, Hoi An.

VIETNAM

864 Have your wedding clothes custom made

Bring photos of your dream wedding dress or suit and spend a morning together in one of Hoi An's legendary tailor shops getting measured and selecting fabrics that will become your own exquisitely custom-made pieces. In just a couple days, with fittings along the way, the tailors will create your ensembles with precision, ensuring you will be saying "I do" in something you could not have gotten elsewhere.

ASIA • VIETNAM

VIETNAM

865 See a kaleidoscope of rainbow lanterns

Ecstatic rainbows of bamboo and silk lanterns are the hallmark of Hoi An, an ancient town threaded with canals and bridges plus a smorgasbord of antique French, Chinese, and Vietnamese architecture. They are vibrant by day, but take a stroll after dark to witness the true enchantment that is a trove of paper lanterns floating on Hoai River each night—hop on a small boat for a full immersion.

VIETNAM

866 Delight in a beach-centric vacation

In mountain- and lagoon-strewn Phu Yen province, find shared bliss on the perfect kilometer-long private beach of luxuriant boutique resort Zannier Bāi San Hô—set on its own lush peninsula of 245 acres (100 ha)—and all it entails. Cocktails on swings at the beach bar, freshly caught seafood with musicians setting the mood on the sand, swims in the turquoise sea, sexy time in your beach villa, and outdoor cinema evenings, too.

VIETNAM

867 Traverse Vietnam by opulent train

Take it all in as you traverse bucolic Central Vietnam on the sumptuous train the Vietage by Anantara, traveling from endearing Hoi An through beachy Quy Nhon to paradisiacal Nha Trang, or the reverse. There are day journeys and overnight ones, in fun little sleeper booths, but all are intimate affairs with mind-blowing cuisine and free-flowing drinks. Included head and shoulder treatments soothe you along the way, too.

865 Hoai River, Hoi An

VIETNAM • ASIA

VIETNAM

868 Hike and cruise before catching a movie

For ultimate seclusion plus your very own water slide, reserve the Rock Retreat villa at Six Senses Ninh Van Bay, set into massive sculptural boulders in the East Vietnam Sea. It is so private that you will arrive into your own bay on speedboat. There is a rustic-chic vibe to the whole resort, where you will hike, relax into colorful cushions of a wooden boat for a sunset cruise, and cozy up for movies on the beach.

VIETNAM

869 Do some high-low feasting in Saigon

Plan a gastronomic trip to the Pearl of the Orient, aka Ho Chi Minh City, where it is easy to feast high and low. Start on a dynamic daytime walking street food, pho, or seafood tour with Saigon Street Eats that is both delicious and enlightening, then finish the night at a low-lit table at Michelin-recommended restaurant Square One. The open kitchen serves enticing dishes drawing from regional traditions and local ingredients.

VIETNAM

870 Start your day with a floating breakfast

On Phu Quoc island, start your day with a swimwear-clad champagne toast to kick off a delectable floating breakfast in your villa's private infinity pool at Regent Phu Quoc. The morning ritual says "vacation" like nothing else except maybe the cushy cabanas that line the resort's pools or the hammocks on its inviting beach. Replace dessert with a seductive bath setup in your bathroom oasis, orchestrated by your butler.

868 Six Senses Ninh Van Bay

351

Virtuous Jungle Adventure

CAMBODIA

871 Harness up for a scintillating zipline arrival and welcome G&Ts

Arrive at your hotel in Cambodia's Cardamom Mountains by hooking into harnesses and streaking above the beryl treetops on a zipline, only to land and be handed refreshing gin and tonics to cheers. At that point the fun has only just begun at Shinta Mani Wild, a luxe, tented, riverside retreat with foraged cuisine, cruises through the rainforest, and infinite adventure. The sweetest part: knowing your stay funds the Shinta Mani Foundation's hospitality training for disadvantaged Cambodians.

ASIA • CAMBODIA

CAMBODIA

872 Experience Khmer healing and Mekong views

Take in Cambodia's Mekong River from a bird's-eye view in your plush suite at Rosewood Phnom Penh, elevated high above the heart of Cambodia's capital, and later soak up sparkling vistas from the river itself on a romantic sunset cruise. In between, treat yourselves to a relaxing dose of traditional Khmer healing in the form of lost remedies incorporated within modern spa therapies.

CAMBODIA

873 Find beauty in the ancient at Angkor Wat

Prepare to be moved by the extraordinary beauty of Angkor Wat—meaning "City of Temples" in Khmer—the largest religious structure on Earth. Arrive at the East Gate of the twelfth-century Buddhist complex with a private guide from your hotel, Amansara, just before dawn. Later, board the hotel's wooden boat for a serene cruise through the floating villages of Tonle Sap lake.

CAMBODIA

874 Spend the day chasing butterflies

Visit one of Southeast Asia's largest butterfly houses, the Banteay Srey Butterfly Centre, where hundreds of colorful tropical butterflies flutter about in a lush, netted garden. You will find this kaleidoscopic ecotourism fantasy just a short drive from Angkor Wat. There is also the outdoor Butterfly Paradise garden even closer to Siem Reap, a serene outdoor space with native Cambodian species.

873 Angkor Wat

876 Six Senses Krabey Island

CAMBODIA

875 Envelop yourselves in luxury in Siem Reap

For a lovely and layered discovery of Siem Reap's temple ruins, waterfalls, and lake, pick the most glamorous and flamboyant home base around: Shinta Mani Angkor. Your suite has its own swimming pool and there is a Khmer restaurant for tasting the delicacies of Cambodia plus a spa where therapists will work their local healing magic on you both.

CAMBODIA

876 Tuck yourselves away on a jungle-covered private island

Hide out from the world on a densely vegetated private island off Cambodia's coast, and disappear into one of Six Senses Krabey Island's lavish ocean-view villas with a backdrop of dense jungle. All provisions can be delivered to you by your GEM (guest experience maker) if you never want to emerge.

CAMBODIA

877 Spice things up with a Kampot pepper farm visit

Add a little heat to your picture-perfect jaunt through Cambodia's south coast with a visit to the sustainable Kampot pepper-growing BoTree Farm. A tour of the farm will reveal all there is to know about the different stages of pepper cultivation, from planting to harvesting, and the organic practices used in the process. It also includes a pepper tasting.

879 Fireworks over the Han River

SOUTH KOREA

878 Get into the bathhouse spirit at a *jjimjilbang* spa

In Seoul, visit a *jjimjilbang* together, a traditional Korean bathhouse. The nude mineral bathing and scrubbing areas are gender separated and heterosexual couples can reunite in the dry part of the spa. Here, you can share a sauna or massage, unwind in a jade or salt room, enjoy snacks, like *patbingsu*, a popular Korean dessert, and even take a nap.

SOUTH KOREA

879 Snuggle close over fireworks on Han River

Spend an evening traveling beneath a canopy of twinkling stars and moonlight on what was once an ancient transportation route through Korea: Han River. In the culturally rich capital of Seoul, steal away on a private yacht or a larger boat for an after-dark cruise, complete with drinks, bountiful food, live music, and even fireworks, lighting up the night and sparking an amorous evening.

SOUTH KOREA

880 Pair romance with a silly, sexy themed park

Hop over to Jeju Island for a loved-up escapade across white sand beaches, volcanoes, and waterfalls, plus a romantic stay at the arresting JW Marriott Jeju Resort & Spa, where private dining experiences and couples spa treatments turn up the romance. Make time for a lighthearted dash of fun at the isle's hilarious Love Land outdoor park full of playful sex-themed sculptures.

JAPAN

881 Sleep high above Tokyo in the plushest environs imaginable

For a seductive sleepover in Japan's capital, book a room with a view so captivating it will be hard to sleep. From your sumptuous soaring room or suite at Bvlgari Hotel Tokyo the glittering nightscape below is worth keeping the curtains wide open for. Do not miss a 400-ft.-high (120-m) swim in the ultraglam pool and exquisite cocktails in the hotel's sultry bar.

JAPAN

882 Experience the lush side of Tokyo with a walk in Yoyogi Park

Discover a flourishing, bordering on otherworldly pocket of forest amid Tokyo's urban sprawl during a stay at the thoughtful, Japandi-leaning boutique hotel TRUNK (HOTEL) Yoyogi Park. Reserve the penthouse suite or a park view room for exclusive access to the hotel's infinity pool and jacuzzi, which look out over a sea of green treetops. After sightseeing and visiting the mystical Meiji Jingu Shrine, relax with handcrafted cocktails.

882 TRUNK (HOTEL) Yoyogi Park

ASIA • JAPAN

883 teamLab Borderless

JAPAN

883 Pair sake tasting with digital art in Tokyo

Take a sommelier-led sake tasting class to compare several varieties of Japan's iconic rice wine—from dry and delicate to rich and fruity. Afterward step into the mesmerizing world of digital art at teamLab Borderless. In this stunning alternative universe, your movements affect the ever-changing images and 360-degree LED lighting, and rooms filled with crystals and reflective bubbles seemingly extend to infinity.

JAPAN

884 Disappear together for the ultimate spa day

Check into one of the most exclusive spots in all of Tokyo: an intimate spa house in Janu Tokyo. There are just two of these ultimate spa suites where you can spend a half or full day immersed together in bathing and spa culture, either hammam or banya style. Food, drinks, and complete relaxation are a given considering the pampering treatments and service that are part of the package.

JAPAN

885 Turn your love into a latte portait

For a creative date idea in Tokyo, go to Cafe Reissue in Shibuya, armed with a favorite photo of the two of you together. There, the artistic baristas will re-create it in 2D, or even 3D, foam on sweet coffee concoctions that you will of course have to photograph before drinking. Another idea: Order a 3D foam engagement ring to help you pop the question.

JAPAN

886 Ski on, play in, and even taste Japan's legendary powder

Feel fluffy flakes of famous "Japow"—Japanese powder—land on your cheeks and eyelashes as you stroll in the sublime snow globe that is Niseko in the wintertime. Stick out your tongues to catch frosty crystals as you build a cute snow-person couple. And, of course, ski and snowboard down impressive mountains coated in it.

JAPAN

887 Canoe beneath Mount Fuji, illuminated by magical morning light

Bask in the calm of drifting soundlessly in a canoe, save for the gentle rhythm of your paddles dipping into Lake Kawaguchi, as radiant early-morning light reflects Mount Fuji on the water's glasslike surface. This 7 A.M. activity is an idyllic way to begin a day at HOSHINOYA Fuji, where the cabins and their balconies offer impeccable viewing of the iconic stratovolcano. During your stay, learn to chop wood, make pizzas in the forest, smoke your own food, hike, and e-bike, spending time each night cozied up with Japanese whiskey around a sparkling bonfire with live musical entertainment.

JAPAN

888 Collaborate on a special ceramic piece in a country known for it

With its exceptional ceramic art traditions, Japan is the place to explore your creative side together. Throughout the country it is possible to arrange a private pottery class, with artisans guiding you through the meditative process of shaping clay by hand. Best of all, you get to collaborate to make a beautiful object that you can take home with you.

887 Lake Kawaguchi

ASIA • JAPAN

890 Bamboo forest, Kyoto

JAPAN

889 Pair pearl harvesting with origami to commemorate an anniversary

Head to seaside Ise-Shima in Japan's Mie prefecture to find amazement in a pearl harvesting experience. You will get to pull up a basket of Akoya pearl oysters, extract the iridescent spherical gemstones, and pick your own to bring home or have set into a piece of jewelry perfect for a thirtieth wedding anniversary gift. Add an origami class if celebrating your first anniversary.

JAPAN

890 Follow a stroll through a bamboo forest with an incense ceremony

Seek to blend in, respectfully, by doing as so many Japanese tourists in Kyoto's quiet and alluring pocket of Arashiyama: dress up in kimono at one of many rental shops, then take a slow stroll through the fairy-tale bamboo forest. Later, step onto a romantic wooden boat to adults-only HOSHINOYA Kyoto and don ensembles provided by the resort for an intricate incense ceremony.

JAPAN

891 Soak up Kyoto's culture—and ceremonies

Alternate between outings to gilded temples, ancient shrines, and Zen botanical gardens, while taking time to simply soak up the golden atmosphere of Roku Kyoto, a resort-like retreat tucked into the foothills of the Takagamine mountains. Focus intently on the rituals involved in a traditional tea ceremony, then let loose in the resort's onsen hot spring pool.

JAPAN

892 Spend the night in downtown Kyoto

Deep-dive into intriguing and delectable Japanese flavors by spending an evening nestled in a dark booth at the seductive speakeasy Nine Tails, where the menu is dedicated to celebrating Japanese spirits. Be sure to start your meal with one of the bar's signature cocktails. You will be within stumbling distance of falling into bed in your chic room upstairs at Six Senses Kyoto.

JAPAN

893 Submerge in your own onsen hot spring

Spend your days and nights surrounded by rice terraces and carpeted mountains, following the pace of nature and steaming things up in your own private hot spring at all hours. The setting: Oita prefecture, a geothermal hot spot, where KAI Yufuin is a spectacular introduction to *ryokan* life, complete with *kaiseki* dinners and a magical Firefly Room for couples.

891 A soothing Japanese onsen

ASIA • JAPAN

JAPAN

894 Travel magnificently across Kyushu island

Explore the absurd beauty of Kyushu from the supreme luxury of Seven Stars, an intimate sleeper train with just ten guest compartment suites for a maximum of ten couples per journey rolling past mountains, shrines, and lovely villages. Dress for the refined three-night occasion that includes stops, of course, but also a tea sommelier for onboard tea ceremonies and live entertainment in the evenings.

JAPAN

895 Find a cherry blossom heart in Hirosaki Park

Travel to Hirosaki Park from mid-April to mid-May to witness the mesmerizing sight of more than 2,500 cherry trees in bloom. Wander through a tunnel of vivid pink Kanzan blossoms, seek out the oldest Somei-Yoshino cherry tree in the park, and take a selfie beneath a huge heart shape created by the overlapping blossom-laden branches.

JAPAN

896 Take in a tiny wonder on Taketomi

Appreciate the little things with your partner by your side on the isle of Taketomi in the Okinawa Islands, as you sit on a flawless beach and dig for the teensiest of treasures: star-shaped sand. Hunt together for the cute grains, a natural phenomenon that never ceases to amaze; take a little vial to bring some home.

895 Hirosaki Park

MALAYSIA

897 Savor the pleasure of having a bath butler

Check into a suite that comes with a bath butler whose role is to draw you divine soaks for two, filled with fragrant botanical salts and oils. When you are not naked in your personal little Eden at Kuala Lumpur's RuMa, venture down to the adults-only sixth floor cantilevered infinity pool for more relaxation.

MALAYSIA

898 Walk the sky and wander the rainforest

Take your spouse for an amble across the 410-ft.-long (25-m) curving suspension bridge on Langkawi, known as the Jewel of Kedah. Some 2,170 ft. (660 m) above sea level, the island's Sky Bridge is an awe-inspiring feat of engineering. Round out the adventure with a JungleWalla tour ensconced in the Gunung Raya rainforest.

ASIA • SINGAPORE

SECRET FOOD TOUR

SINGAPORE

899 Trade bites with each other while on a foodie trip

Switch on your senses for an in-the-know excursion on foot with Secret Food Tours, the very best way for a couple of gourmets to venture through a new city. There are offerings across nearly all the continents, so the foodie fun can be had almost anywhere you roam, but Singapore's melting pot of Asian cultures and culinary traditions makes it especially stimulating for the taste buds while adding depth to your vacation together.

Smith Street, Chinatown

Lau Pa Sat hawker market

SINGAPORE • ASIA

Market Street Hawker Center

SINGAPORE

900 Canoodle inside a wildly provocative bar

Start an after-dark caper with some clandestine canoodling in the LED-lit glow of Singapore's photogenic Henderson Waves pedestrian bridge. Continue onward to the unabashedly sexy Tokyo-styled speakeasy Here Kitty Kitty and pick your poison between the concept rooms. Go for the Cathouse or Mamasan lounge spaces for entrancing decor and potent libations or, if you are feeling naughty, reserve the private Shibari room inspired by Japanese bondage.

SINGAPORE

901 Write each other a poem or letter

In one of the most iconic hotel bars there is, Raffles Singapore's Writers Bar, order a pair of Singapore Slings—the cherry-tinged tropical cocktail was created there in 1915. Then take out a couple pens and some paper, and craft a poem or letter for and about your love, paying homage to bygone literary greats who once drank there.

ASIA • SINGAPORE

SINGAPORE

902 Admire your date alongside Singapore's most iconic building

Take in one of the world's most recognizable skyscrapers, Marina Bay Sands, from afar and then near, during a romantic afternoon. Admire it from inside the intimate rooftop pool of 21 Carpenter, a design-forward boutique hotel at the junction of historic Chinatown and Clarke Quay. Later, gussy up and head over to the triple towers for a decadent dinner with the city at your feet at Spago Dining Room by Wolfgang Puck.

SINGAPORE

903 Be immersed in a real-life wonderland at Gardens by the Bay

After an evening on the town, take your partner on an epic post-dinner walk at Gardens by the Bay. This famous urban park of 260 acres (105 ha) is open until 2 A.M., and in perennially steamy Singapore it is most pleasant under the stars. The lush flora crawling up and down indoor waterfalls and conservatories stuns, but be sure to engage in a little PDA beneath or between the gargantuan lit-up Supertrees.

903 Supertrees at Gardens by the Bay

SINGAPORE • ASIA

905 Luxury Tall Ship *Royal Albatross*

SINGAPORE

904 Treat yourselves to an innovative hands-on cooking class

Stroll an urban garden and sign up for the Air CCCC Cooking Club where you can both quench your love of cooking and food with a storytelling farmer talk or hands-on class to practice offbeat techniques from the circular campus' innovating chefs. The leafy dining destination that wastes absolutely nothing makes for an unforgettable and dynamic date day or night, especially once you share bites of the palate-pleasing fare.

SINGAPORE

905 Sail through the sunset together on the *Royal Albatross*

Set out before the sun drops into the sea for a majestically romantic evening on a gracious tall ship with an impressive twenty-two sails. On the one-of-a-kind *Royal Albatross* superyacht, you can expect to sail through the sorbet-colored sunset off Sentosa Island, breezing past photo-worthy bays and Singaporean landmarks. With surreal scenes as your backdrop, feast on a four- or seven-course dinner while sipping champagne.

ASIA • INDONESIA

INDONESIA

906 Meander on a private riverboat safari

Charter your own riverboat on the island of Borneo for a very special excursion in search of some of Earth's rarest species: endangered orangutans and vulnerable Bornean clouded leopards. Feel pampered on what is essentially a miniature floating hotel and visit a place where the primates are treated well, too, an orangutan rehabilitation center.

INDONESIA

907 Immerse yourselves in culture with splendor

Find yourselves endlessly fascinated on an itinerary that blends culture with grandeur and warm hospitality on the island of Java. In the vibrant artistic city of Yogyakarta, board a plush train car bound for Borobudur, the world's largest Buddhist temple. As you travel toward the ornate eighth-century monument and Amanjiwo, your temple-like resort nearby, a historian will regale you with stories.

INDONESIA

908 Try something new: sleeping without walls

In the thick jungles of central Bali, go out on a limb and spend a few nights in a very revealing situation. At Buahan, a Banyan Tree Escape, your secluded villa has zero walls and no doors, so you will be totally at one with nature amid ephemeral curtains as you soak and swim in supreme peace. Enhance the experience by signing up for the resort's Insight Journey in the wilds.

INDONESIA

909 Experience the apex bedtime tuck-in together

At the conclusion of an illuminating day exploring Bali, blissfully perched in your fabulous Capella Ubud tent in Keliki, invite a pair of spa therapists into your bed for the literal dreamiest massages of your lives. They will deliver you deep sleep therapy, incorporating a magnesium oil and salt foot massage and a slow, deliberate head and shoulder rubdown, then play a Tibetan sound bowl and tuck you both in.

907 Borobudur Temple

910 Four Seasons Resort Bali at Sayan

INDONESIA

910 Embark on a sensual shared chakra ritual

Tap into the chakra that is most linked to desire and intimacy at Four Seasons Resort Bali at Sayan, where the two-and-a-half hour Swadhisthana Chakra Ceremony promises to unlock and increase your capacity for pleasure. Feel sensitivities build as you undergo a heavenly scented scrub and bathing ritual, flowing massage, and meditation during the sensuous experience. Alternatively, enjoy a Night Spa ritual by the riverside.

INDONESIA

911 Taste the root-to-leaf flavors of Bali

Duck inside a woven pod overlooking the rushing Ayung River for an atmospheric candlelit multicourse dinner that is more than nature inspired—it is dictated by it. The true flavors of Bali's bountiful homegrown ingredients come through in chef Eka Sunarya's menus, every element of which comes from within 62 mi. (100 km). Go for all plants (root to leaf) or sample sustainable fish, too—either way, it is zero-waste cuisine to savor.

ASIA • INDONESIA

912 Bambu Indah, Bali

INDONESIA

912 Cuddle up in an imaginative tree house over humming jungle

Channel your inner adventurers when you book a fanciful bamboo tree house or fantastic villa complete with a boho open-air bed draped in netting and perched above flowing water. At Bambu Indah, vacation happens outside and might include baths in a copper tub under moonlight, plunging into natural pools, and swinging in a pod over the river.

INDONESIA

913 Incite a more sustainable life at a "good times, do good" hotel

Feel compelled to live more sustainably at home after a mind-blowing stay at Bali's hands-down coolest beach resort, Desa Potato Head. Choose a textural contemporary Balinese suite or modern brutalist studio for your foray into all things zero waste, circular, and stunning, where "good times, do good" from morning through night.

INDONESIA

914 Scope out eagle and manta rays during a spoiling meal at Koral

At the Apurva Kempinski Bali, Koral is Bali's first underwater restaurant. Your table for two sits inside a clear tunnel, beneath a vast saltwater pool, where you can watch manta rays and eagle rays glide silently by as you eat. Dine on a mouthwatering Michelin-level meal of caviar, blue crab, and lobster alongside mystical cocktails.

INDONESIA • ASIA

INDONESIA

915 Make a meaningful wish together during a Balinese Hindu ceremony

Experience the only-in-Bali ritual of a *melukat* ceremony in the most spectacular of settings: an ancient waterfall temple far beyond the well-beaten tourist track. Guided by a local from Sala village, the Balinese Hindu tradition will get you both very wet and very purified in the most beautifully spiritual way.

INDONESIA

916 Help save Bali's fireflies

Head to Taro, or another flourishing village on Bali, for a firefly immersion, first learning about the luminous insects, their behavior, and meaning in Balinese culture, before helping with conservation efforts. Later, after sunset, step into the night to watch them glow, and enjoy a local dinner in their supernatural presence.

INDONESIA

917 Witness Marapu traditions on Sumba

From sustainable French-meets-Indo resort Cap Karoso, ride on e-bikes to a Marapu village with its impressive roofs. Locals follow the Bronze Age animist culture, and you will have a chance to observe their ancestral traditions. Take a guided tour or sign up for the resort's Shamanic Healing Journey to meet personally with a Marapu shaman.

INDONESIA

918 Ride off into the ocean on horseback

On the island of Sumba, check into the Sanubari for a one-of-a-kind adventure, forging trusting relationships with a pair of horses. You will groom the magnificent animals before hopping on them bareback for an extraordinary ride along the resort's powdery white beach. There is every chance your horse will crave a refreshing swim, so off you will go into the aquamarine ocean, feeling more relaxed with every wave.

917 Marapu village, Sumba

ASIA • INDONESIA

WILD WELLNESS

INDONESIA

919 Take a full-day couples wellness safari on Sumba

On a full-day Spa Safari at NIHI Sumba, you start early, hiking or horse riding through divine landscapes to your own spa villa with a pool and sublime views. Thanks to well-placed mirrors, the ocean is even visible when you are face down on the massage beds for hours of treatments tailored to your requests, organic facials, cooling wraps, and full body massages among them. There are breaks for tantalizing meals and exploring the surrounding beaches and forests.

INDONESIA/PHILIPPINES • ASIA

INDONESIA

920 Swim with breathtaking megafauna on a Komodo cruise

Charter a traditional *phinisi* yacht, such as *Vela*, for a once-in-a-lifetime experience in Komodo National Park. Donning snorkels, you will slip into tropical waters to swim with graceful spotted whale sharks, who glide gently beneath you. Balletic manta rays might also be your aquatic companions. Your days will follow completely bespoke itineraries, featuring delicious Indonesian cuisine with occasional stops along the Jurassic coast and onboard massages.

INDONESIA

921 Combine Komodo dragons with fascinating Flores culture

Discover the uniqueness of each and every Indonesian island—and there are more than 17,000 of them—while luxuriating at, and tasting your way through, TA'AKTANA, a Luxury Collection Resort & Spa, Labuan Bajo, a gateway to idiosyncratic culture and wildlife. During your stay, take a boat trip to see prehistoric Komodo dragons and sign up to watch, and perhaps try, the Manggarai signature *caci* dance.

PHILIPPINES

922 Pair a chocolate extravaganza with a city tour in Manila

Go all out for an anniversary or honeymoon trip to the Philippines, starting in buzzy Manila with a celebration in chocolate form. Let the Peninsula Manila know it is a special occasion and allow their pastry team to work their magic for a wildly creative and artful chocolate display personalized for you and your partner. Make time for a fun private city tour in the hotel's iconic vintage Jeepney or their Rolls-Royce.

PHILIPPINES

923 Get up close and personal with spectacular sea life

Take an underwater walk on a seabed in Boracay, where air-pumped helmets allow you and your partner to serenely stroll and bob along under the surface. Unlike scuba diving, no training is needed in order to engage in the thrilling act of breathing in lucid cerulean saltwater, so you can focus solely on the eye-catching marine life. You can see colorful clownfish, parrotfish, and angelfish, among others.

PHILIPPINES

924 Explore an ancient subterranean river and cave system

Hire a private guide to show you all the most marvelous spots in Puerto Princesa Subterranean River National Park, one of the New Seven Wonders of Nature. Here, the world's second-longest underground river flows through an ancient limestone cave system before emptying into the West Philippine Sea. Traveling by canoe, you will see huge stalactites as you explore the vast network of caves.

PHILIPPINES

925 Stroke in sync in a transparent kayak

The color of Coron's water is practically mythical, it is that luminous, clear, and startlingly turquoise. It sets the scene for excellent snorkeling and diving, but even more so, admire it in a totally transparent tandem kayak. Enjoy the surreal experience of sitting in the vivid liquid while paddling together over a pristine coral reef.

PHILIPPINES

926 Hold a golden hour SUP race at Amanpulo

Challenge your partner to a fun-spirited race on stand-up paddleboards around the dreamy private island of Pamalican, home to the exclusive resort Amanpulo. Start your scenic journey late in the afternoon when everything is bathed in striking golden light, and hop onto the same board to watch the sun drop before a memorable bountiful dinner.

PHILIPPINES
927 Do nothing but relax together

Escape all signs of civilization at the intimate island paradise Nay Palad Hideaway, oozing with romance. With an all-inclusive model that truly includes everything, it is easy to achieve the most laid-back of routines simply waking, eating, boating, eating, getting massaged, and eating some more before falling into a sumptuous bed together.

MICRONESIA
928 Honor folktale lovers with a kiss

Connect with a slice of the island of Guam's history and your partner all at the same time by taking a picturesque walk up to Two Lovers Point just before the sun sets. There, take in the impeccable South Pacific seascape and exchange a kiss in honor of the lovers from the romantically tragic old folktale for which it is named. Bring a bottle of wine and toast to your own happy ending.

928 Two Lovers Point, Guam

6
OCEANIA

OCEANIA • AUSTRALIA

933 Purnululu National Park, Kimberley

AUSTRALIA, WESTERN AUSTRALIA

929 Explore Perth on an engrossing walking tour

There is more to Western Australia's capital city than meets the eye, and couples who harbor intense curiosity would do well to dig deeper with the help of a knowledgable, soulful guide from homegrown company Two Feet & a Heartbeat. Pick a theme for your tour: coffee, culture, and art; cuisine, true crime, or whiskey, and expect an illuminating ramble through Perth's alluring laneways and alleys.

AUSTRALIA, WESTERN AUSTRALIA

930 Get a little giddy blending gin

Use your partner as your aromatic inspiration while selecting botanicals to combine for a spirit that captures their essence during a Giniversity Gin Blending Class in the cool western surf town of Margaret River. During the session you will learn all about distilling gin and ways to drink it, and you will go home with your own full-size bottles of flavorful nectar with which to toast for many years to come.

AUSTRALIA, WESTERN AUSTRALIA

931 Follow a black truffle hunt with a picnic

Venture out to Australia's truffle country, the bucolic Manjimup region, for a heady dose of the famously rich fungi. Visit from June through August for your own private black truffle hunting experience, during which you will get to follow the cute truffle dog's nose to dig up the fragrant gastronomic treasures. Check in to the region's seductive Cape Lodge and settle into a wine-pairing picnic featuring standout local ingredients.

AUSTRALIA, WESTERN AUSTRALIA

932 Be spellbound by Ningaloo Reef's subaquatic magic

Escape to the always warm, sunny, and turquoise Ningaloo Reef Marine Park—a heritage-listed fringing reef of 1,930 sq. mi. (5,000 km^2)—for phenomenal aquatic adventures. The destination is literally swimming with rainbows of special species all year long. April to July is prime time for spotting migrating whale sharks, a once-in-a-lifetime experience.

AUSTRALIA, WESTERN AUSTRALIA

933 Share a sense of wonder in the Kimberley wilderness

Coordinate a combination of rugged road-tripping and river- or ocean-cruising to take in the jaw-dropping beauty of the distinctive Kimberley region of Western Australia, where the Indian Ocean and Timor Sea meet. Between horizontal waterfalls, ancient domes, cave-swimming, mountain-view picnics, rare species, and rock art, every excursion will surely look different.

931 Cape Lodge

AUSTRALIA, NORTHERN TERRITORY

934 Witness Australia's Red Heart, the iconic Uluru

Experience the unique gravitational pull of Uluru, the sacred Aboriginal site and half-billion-year-old sandstone monolith rising out of the outback desert known as Australia's Red Heart. Check into a dune pavilion at the inimitable Longitude 131° for a wildly romantic expedition involving privileged vistas of the ever-color-changing rock and awe-inspiring Kata Tjuta from your bed, either inside the glass and canvas structure or on its deck, where you can linger through sunset and moonlight. Guided tours and cocktail hours in Uluru's shadows, Indigenous art classes, and native cuisine spark all your senses.

AUSTRALIA, SOUTH AUSTRALIA

935 Spy on koalas and wallabies at night during a stay on Kangaroo Island

Couples seeking remote beauty will feel as though they hit the jackpot with a stay at the award-winning Southern Ocean Lodge. The clifftop panoramas from this plush and wonderfully low-impact hotel on Kangaroo Island are film worthy, and relatively few get to sear them into their memory. A true highlight here is a nocturnal exploration at the Hanson Bay Wildlife Sanctuary to observe Australian animals that come alive at nighttime, especially kangaroos, wallabies, owls, and koalas. Take it all in beneath southern hemisphere constellations that include the Crux, Centaurus, and Carina.

934 Longitude 131°

937 The Ghan

AUSTRALIA, SOUTH AUSTRALIA

936 Pedal, sip, and nibble through wine country

Hire a couple of e-bikes for an unhurried, idyllic ride through South Australia's acclaimed Barossa Valley, northeast of Adelaide. Take the super scenic 17-mi. (27-km) Jack Bobridge Bike Trail as you wind through sought-after wineries and bountiful farms, stopping along the way for tastings. Collect provisions for a picturesque picnic when you find the most beautiful setting to stop.

AUSTRALIA, SOUTH AUSTRALIA

937 Step back in time on a lavish train journey

Experience the outback from the sumptuous comfort of the Ghan, a train expedition that defines the word *epic*. It is pricey, but worth the expense to reserve a suite or Platinum cabin, which include perks to make the trip all the more alluring: free-flowing Bollinger champagne, turndown nightcaps, divine linens, and artisanal chocolates. Prepare to hop off for exhilarating excursions that include camel riding and hiking amid endemic flora and fauna.

AUSTRALIA, QUEENSLAND

938 Focus affections on Gold Coast koalas

Direct your combined energies to endemic species of Australian wildlife that are endangered and need protection. The country's beloved koalas take particular skill to assist with, but there are nonprofits and organizations stretching across Queensland that care for the fluffy mammals—or kangaroos, wallabies, and more—and take volunteers who can make a difference planting much-needed koala trees, for example.

AUSTRALIA, QUEENSLAND

939 Dig into regenerative farming at an off-grid tiny home

Move into a tiny eco-friendly home on a farm with a stay at the Edenic 140-acre (57-ha) High Valley Dawn Permaculture Farm. Your teeny off-the-grid abode will introduce you to key concepts of truly sustainable living, such as using composting toilets and recycling rainwater for drinking. During your stay, you will also learn permaculture principles, bird-watch, and practice yoga in nature.

AUSTRALIA, QUEENSLAND

940 Take in the Whitsundays from above—including the iconic Heart Reef

Experience the Great Barrier Reef from a new perspective on a scenic helicopter flight over the Whitsundays. You will spot the naturally formed, heart-shaped coral formation known as Heart Reef, a striking symbol of nature's artistry best seen from the air. Many tours include a landing on a floating pontoon, where you can snorkel the reef's vibrant underwater world.

AUSTRALIA, QUEENSLAND

941 Have a couples massage in the midst of a rainforest

At InterContinental Hayman Great Barrier Reef, book a couples massage in an open-air pavilion embraced by rainforest for the most peaceful treatment of your lives. During your stay here, you can leap into a massive pool directly from your suite and spot wallabies on morning hikes.

AUSTRALIA, QUEENSLAND

942 Gain privileged access to pristine white sand beaches

Escape the tourist throngs at the über-exclusive Lizard Island Resort, an elegant playground of blindingly white powdery beaches, unspoiled wilderness, and abundant reefs. The latter are best explored privately, on your own motorized dinghy. Make your way to secluded spots for snorkeling and picnicking, one of abundant options.

AUSTRALIA, NEW SOUTH WALES

943 Hone your seafood cooking skills for future special meals

Sign up for a riveting master class at state-of-the-art Sydney Fish Market, which underwent an impressive overhaul to become a true destination for seafood lovers. Learn from the pros how to cut fish, prepare seafood, and cook succulent treats from the ocean. All that fun translates to a lifetime of elevated home-cooked meals for each other.

942 Lizard Island Resort

OCEANIA • AUSTRALIA

AUSTRALIA, NEW SOUTH WALES

944 Join Sydney's Gay and Lesbian Mardi Gras

For couples who love boldly and live joyfully, the annual Gay and Lesbian Mardi Gras is an outrageously spirited setting in which to express just that. Lose yourselves in a truly exuberant program of festivities that features a constant flow of dance parties, live music, and flashy costumes. Enjoy dressing up together for the extravagant grand finale Pride parade.

AUSTRALIA, NEW SOUTH WALES

945 Take a coastal walk from Coogee to Bondi

Follow Sydney's celebrated coastal trail, a 3.7-mi. (6-km) route that takes two to three hours at a leisurely pace, with sweeping views of the Pacific, sandstone cliffs, and picturesque beaches. Along the way, play a round of lawn bowls at the historic Clovelly Bowling Club and cool off with a swim in the Bondi Icebergs ocean pool, a local institution since 1929.

AUSTRALIA, NEW SOUTH WALES

946 Sail Sydney Harbour on a vintage yacht

You will be the only two passengers on the 1950 *Southwinds* racing yacht when booking Capella Sydney's Sail Away excursion, which involves an amuse bouche of local oysters and champagne while cruising glowy Sydney Harbour. The unique experience continues on Shark Island, where a private chef is waiting to get you both involved preparing an exquisite wine-paired lunch.

945 Bondi Icebergs ocean pool

AUSTRALIA • OCEANIA

AUSTRALIA, NEW SOUTH WALES

947 Capture your love on film in the Blue Mountains

Bring your old-school camera for a Blue Mountains escapade filled with gentle bushwalks, cascading waterfalls, and jaw-dropping cable-car rides. Often shrouded in mist, this rugged region presents a naturally romantic backdrop, and will feel all the more so when you take an analog approach to capturing the fleeting moments and then must wait anxiously to develop them and relive your caper.

AUSTRALIA, NEW SOUTH WALES

948 Head to Byron Bay's famous lighthouse

Strike out early in the laid-back surf paradise of Byron Bay for a glutes-burning hike up to the iconic Cape Byron lighthouse—the continent's most easterly point—to savor sunrise and 360-degree panoramas. See if you can spot a whale or pod of dolphins. Return to your home base, the cool, cozy Hotel Marvell, for a long, decadent breakfast and, later, a cooling dip in the rooftop pool.

AUSTRALIA, NEW SOUTH WALES

949 Sleepover at the perfect beach hotel

Spend several days in residence at the ravishing beach hotel Raes on Wategos, which feels like an amazing secret known by all the right people. It is mere steps to Byron Bay's most inviting beach for swimming and surfing, or slow beach walks with your spouse, but the generous Moroccan-inspired suites with bespoke amenities—plus delectable cuisine in the dining room—will seduce you back inside.

948 View from Cape Byron lighthouse

AUSTRALIA, CANBERRA

950 Celebrate five years of marriage with wood carving

Ring in five years of wedded bliss with a wood-carving class. In Canberra, hire a green woodworker to train you both how to wield knives and carve a pair of beautiful spoons for cooking or eating. As well as learning the principles of carving, you will pick up tips on knife safety and choosing wood.

AUSTRALIA, VICTORIA

951 Try a classic afternoon date on the sand

When in Melbourne, opt for a classic afternoon date idea: eating takeout fish and chips with the ocean providing your soundtrack. Take your partner to the hidden-gem Half Moon Bay—once a nude beach—for this delicious ritual. Don't miss slowly strolling down the sand to striking Red Bluff.

AUSTRALIA, VICTORIA

952 Steam up the windows during a night of passion

Let the dark, sexy moodiness of the QT Melbourne inspire a passionate night with your true love. Book one of the rooms with a bathtub designed for two—it is placed right beside a large window that will surely steam up during your cheeky soak that may incite exhibitionist fantasies.

AUSTRALIA, VICTORIA

953 Pair axe-throwing with a moonlight movie

Release some energy during an adrenaline-producing axe-throwing session at Melbourne's Maniax facility, then settle into beanbags to watch a flick together at the Moonlight Cinema in the city's fairy-tale Royal Botanic Gardens. Pack a picnic to graze on and a bottle of Yarra Valley wine.

AUSTRALIA, VICTORIA

954 Follow an art trail on the Mornington Peninsula

Indulge in a shared enthusiasm for quirky art and singular design at the striking Mornington Peninsula boutique hotel Jackalope, with a pool that looks out over vineyards and a geode-like massage pavilion. Follow the on-site art trail to encounter striking works—including a towering jackalope sculpture.

AUSTRALIA, VICTORIA

955 Take a journey on and over the Great Ocean Road

Pack in as much beauty as possible on Acacia Tours' private Great Ocean Road experience. The drive features pristine beaches, verdant rainforests, wild koalas, kangaroos, and the iconic Twelve Apostles limestone stacks. And to finish: a spectacular helicopter flight back to Melbourne.

955 Twelve Apostles

OCEANIA • TASMANIA

957 The southern lights in Tasmania

TASMANIA

956 Taste your way across Bruny island

Hop on a ferry from Hobart, Tasmania, to dramatic, ancient feeling Bruny Island for mind-blowing scenery alongside a luscious day of incredible food. You will be in heaven, sampling gourmet artisan treats the island is known for, from cheese and beer tasting to local oysters, fudge, and honey ice cream. Take time from all that indulgence to walk part of the serene 3-mi. (5-km) Cloudy Bay beach.

TASMANIA

957 Rent your own island to sleep over the sea

If privacy is the ultimate goal, save up for a stay on a secretive 76-acre (30-ha) Tasmanian gem that will be exclusively yours: Satellite Island. Your dream of a vacation starts with a racy speedboat or helicopter flight to reach it. Once there, you will have the place to yourselves to hike and shuck oysters straight from the water. Come nighttime, you will sleep over the sea, under the neon southern lights.

TASMANIA

958 Catamaran-cruise Tasmania's remote fringes

Join just a few other guests aboard a plush 78-ft. (24-m) catamaran to cruise the remote fringes of Tasmania, which is rugged and striking, with brilliant blue waters, giant sand dunes, forests, and granite mountains. On Board Tasmanian Expedition Cruises' multiday adventures pair comfortable accommodations with daily excursions to historic sites and wildlife habitats.

DELUXE ISLAND STAY

TASMANIA

959 Pluck and shuck oysters; dream inside deluxe digs

Check in to the most deluxe design digs imaginable at Saffire Freycinet, an all-inclusive resort on Tasmania's east coast. The lodge, whose architecture bends and moves in response to the landscape, is home to a free-range Tasmanian devil enclosure for research and conservation efforts where guests can observe the actually timid creatures. With the rest of your escape, balance time enjoying the views from your ultra-private suite with only-at-Saffire experiences such as requiring waders so you can pluck and shuck Pacific oysters to slurp with sparkling wine.

OCEANIA • NEW ZEALAND

962 Hobbiton

NEW ZEALAND

960 Savor a chef-in-the-wild picnic in New Zealand

Hop on a Land Rover at the 3,000-acre (1,200-ha) Wharekauhau Country Estate for the ultimate destination dining affair: a chef-in-the-wild picnic. Inhale the clean country air as you explore your pastoral "dining room" and chef prepares your sumptuous meal at the source.

NEW ZEALAND

961 Stroll from beach to beach and winery to winery

On the charming and highly walkable island of Waiheke—it has a 62-mi. (100-km) network of connected coastal trails for ultra-ambitious couples—take a simple approach: just stroll. Wander from beach to winery (there are dozens) to beach and back.

NEW ZEALAND

962 Make a pilgrimage to Hobbiton for a banquet feast

Lord of the Rings devotees can gratify their shared love of the trilogy and lore around it by making a pilgrimage to Middle-earth™ itself or, at least, the illustrious Hobbiton film set on New Zealand's North Island. Take a private behind-the-scenes tour before sitting down to a candlelit banquet feast to finish off the fantasy day.

NEW ZEALAND

963 Fly or ferry to off-the-grid Aotea island

On the entirely off-grid Aotea Great Barrier Island, nature is prized over technology. Take your pick of activities guaranteed to show you the best of the wildlife: kayaking through coves frequented by bottlenose dolphins; hiking sections of the Te Ara Hura; bird-watching for endangered species such as the North Island brown kiwi.

NEW ZEALAND

964 Explore Maori culture before taking a mud bath

Spend a morning immersed in native culture and arts in Rotorua, the traditional lands of the Te Arawa Māori people, in a living village and craft institute. Then share an afternoon together, fully engulfed in Rotorua's famously steamy lake's geothermal mud baths, mineral pools, and sulfur springs.

NEW ZEALAND

965 Hop in the backseat of a classic car

With your spouse, slide into the backseat of a cool, vintage, chauffeur-driven automobile and be whisked away for a tour of dazzling Hawke's Bay and its attractions, both natural and man-made. Enjoy impressive art deco architecture that transports you back in time, before taking a peaceful walk in the Sunken Gardens and then sharing a bottle of local wine.

964 Lake Rotorua

OCEANIA • NEW ZEALAND

NEW ZEALAND

966 Book a scenic two-part escapade by air and on boat

It is hard to understand the staggering beauty of what's around Queenstown—threaded with the braided rivers, snowcapped peaks, and glaciers of Fiordland National Park—until you see it from the sky. Climb aboard what looks like a VW bus with wings for a gorgeous flight over the Southern Alps to Milford Sound. On landing, step aboard a vessel for a cruise beneath sheer mountains and waterfalls.

NEW ZEALAND

967 Declare your love before taking a bouncy leap of faith

There is no better time to make a public declaration of love than the moment before you take a massive leap of faith—off a 141-ft. (43-m) bridge. The AJ Hackett Kawarau Bridge Bungy in Queenstown is the place bungee jumping was invented. Choose to take the plunge together in tandem, or one after the other. Either way, your heart will end up in your stomach and you may just be giddy for more.

NEW ZEALAND

968 Pair parasailing over dazzling Wakatipu with a lakeside picnic

Harness up for a tandem parasailing outing on lapis-hued Lake Wakatipu, pulled behind a motorboat with a giant parachute giving you the sensation of flying. Sit side by side while taking in the breathtaking body of water below, framed by Queenstown's impressive mountains. After touching down, settle in for a magical lakeside picnic—think soft blankets, local delicacies, and a bottle of Central Otago wine.

NEW ZEALAND · OCEANIA

NEW ZEALAND

969 Take a private landscape photography tour at Doubtful Sound

Whether you are experienced or amateur photographers, take the opportunity to hone your skills when booking a private landscape photography workshop for two in Doubtful Sound. Not only will you be experiencing a fairy-tale place together—waterfalls, ridges, rainforests, and reflective, mirror-like water—but you will also learn to capture it. When it comes time to leave New Zealand, it will be with beautiful photo proof of the indelible memories you made there together.

NEW ZEALAND

970 Drink your way through a bespoke wine tour

Oenophiles will find plenty of happiness in the South Island's iconic Central Otago, a wine region with roads treacherously winding around breathtaking lakes, flower fields, river gorges, mountains, and, yes, vineyards. There are more than 140 wineries in the famous Pinot Noir destination, so leave the picking—and the navigation—to an expert and book a bespoke wine tour for two, either by helicopter or chauffeured car.

966 Milford Sound

OCEANIA • NEW ZEALAND/PALAU

NEW ZEALAND
971 Spend a night fancy camping at Mount Aspiring

New Zealand's Southern Alps are remarkable, but the wonderfully named Mount Aspiring is particularly staggering with its pyramidal silhouette. It lies at the heart of a national park in the Wanaka region where outdoorsy couples will thrive while camping in an offbeat structure—think tepee, yurt, safari tent, or geo-dome—and spending unlimited time immersed in one of the most pristine environments there is.

NEW ZEALAND
972 Taste New Zealand while traversing it on a train journey

If you and your partner cannot choose between sightseeing and eating your way through the South Island, book tickets for the TranzAlpine Scenic Plus Experience in the premium carriage and do both. You will taste seasonal, regional, farm-fresh ingredients from the West Coast and Canterbury areas—paired with drinks and fascinating storytelling—while living one of the world's most beautiful train journeys.

PALAU
973 Go island hopping and deluxe camping together via kayak

Work as a team as you kayak your way through surreal lagoons, around island coves, and past rugged, rocky coastlines in Palau on a grand guided paddling adventure that becomes a plush and cozy camping setup each night. Besides the extraordinary environs you find yourself navigating, the trip involves equally amazing wildlife during snorkeling, from turtles and baby eagle rays to a marine lake full of stingless golden jellyfish.

973 Island hopping, Palau

975 Mount Yasur, Vanuatu

PALAU

974 Set sail side by side on a wildly romantic five-star floating resort

If you have not heard "cruising resort" before, you are not alone. The Four Seasons Explorer, Palau, may be the only one, and it is as dreamy as it sounds. Book one of ten cabins (for as long or short a stay as you wish) on the ultra-lavish 129-ft. (39-m) catamaran with your spouse to celebrate something special and let the floating resort's daily embarkations guide your soulful trip through Micronesian culture and the underwater world.

VANUATU

975 Hike through a moonscape to see Mother Nature's fireworks

Embark on a trip you will never forget when you take on Vanuatu's Mount Yasur volcano, one of the world's most active. Hike through an unearthly moonscape at night—with a guide leading you confidently forward—to the rim of the crater for a potential crashing lava display that is the closest thing to fireworks in nature. If you do not fancy the hike, book a scenic flight over the steamy drama.

VANUATU

976 Pair snorkeling in crystal waters with a picnic on the beach

Snorkel in sync with your partner as you explore the warm, turquoise waters of Espiritu Santo, swimming among colorful coral reefs teeming with tropical fish. As the afternoon starts to drift into evening, dry off under the palms and settle into a secluded beach picnic of island delicacies, fresh tropical fruits, and a chilled drink to toast each other as the sun starts to dip.

OCEANIA • TONGA/FIJI

TONGA

977 Share thrills and chills in a subterranean natural pool

Descend into a world of impressive stalactites and stalagmites at Anahulu Cave in eastern Tongatapu island. The run of several interconnected caves has been around for thousands of years, and its age shows in the most magical way possible. Wear bathing suits for a refreshing subterranean swim in the deep, crystal-clear limestone pool at the end of the tour.

TONGA

978 Try to keep up with colossal humpback whales in Tonga

Marine life advocates and admirers know that the Kingdom of Tonga is an ideal place to complete a bucket-list mission: sharing an ocean with colossal cetaceans. It is one of the few places on the planet where couples can swim intimately with humpback whales (legally); that is, if you can kick strong enough to keep up when they are around, July to October.

FIJI

979 Kick back on a carbon-neutral floating bar in the Pacific

Sip, dine, and savor a sun-drenched day aboard the carbon-neutral bar and kitchen Seventh Heaven, which floats in the middle of the Pacific Ocean. Gentle rocking and the surrounding aquamarine expanse invite doing little more than lounging on sun beds and sharing pizza. Plunge into the blue together for a swim whenever the mood strikes.

FIJI

980 Start a new tradition at a resort made for romance

Plan your wedding in true paradise at Nanuku Resort, one of the most romantic island resorts on Earth, sprawling across 500 acres (200 ha) of Viti Levu. In saying "I do" to your beloved there, you will be starting a new tradition because couples who are married at Nanuku stay for free on their anniversary night forever. That means you can take endless trips back for pampering and seductive escapades.

FIJI

981 Let love drive you to preserve Fiji's magic

Get acquainted with Fiji by participating in the nation's Loloma Hour, a responsible tourism initiative whose name means "acting generously, with love." Join activities that include planting coral and learning a traditional craft to help preserve the environment and cultural heritage.

FIJI

982 Find enchantment on an ephemeral ocean sandbar

Your love may last into eternity, but the sandbar in the middle of the Pacific Ocean on which you and your companion will sunbathe, picnic, and toast to sublime seclusion? Not so. Several resorts offer private outings to fleeting, intimate locations where part of the pleasure comes from knowing they will never again exist the same way.

980 Nanuku Resort

OCEANIA • FIJI

FIJI

983 Go wild swimming in a waterfall pool

On Fiji's northern islands, many waterfalls are easy to reach, yet feel remote and deeply romantic. If you find one all to yourselves, act on the moment. Slip out of your clothes and into the water for a spontaneous dip that is wildly free.

FIJI

984 Indulge in an A-list getaway on Laucala Island

Take the most indulgent vacation of your lives at self-sustaining COMO Laucala Island, where you might sleep in a bed that once held George Clooney, in one of just twenty-five tropical-cool residences on 3,500 acres (14,000 ha). With private butlers and pools, spa treatments, and sailing trips, this is real movie star stuff.

FIJI

985 Unwind and reconnect at a resort without WiFi

Put down your devices, ease into island time, and reconnect with each other at a beach retreat designed for twosomes. At Turtle Island, there is no WiFi—or kids—to distract, but there is a guest whisperer, whose job is making all your dreams come true.

PRIVATE ISLAND LIFE

FIJI

986 Experience total togetherness on a private island

For an even more exclusive escape, let Kokomo's boat whisk you and your partner to the secluded shores of Namara Island for your own private beach picnic and a day of unbridled bliss. Awaiting you is a lavish spread of food and refreshing drinks, with plush loungers and snorkelling gear at the ready for when the turquoise sea calls. Beyond the kaleidoscope of marine life, there won't be another soul in sight.

SAMOA

987 Commit to a permanent symbol of your affection

Ink a lovestruck ode to your partner—or perhaps matching symbols of your affection—with a traditional hand-tapped tattoo in Samoa. In the Polynesian island country, *tatau* are considered sacred, making this an appropriate way to consecrate your relationship. If you are not prepared for the pain, watch a traditional *tatau* ceremony at a cultural village to appreciate the deep meaning in the act.

SAMOA

988 Be intoxicated by Samoa's beauty on an eco tour

Eco-tourism encourages sustainable travel practices and offers enriching, low-impact ways to explore unique ecosystems. On Samoa, book a zero-carbon tour that will first take you across lucid water on a stand-up paddleboard or glass-bottomed kayak. Then, stretch your legs on a treetop walking tour of the hanging Falealupo Canopy Walkway, which reaches between giant banyan trees.

COOK ISLANDS

989 Get your passports stamped on One Foot Island

Escape from it all in the most complete way possible in the Cook Islands, where there is a tiny isle encircled with pristine beaches and just a single self-catering cabin to rent overnight. Day trip to One Foot Island in the idyllic Aitutaki Lagoon via boat tour for snorkeling and dream-come-true beach walks, or relax with your loved one in the exclusive accommodation. Either way, swing by the island's one little post office for a cute passport stamp of a bare foot to commemorate your trip, since the native name, Tapuaetai, means "footprint."

989 Beach at Cook Islands

OCEANIA • FRENCH POLYNESIA

FRENCH POLYNESIA

990 Enjoy the sweetest breakfast delivery ever in Bora Bora

The only thing better than breakfast in bed is breakfast delivered by outrigger canoe gliding across a sea of electric blue. Reserve your villa perched above Conrad Bora Bora Nui's spectacular lagoon, then add on a Tahitian canoe breakfast. Linger in bed together before slipping on your bathrobes and awaiting the picture-perfect arrival of your deliciously fresh breakfast to your deck.

FRENCH POLYNESIA

991 Soar over lagoons before dinner on a private islet

Set out on an unforgettable parasailing escapade with your spouse over the most magical of seascapes around Bora Bora, which may have the world's most luminous water. When you return to Earth, do a quick wardrobe change, tuck Tahitian tiare flowers behind your ears, and hop into a canoe for the short journey to Four Seasons Resort Bora Bora's intimate islet for a customized candlelit dinner of tempting Tahitian specialties.

FRENCH POLYNESIA

992 Pop a bottle at the top of Bora Bora's Mount Mata Pupu

Pack a bottle of bubbles to open with a celebratory pop at just the right moment—perhaps the top of Mount Mata Pupu on Bora Bora island. The hike is relatively short yet demanding and steep in parts, so make it more of a stroll than a race, taking time to admire jaw-dropping views along the way. These are as much the reward as the champagne.

990 Conrad Bora Bora Nui

FRENCH POLYNESIA • **OCEANIA**

993 Bora Bora romance

FRENCH POLYNESIA

993 Wake up in a place where love is always in the air

Lovers seeking all-day—and all-night—romance will find it on one of the planet's most seductive islands. Famously fabulous for lavish weddings and honeymoons, the St. Regis Bora Bora is a place where bucket lists become reality. You will wake to a heavenly scene for swimming in crystal-clear water, dining decadently, and indulging in gold-flecked couples massages, with surprises in between.

FRENCH POLYNESIA

994 Hire a catamaran captain to catch lunch for you

In the saturated turquoise panorama of French Polynesia, charter a catamaran for a majestic day sail in paradise, complete with tipples to make you tipsy. Request a captain or crew who can fish—or has access to the freshest catch—and snag some delicacies from the sea, such as tuna or parrotfish. Meanwhile, the pair of you can swim or snorkel in the surreal water surrounding the gleaming boat.

FRENCH POLYNESIA

995 Check into an overwater bungalow by a pink beach

Head off the beaten path to the small, sublimely peaceful atoll of Tikehau, in the Tuamotu Archipelago. There, you will rest up under clear night skies in one of Le Tikehau by Pearl Resorts' charming overwater bungalows built of natural materials, and spend your blue-sky days frolicking on the hotel's pink sand beach. Up the seclusion on a private motorboat jaunt to snorkel and savor a motu picnic.

FRENCH POLYNESIA/MARSHALL ISLANDS/SOLOMON ISLANDS • **OCEANIA**

FRENCH POLYNESIA

996 Drift together through a vivid underwater dream

Step into two sets of flippers and snorkel masks before entering the crystalline shallows beside Le Taha'a resort for the waking version of a mermaid dream. Following a guide, the incoming tide will carry you both rapidly—it is a true thrill—through explosions of rainbow fish, giant colorful clams, and Technicolor corals. Moving through the wondrous coral garden is an unforgettable experience, best timed for mid- to high tide when the current helps you along.

FRENCH POLYNESIA

997 Witness mating and calving humpback whales

Couples with a thing for megafauna will discover a worthwhile excursion in the azure South Pacific at the Brando, a plush retreat with a ritzy guest list yet gorgeously down-to-earth vibe. The sustainable private island resort's surrounding waters of the Tetiaroa Atoll are a hot spot for humpback whales who visit from August to October to mate and have their babies, and it is possible to watch it all from a private boat.

FRENCH POLYNESIA

998 Tour the island of Moorea by e-bike

The fifty shades of blue swirling around French Polynesia are especially intense in Moorea, where thriving mountains meet crystal lagoons full of stingrays and (harmless) sharks. Admire it all from the saddles of two bright e-bikes as you take a tour of the island, either on your own or guided. Depending on your interests, you can plan stops at ancient temples, pineapple plantations, panoramic lookouts, and hidden coves for picnics.

MARSHALL ISLANDS

999 Sail an outrigger canoe then learn Marshallese weaving

A romantic escapade in the Marshall Islands is incomplete without a ride in a fine-tuned Marshallese traditional outrigger canoe. Hang on tight once you are on board, because the boats speed quickly across the vibrant elliptical Majuro Lagoon. After that dopamine hit, settle into a weaving workshop led by an artisan at a local cultural center while making something special, side by side, to take home.

SOLOMON ISLANDS

1000 Propose to your scuba-diving sweetie under the sea

With excellent visibility so there is no mistaking the underwater sign language, plus pleasant water temperatures, several feet down in the world's largest saltwater lagoon, Marovo, is a picture-perfect place to pop the all-important question—if you are both scuba divers, that is. Work out the hand signals ahead of time and coordinate with the dive shop to orchestrate a truly awe-inspiring proposal.

996 Le Taha'a

405

INDEX

A
Alaska
 Alaska Railroad 24
 coastal cruise 24
 Glacier Bay National Park and Preserve 25
 sea kayak adventure 25
Albania
 Adriatic sailing tour 264
Anguilla
 AMA Center 125
 Maundays Bay 125
Antarctica
 Drake Passage cruise 179
 polar scientist trip 179
 Southern Ocean dip 178
 tandem kayak trip 178
Antigua
 glass canoe adventure 126
Argentina
 Buenos Aires 177
 El Calafate 177
 Gran Chaco forest 178
 Patagonia Azul 176
 horseride with gauchos 178
 Rio de la Plata 177
 wine experience 178
Aruba
 Butterfly Farm 134
 Donkey Sanctuary 134
 Quadirikiri Cave 134
Australia
 Canberra
  wood-carving class 386
 New South Wales
  Blue Mountains 385
  Bondi Beach 384
  Byron Bay 385
  Cape Byron lighthouse 385
  Clovelly 384
  Mardi Gras 384
  Shark Island 384
  Sydney 383–4
  vintage yacht sail 384
 Northern Territory
  Kangaroo Island 380
  Uluru 380
 Queensland
  Gold Coast 381
  Great Barrier Reef 382, 383
  Lizard Island 383
  off-grid farm stay 382
  Whitsundays 382
 South Australia
  Barossa Valley 381
  outback 381
 Tasmania
  Bruny Island 388
  Hobart 388
  Satellite Island 388
 Victoria
  Great Ocean Road 386–7
  Melbourne 386–7
  Mornington Peninsula 387
  Twelve Apostles 386–7
 Western Australia
  Kimberley 378–9
  Manjimup 378
  Margaret River 378
  Ningaloo Reef Marine Park 378
  Perth 378
Austria
 Alpine forage 251
 Lake Fuschl 251
 Lech 251
 Vienna 249
 Wiener Eistraum 249

B
Bahamas
 Baha Mar 114
 Compass Cay 116
 Eleuthera 114
 John McEnroe Tennis Center 114
 Potlatch Club 114, 115
Bahrain
 Muharraq 280
 Pearling Path 280
Bangladesh
 Sreemangal 340
Barbados
 botanical gardens 132
 eco-adventure park 132
 rum-tasting 132
Barbuda
 Princess Diana Beach 127
 sushi-making workshop 127
Belgium
 Antwerp 244
 Bruges 244
 Brussels 244
 Flanders 244
Belize
 beach hideaway 146
 Belize Barrier Reef 146
 forest reserve river lodge 146
Benin
 Ganvié 292
Bermuda
 cave spa 114
Bhutan
 hot river stone bath 338
 star reading 339
 Tiger's Nest monastery 340
 Paro Valley 340
Bolivia
 Salar de Uyuni 174
Borneo 368
 firefly immersion 371
 Flores 373
 Java 368
 Komodo National Park 373
 Sumba 371, 372

Botswana
 baobab treehouse 307
 Okavango Delta 307, 308
Brazil
 Emerald Coast 173
 Iguazu Falls 173
 Lençóis Maranhenses National Park 172
 Pantanal 174
 Rio de Janeiro 171
 São Paulo 173
British Virgin Islands
 Anegada 125
 Norman Island 123
 Virgin Gorda 124, 125
Bulgaria
 Nessebar 264

C
Cambodia
 Angkor Wat 354
 Cardamom Mountains 352–3
 Kampot 355
 Khmer 354
 Krabey Island 355
 Phnom Penh 354
 Siem Reap 355
Canada
 Alberta
  Banff National Park 15
  Lake Louise 15
  Rocky Mountains 15
 British Columbia
  Capilano Suspension Bridge 15
  forest bathing 13
  Hot Springs Cove 11
  ice caves 13
  Kitsilano Beach Park 11
  Maquinna Marine Provincial Park 11
  Stanley Park 11, 13
  surfing 11

INDEX

Vancouver 11, 14, 15
Whistler 12–13
Calgary
  scent workshop 16
Manitoba
  Riding Mountain National Park 16
New Brunswick
  Bay of Fundy 20
Newfoundland
  Fogo Island 20, 21
  Newfoundland Island 20
  road trip 20
Nova Scotia
  Bay of Fundy 22
  Halifax coast 22
Ontario
  Lake Ontario 18
  Prince Edward County 18
  maple syrup workshop 16
  Niagara-on-the-Lake 18
Prince Edward Island
  seafood dining 23
  treetop pod 23
Quebec
  Heart Lake 20
  Montreal 19, 20
  St. Lawrence River 19, 20
Saskatchewan
  Opimihaw Valley 16, 17
  Saskatoon 16
Yukon 10
  aurora borealis 10
  Marsh Lake 10
  Whitehorse 10
Canary Islands
  Lanzarote 231
  Tenerife 231
Cape Verde
  luxury yacht adventure 289

Cayman Islands
  Bloody Bay Wall Marine Park 120
  island flyover 120
  Owen Island 120
Chad
  Zakouma National Park 293
Channel Islands
  La Rocque Harbour 211
Chile
  Atacama Desert 168, 169
  Cachapoal Valley 168
  Easter Island (Rapa Nui) 171
  Huerquehue National Park 168
  Nordenskjöld Lake 170
  Patagonia 168, 170
  Puerto Williams 170
  Torres del Paine National Park 170
China
  Beijing 326
  Chengdu 328
  Great Wall 326
  Hong Kong 328, 329
  junk boat cruise 329
  Lijiang 328
  Shanghai 326–8
Colombia
  Bogotá 158–9
  Cartagena 159, 160
  Islas del Rosario 158
  Magdalena River 160
  Monserrate 158–9
Cook Islands
  One Foot Island 400–1
Costa Rica
  canopy zipline 151
  Culebra Bay 151
  Punta Islita 151
  Nicoya Peninsula 151
  Rio Perdido 151
  Santa Teresa 152
  Talamanca Mountains

153
  whitewater rafting 150
Cote D'Ivoire
  Abidjan 290
Croatia
  Biševo 262
  Brač 262
  Dalmatian Coast 262
  Dubrovnik 262
  Hvar 262
  island hopping 262
  Istria 262
  Korčula 262
  Lopud Island 263
  Plitvice Lakes National Park 262
  Split 262
  sunset SUP tour 262
Cuba
  Havana 119, 120
  salsa class 119
  Santa Clara 118
  Trinidad 120
  Viñales Valley 118
Cyprus
  Lefkara 271
Czech Republic
  Prague 256, 257
  spray can workshop 257

D
Denmark
  Copenhagen 191
  Noma 191
  polo lesson 191
Dominica
  Coulibri Ridge 12
  sperm whale-watching 128
Dominican Republic
  Cabarete 122
  kitesurfing lesson 122
  Tortuga Bay 123
Dutch Antilles
  St. Eustatius 135

E
Ecuador
  eco-snorkeling trip 161
  Galapagos 161, 162–3
  giant tortoise reserve 162
Egypt
  Mount Sinai 293
  Nile cruise 293
Estonia
  Soomaa National Park 254
Eswatini
  horseback safari 310
Ethiopia
  Addis Ababa 293
  Danakil Depression 294, 295
  Lake Bishoftu 294
  Lalibela 294

F
Faroe Islands
  Sandoy Tunnel 184
  waterfalls 184
Fiji
  Laucala Island 398
  Kokomo Island 398–9
  Viti Levu 396–397
  Turtle Island 398
  waterfall swimming 398
Finland
  Helsinki 188
  Lapland 189
  northern lights 191
  Urho Kekkonen National Park, 190–1
France
  Alps 215
  Arc de Triomphe 210, 211
  Bordeaux 214
  Burgundy 214
  cabaret 211
  caviar 211
  champagne tour 214
  Corsica 216

INDEX

Eiffel Tower 211, 212–13
Gorges du Verdon 215
Grasse 216
Île de Ré 215
Musée Rodin 212
Nice 216
Palace of Versailles 213
Paris 210–13
Ritz Paris 213
French Polynesia
 Bora Bora 402–3
 catamaran cruise 403
 Moorea 405
 Tetiaroa Atoll 405
 Tikehau 403

G
Georgia
 Caucasus Mountains 264
 Gergeti Trinity Church 264
 Mount Kazbek 264
 Tbilisi 264
Germany
 Baden-Baden 245
 Bavaria 246
 Berlin 244, 245
 Dresden 244
 museum-hopping 245
 Neuschwanstein Castle 246–7
 Romantic Road 247
 Rothenburg ob der Tauber 247
 Sylt 248
Ghana
 Gold Coast 292
Greece
 Acropolis 265
 Antiparos 269
 Athens 265–6
 Cali Mykonos 268
 catamaran cruise 267
 Chios 267
 Hydra 267

Ios 269
Kefalonia 266
Milos 266
Mykonos 268
Naxos 266, 271
Parthenon 266
Santorini 270, 271
Saronic Gulf 267
Sifnos 266, 271
Greenland
 Disko Bay 24
 kayak adventure 22–23
 wildlife tour 24
Grenada
 Belmont Estate 133
 catamaran champagne cruise 133
 chocolate tour 133
 underwater sculpture garden 133
Guadeloupe
 Cousteau Reserve 128
 waterfall hike 128
Guatemala
 Antigua 147
 Lake Atitlán 146–7
 Santa Catarina Palopó 147
Guinea-Bissau
 Bijagós Islands 289

H
Hawai'i
 Haleakala Crater 28, 29
 helicopter tour 26
 Hualalai knife workshop 28
 hula lesson 26
 Keahiakawelo 31
 lei workshop 26
 lomilomi massage 26
 Maui 28, 30, 31
 Napali Coast 26, 27
 Oahu 28
 outrigger canoe tour 31
 plant a tree 28
 sailing canoe 28

sunset supper 26
surf lesson 28
Volcanoes National Park 31
voluntourism 26
Waikiki 28
whale-watching 28
Hungary
 Budapest 260
 Danube 260, 261
 Lake Balaton 261
 Margaret Island 260
 sleeper train 261
 Széchenyi Thermal Bath 260

I
Iceland
 geothermal lagoon 182–3
 Reykholt 182
 Reykjavik 182
 Silfra Fissure 183
 Trollaskagi Peninsula 183
 Vatnajökull glacier 183
India
 Bandhavgarh National Park 333
 Holi 330
 Jaipur 332
 Kerala 333
 Ladakh 330
 Mumbai 330
 Ranthambore National Park 332–3
 Rajasthan 332–3
 Taj Mahal 330–1
 Udaipur 333
 Uttar Pradesh 330
Indonesia
 Ayung River 369
 Bali 368–71
 Balinese Hindu ceremony 371
Ireland, Republic of
 Ashford Castle 208–9

Blarney Castle 207
Cliffs of Moher 208
County Clare 208
County Cork 207
County Mayo 208
Dromoland Castle 208
Dublin 206, 207
Dublin Pride 206
Northern Ireland see under United Kingdom
Ring of Kerry 207
Skellig Michael 207
Italy
 Alberobello 228, 229
 Alps 222
 Amalfi Coast 226, 227
 Capri 227
 Cinque Terre 224
 Dolomites 218, 221
 Florence 225
 Lake Como 221, 222–3
 Lake Garda 222
 Lombardy 222
 Lucca 225
 Matera 229
 Matterhorn 222
 Milan 222
 pasta-making workshop 218
 Puglia 228, 229
 Ravello 226
 Rome 217–19, 230
 Sicily 219
 Sistine Chapel 220
 sleeper train 218
 Sorrento 226
 Spanish Steps 219
 Tuscany 225
 Umbria 225
 Vatican City 220
 Venice 224
 Verona 222
 Villa Borghese 219

J
Jamaica
 Caymans' Seven Mile

INDEX

Beach 120
GoldenEye 120, 121
Martha Brae River 122
Montego Bay 120
Trelawny Parish 122
Japan
  digital art experience 358
  Hirosaki 362–3
  hot spring 361
  Ise-Shima 360
  Kyoto 360–1
  Kyushu island 362
  Lake Kawaguchi 359
  latte portrait 358
  Mie prefecture 360
  Niseko 359
  Oita prefecture 361
  Okinawa Islands 362
  pottery class 359
  sake tasting 358
  spa house 358
  Takagamine mountains 361
  Tokyo 357–8
Jordan
  Dead Sea 278, 279
  desert glamping 278, 279
  Petra 278
  Wadi Rum 278, 279

K

Kazakhstan
  Almaty 324
  Ile-Alatau National Park 324
Kenya
  cave restaurant 300
  Chyulu Hills 299
  Diani Beach 300
  Great Rift Valley 299
  hot-air balloon safari 299
  horseback safari 299
  Lamu 299
  Lewa Conservancy 298

Mount Kenya 298
Mount Kilimanjaro 299
Singing Wells ritual 297
tea with a giraffe 297
Kosovo
  Prizren 264
Kyrgyzstan
  horseback tour 324
  Issyk-Kul Lake 324

L

Laos
  Amantaka 341
  Kuang Si Falls 342
  Luang Prabang 342
Latvia
  Riga 255
Liberia
  eco-lodge stay 290–1
Lithuania
  Vilnius 254

M

Madagascar
  Avenue of the Baobabs 314–15
  lemur safari 316
  Miavana 317
  Tsingy de Bemaraha National Park 316
Malaysia
  Kuala Lumpur 363
  Langkawi 363
Maldives
  champagne sabering 337
  coral conservation dive 336
  floating villa 336
  Hanifaru Bay 338
  Noonu Atoll 336
  observatory trip 337
  overwater bungalows 337
  Rangali Island 338
  snorkeling expedition

336
  subaquatic dining 338
  submarine experience 336
  tree-house dining 336
  tropical fish massage 336
  underwater villa 338–9
Malta
  Comino Island 231
  Gozo 231
  Valletta 230
Marshall Islands
  Majuro Lagoon 405
Martinique
  Mount Pelée 129
Mauritius
  Anahita 318–19
  Black River Gorges National Park 317
  Île aux Cerfs 318
  golf playground 318
  waterfall trail 317
Mexico
  Baja California 136–8
  Cabo San Lucas 136, 137
  Careyes 138, 139
  Celestún 143
  Chichen Itza 144
  Costalegre 140
  Day of the Dead parade 140
  Guerrero 142
  Isla Holbox 145
  Isla Mujeres 145
  Jalisco 140
  jungle retreat 143
  Mayapan 144
  Mexico City 141, 142
  Nayarit 138
  Oaxaca 142, 143
  Puerto Escondido 143
  Punta Mita 138
  Quintana Roo 144-5
  Riviera Maya 144
  San Miguel de Allende

140
  sea turtle release 138
  scuba dive 144, 145
  temazcal ritual 145
  Todos Santos 136
  Tulum 144
  Valle de Guadalupe 136, 138
  Yucatán Peninsula 143
Micronesia
  Guam 374–5
Monaco
  Monte Carlo 216
Mongolia
  dune sledging 325
  Gobi Desert 325
Montenegro
  Bay of Kotor 263
  Black Mountains 264
Morocco
  Atlas Mountains 283
  Chefchaouen 284–5
  Essaouira 286
  Fès 286
  Imsouane 286
  Jardin Majorelle 286–7
  Marrakesh 7, 286
  Sahara camel camp 288
Mozambique
  Benguerra Island 308
  Maputo 308
  Santorini Mozambique 308
Myanmar
  Bagan 341
  Inle Lake 341

N

Namibia
  4x4 safari 307
  Big Daddy dune 305
  dark sky reserve 306
  Deadvlei 305
  Namib desert 306
  Skeleton Coast 305
  wild rhino chase 305
Nepal

INDEX

Chitwan National Park 330
countryside tour 330
Netherlands
 Amsterdam 240–3
 Rotterdam 243
 Tulip Festival 243
 Zaanse Schans 243
New Zealand
 Aotea Great Barrier Island 391
 Central Otago 393
 Doubtful Sound 393
 Fiordland National Park 392
 Queenstown 392
 Hawke's Bay 391
 Lake Wakatipu 392
 Milford Sound 392–3
 Mount Aspiring 394
 North Island 390
 Rotorua 391
 Southern Alps 392–3
 South Island train tour 394
 Waiheke 390
 Wanaka 394
Nicaragua
 Emerald Coast 148
 Lake Nicaragua 149
 Popoyo 148
 San Juan del Sur 148
Norway
 Ålesund 185
 glacier cruise 187
 Hessa 185
 Longyearbyen 187
 Oslofjord 185
 Salmon Eye 186
 Sukkertoppen 185

O
Oman
 Arabian Sea scuba dive 283
 Muscat 283

P
Palau
 floating resort 395
 island hopping 394
Panama
 Casco Viejo 154
 Nayara Bocas del Toro 154
 Panama Canal 154
 Quebrada Sal 155
 Starfish Cay 155
Peru
 Amazon rainforest 164, 167
 Cordillera Escalera 164
 Colca Canyon 168
 Cusco 165
 Lake Titicaca 165
 Lima 163, 164
 Machu Picchu 165, 166, 167
 Parque del Amor 163
 Rainbow Mountain 167
 Sacred Valley 165
 Vinicunca 167
Philippines
 Boracay 373
 Coron 374
 Manila 373
 Pamalican 374
 Puerto Princesa Subterranean River National Park 373
Poland
 Chelmno 255
 Kazimierz Dolny 256
 Krakow 256
 Warsaw 255
Portugal
 Algarve 237, 238
 Azores 238
 Douro Valley 238
 Lisbon 237
 Madeira 240
 Sintra 238, 239
Puerto Rico
 catamaran charter 110, 111
 Condado Beach 111
 El Yunque National Forest 112
 Icacos 111
 San Juan 111
 wing foiling 111

Q
Qatar
 camel-racing 281
 Doha 280

R
Republic of Congo
 Odzala-Kokoua National Park 294
Réunion
 Piton des Neiges 321
Romania
 Bran Castle 259
 Bucegi Mountains 259
 Carpathian Mountains 258
 Transylvania 259
Rwanda
 Akagera National Park 301
 Virunga Mountains 300

S
Saint Lucia
 Gros Islet 131
 Gros Piton 131
 Pitons 129, 130–1
 Soufriere Bay 129
 Sugar Beach 129
Samoa
 eco-tour 400
 hand-tapped tattoo 400
São Tomé & Príncipe
 marine safari 292
Saudi Arabia
 Bedouin traditions 280
 desert resort 280
 Red Sea by horseback 279
Senegal
 Dakar 288
 small-boat bird safari 288
Serbia
 Belgrade 261
 Vrnjačka Banja 261
Seychelles
 Anse Source d'Argent 320
 Félicité 320
 Fregate Island 321
 padel and surf 319
 Sainte Anne Marine National Park 319
 tortoise conservation island resort 321
 yacht charter 319
Sierra Leone
 chimpanzee sanctuary 289
Singapore
 Chinatown 366
 cookery class 367
 food tour 364
 Sentosa Island 367
 Singapore Slings at Raffles 365
 superyacht cruise 367
Slovakia
 Bratislava 257
 Mirror Cocktail Bar 257
Slovenia
 gastronomic food tour 257
 Goriška Brda 258
 Julian Alps 257
 Lake Bohinj 257
 Ljubljana 257
 wine safari 258
Solomon Islands
 Marovo Lagoon 405
South Africa
 Boulders Beach 312
 Cape Dutch farm stay 312
 Cape Town 310–12,

INDEX

314
Forgotten Mountains 313
Franschhoek 313
Garden Route 314
Kalahari Desert 314
Sabi Sand Game Reserve 314
Tswalu 314
Victorian farm experience 312
South Korea
  Han River cruise 356
  Jeju Island 356
  Seoul 356
Spain
  Alhambra 234
  Basílica de la Sagrada Família 232–3
  Barcelona 232–3
  Basque coast 232
  Formentera 237
  Granada 234
  Ibiza 236–7
  Madrid 232
  Majorca 234
  Menorca 234
  Priorat 234
Sri Lanka
  Ayurvedic retreat 335
  Central Highlands 335
  Galle 334
  Kandy 334, 335
  Ratnapura 334
  Yala National Park 334
St. Barts
  Grand Cul-de-Sac 128
  Nikki Beach 126, 127
  piscines naturelles 126, 127
St. Kitts and Nevis
  Scenic Railway tour 126
  Spa Under the Stars 125
St. Martin
  Orient Bay 135
St. Vincent and the Grenadines
  Mustique 132
  Sandals resort 132
Suriname
  Paramaribo 161
  Voltzberg Dome 160
Sweden
  Icehotel 188
  Lapland 188
  Stockholm 188
  Stockholm Archipelago 188
Switzerland
  Andermatt 251
  Lake Lucerne 251
  St. Moritz 252, 253
  Tour du Mont Blanc 252–3
  Vals 252
  Zermatt 253
  Zurich 251

T
Tanzania
  Devil's Pool 302–3
  dolphin conservation project 301
  helicopter safari 301
  Ngorongoro Crater 302
  Serengeti 302
  Victoria Falls 302–3
  Zanzibar 301
Thailand
  Bangkok 342–4
  cooking class 343
  Chiang Rai 344–5, 346
  Hua Hin 346
  Kamala Beach 347
  Krabi 347
  Mahanakhon Skywalk 343
  mangrove-tree planting 346
  Phuket 346–7
  Thai massage 344
  Trat 347
Tonga
  Tongatapu Island 396
Trinidad and Tobago
  Bamboo Cathedral 133
Tunisia
  Djerba 293
Turkey
  Bodrum 273
  Bosphorus Strait 272
  Cappadocia 274–5
  cave hotel 275
  hammam 273
  hot-air balloon trip 274–5
  Istanbul 272
  yacht trip 273
Turks and Caicos
  Amanyara 117
  coral restoration expedition 118
  Grand Turk 117
  Parrot Cay 116
  Providenciales 117
  Salt Cay 118
  submarine tour 117

U
Uganda
  basket-weaving lesson 297
  Bwindi Impenetrable Forest National Park 296
  Nile safari 296
  Rwenzori Mountains 296
United Arab Emirates
  Dubai 282
  dune bashing 281
  eco sanctuary 281
  Ras Al Khaimah 281
United Kingdom
  England
    afternoon tea 200
    Barbican Conservatory 196
    Blenheim Lake 204
    Blenheim Palace 202
    Borough Market 196–7
    Cotswolds 202
    Dover 202–3
    Globe Theatre 199
    Greenwich Royal Observatory Planetarium 200, 201
    Hampton Court 199
    Kent 202
    Kew Gardens 199
    Lake District 4-5, 202
    London 195–201
    London Eye 198–9
    London Zoo 196
    New Forest 202
    Oxfordshire 202, 204
    pole-dancing class 195
    pottery class 195
    River Thames 198–9
    Royal Philharmonic Orchestra 200
    sex club retreat 201
    Shard, The 196
    Tube supper club 195
    Westminster 199
    West Sussex 204
    Windsor 199
    Yorkshire Dales 202
  Northern Ireland
    County Antrim 206
    Giant's Causeway 206–7
    Portrush 206
  Scotland
    Caledonian Forest 192
    Dalhousie Castle 194
    Edinburgh 192
    Eilean Donan Castle 192, 193
    Glasgow 194
    Glenfinnan Viaduct 194–5
    Scottish Highlands 192

INDEX

West Highland Way 192
Wales
  Black Mountains 205
  sleeper train 205
  Tenby 205
United States
  Alabama
    Appalachian Mountains 80
    Huntsville 80
    Space & Rocket Center 80
    wine trail 80
  Arizona
    Antelope Canyon 52
    astrophotography class 56
    Boynton Canyon 52
    Grand Canyon 56
    Sonoran Desert 54–55, 56
    Via Ferrata 54–5
  Arkansas
    Crater of Diamonds State Park 73
    diamond dig 73
    Ozark forest 73
  California
    Beverly Hills 43
    Big Sur 39, 40
    Calla Lily Valley 38, 39
    Highway 1 road trip 39
    Hollywood 43
    Joshua Tree National Park 44, 45
    Keyhole Arch 40
    Los Angeles 43–4
    Malibu 41, 42
    Napa Valley 36
    Palm Desert 44
    Palm Springs 44
    Pfeiffer Beach 40
    San Diego 44
    San Francisco 36
    Santa Monica 41
    Sausalito 36
    Sonoma 36, 37
    wine train 36
    Yellowstone National Park 41
    Yosemite National Park 40
  Colorado
    Aspen 59
    Breckenridge 60
    Denver 61
    fly-fishing trip 59
    puppy yoga class 58
    Red Rocks Amphitheatre 60
    Telluride 61
    Tennessee Pass 60
    Vail Valley 59
  Connecticut
    drive-in movie 105
    Mystic 105
    sunset sail 105
  Delaware
    Red Clay Valley 100
    White Clay Creek State Park 100
  Florida
    clay shooting 86
    Disney's Magic Kingdom 86
    Everglades 87
    golf round 86, 87
    Hemingway Home and Museum 90, 91
    Key West 90
    Little Havana 88
    Miami 88
    Miami Beach 88
    Palm Island 90
    neon painting workshop 88
    Skydive Space Center 88
    South Beach 88, 89 90
    swim with dolphins 90
    Titusville 88
  Georgia
    Atlanta 84
    Savannah 84–5
  Idaho
    Central Idaho Dark Sky Reserve 46
    stargazing tour 46
    Sun Valley 46
  Illinois
    Chicago 71
    thermal baths 70
  Indiana
    Brown County 78
    Indianapolis 78
    woodland retreat 78
  Iowa
    Field of Dreams movie site 70
    Madison County 70
  Kentucky
    bourbon trail 79
    Kentucky Castle 79
    Louisville 78
  Louisiana
    New Orleans 73, 74
  Maine
    Kennebunk River 107
    lobster shack ramble 107
    Penobscot Bay 107
    puffin-watching 106
  Maryland
    Chesapeake Bay 99
    Miles River 99
  Massachusetts
    Berkshires 103
    Boston 104
    Cape Cod 104
    Martha's Vineyard 105
  Michigan
    Detroit 74
    Mackinac Island 76–7
    Saugatuck 74, 75
  Minnesota
    Cuyuna Lakes 68
    Minneapolis 68
    Twin Cities distillery tour 68
  Mississippi
    Blues Trail road trip 74
    Oxford 74
  Missouri
    Dogwood Canyon Nature Park 72
    Mississippi paddleboat tour 72
    St. Louis 72
  Montana
    Gem Mountain 47
    Grand Prismatic 47
    helicopter tour 47
    Rock Creek 47
    sapphire panning 47
    Yellowstone National Park 47
  Nebraska
    Fontenelle Forest 63
    Kansas City 64
    Lincoln 64–65
  Nevada
    Lake Tahoe 52
    Las Vegas 50–51, 52
    Mojave Desert 52, 53
    Red Rock Canyon 52, 53
  New Hampshire
    Laconia 103
    White Mountains 103
  New Jersey
    Bayville 100
    Cape May 100–1
  New Mexico
    Carlsbad Caverns National Park 63
    Ghost Ranch 62
    Vermejo 62
  New York
    breakfast at Tiffany's 94, 95

INDEX

Brooklyn 96
Buffalo 92
Catskills Mountains 92
Central Park 93, 94
Coney Island 97
cookery class 96
Empire State Building 94
Fire Island 92
Hudson Valley 90, 97
New York City 93, 94–6
Niagara Falls 92
Roosevelt Island 95
Saranac Lake 90
North Carolina
 Asheville 82
 fishing trip 82
 intimacy retreat 82
 Mountain Snorkel Trail 82
 Outer Banks 82
North Dakota
 Medora 63
Ohio
 Columbus 81
 NFL matchup 80
Oklahoma
 Oklahoma City 65
Oregon
 Dundee 34
 Eagle Cap 35
 Portland 34, 35
 sparkling wine tour 34
 wilderness retreat 35
 Willamette Valley 33
Pennsylvania
 Philadelphia 98
 metalworking workshop 98
Rhode Island
 Newport 106
 Providence 106
South Carolina
 Charleston 84
 Kiawah River 84
South Dakota

Black Hills 63
Tennessee
 country music concert 79
 farm retreat 79
 Franklin 79
 Great Smoky Mountains National Park 79
Texas
 Austin 67
 Barton Creek Greenbelt 68
 Dallas 67
 Houston 67
 Marfa 66, 67
 San Antonio 67
Utah
 Arches National Park 56–7
 Bryce Canyon 57
 desert camp 58, 59
 Moab 58
 mountaintop yurt 56
 Sarika 58, 59
Vermont
 Stowe 102, 103
Virginia
 Blue Ridge 82
 Chesapeake Bay 82
 Monticello Wine Trail 82
Washington
 doughnut tour 33
 glassblowing workshop 32
 Orcas Island 33
 San Juan Islands 33
 Seattle 32, 33
Washington, DC
 cherry blossoms 98–9
West Virginia
 Berkeley Springs 81
 Lewisburg 81
 Paranormal Trail 81
Wisconsin
 lavender farm 68, 69

thermal spa 68
 Wisconsin Dells 68
Wyoming
 Grand Teton National Park 48–9
 Jackson Hole 48
 mountain wellness retreat 49
 Snake River 48
 wildlife safari 49
 Wild West cookery class 49
Uruguay
 Garzón 176
 José Ignacio 176
 Punta Ballena 175
 wine lodge 174
Uzbekistan
 Samarkand 325

V
Vanuatu
 Espiritu Santo 395
 Mount Yasur volcano 395
Vietnam
 Bai Tu Long Bay 348–9
 cookery class 349
 Hanoi 347
 Hoi An 349, 350
 Hoi An to Nha Trang by train 350
 Hoai River lanterns 350
 Hue 348
 Mekong river cruise 349
 Phu Quoc 351
 Phu Yen 350
 private island villa 351
 Saigon 351
 sleeper train 350
Virgin Islands
 Buck Island Reef National Monument 113

Z
Zambia

Lake Malawi 304–5
Mzuzu 305
North Luangwa National Park 305
Zimbabwe
 elephant camp 308
 Kafue National Park 308
 vintage train safari 309

413

PICTURE CREDITS

The publisher would like to thank the following for the permission to reproduce copyright material.

Front cover: Pakin Songmor/Getty Images
Back cover (top to bottom): Row 1L David Madison/Getty Images; Row 1M givag/Shutterstock; Row 1R Roberto Moiola / Sysaworld/Getty Images; Row 2L Mark Meredith/Getty Images; Row 2R Angel Villalba/Getty Images; Row 3L fokke baarssen/Shutterstock; Row 3R Mystockimages/Getty Images; Row 4L © Cvandyke/Dreamstime.com; Row 4M tolobalaguer.com/Shutterstock; Row 4R PamelaJoeMcFarlane/Getty Images; Row 5L INNA FINKOVA/Alamy; Row 5M Tom Nebbia/Getty Images; Row 5R Quang Ngoc Nguyen/Getty Images.

Alamy: 11 All Canada Photos / DEDDEDA; 21 Ryan Carter; 39 Cannon Photography LLC/BrownWCannonIII; 51 Robin Utrecht/Sipa USA; 58 Dan Leeth; 70 Westend61 GmbH / Martin Benik; 71 © Bill Bachmann; 84-85 Wolfgang Kaehler; 110 Irina Brester; 112 Gillian Pullinger; 119t Guy Midkiff; 119b Hemis / SOULARUE / Hemis.fr; 135 Frans Lemmens; 139 Douglas Peebles Photography / © Douglas Peebles; 141l Paul Barbera; 141r Paul Barbera; 142 Cavan Images; 175 Emiliano Rodriguez; 177 Jon Arnold Images Ltd / Demetrio Carrasco; 179 Ralph Lee Hopkins; 216 Hemis; 217 Ivoha; 218 Susan Wright; 219r Hercules Milas; 233t Chad Ehlers; 243 frans lemmens; 248 Image Professionals GmbH / Schmitz, Walter; 250 Hemis / MATTES Ren☒ / hemis.fr; 263 INNA FINKOVA; 282 Robin Weaver; 292 Gerhard Pettersson; 303 Allen Brown; 309t Africa Media Online / Marinda Louw; 311 guy oliver; 325 Danita Delimont / Tom Norring / DanitaDelimont.com; 326-327 Xinhua; 355 Keith Mundy; 362-363 Navapon Plodprong; 364l JS Callahan/tropicalpix; 366 Efired; 380 imageBROKER.com / White Star / Monica Gumm

Getty Images: 4-5 Matt_Gibson; 7 Thomas Barwick; 8-9 William Reagan; 14 Andrew Chin; 19 Vincent Demers Photography; 22-23 Sean Gallup / Staff; 25t Betty Wiley; 25b David Madison; 38 Photo by Chris Axe; 40 Andy Ryan; 43 Bohemian Nomad Picturemakers; 45 Images by Steve Skinner Photography; 46 Cavan Images; 48-49 Deborah Garber; 53 Cavan Images; 55t Francesco Riccardo Iacomino; 55b AscentXmedia; 56-57 Greg Jacobs/ Ascent Xmedia; 60 RJ Sangosti; 66 Cavan Images; 72 BackyardProduction; 73 Walter Bibikow; 75 Aaron McCoy; 76b corfoto; 79 Zhuokang Jia; 87 Ryan McVay; 91 ullstein bild; 93 Barry Winiker; 94 Stacey Bramhall; 102 Carl D. Walsh / Aurora Photos; 109 PamelaJoeMcFarlane; 111 Carlos Gotay; 113 Don Hebert; 117 Stephen Frink; 118 danm; 121 Jan Abadschieff / 500px; 129 The-Vagabond; 130-131 ThomasFluegge; 134t Ascent/ PKS Media Inc.; 134b Smithlandia Media; 144 Thomas Barwick; 145 Thomas Barwick; 150t MB Photography; 150b THEPALMER; 152 Kryssia Campos; 156-157 Cesar Okada; 158-159 holgs; 160 Mystockimages; 161 Michael Nolan/ robertharding; 165 Westend61; 169 Simon Dubreuil; 173 Mark Meredith; 176 Peter Macdiarmid / Staff; 180-181 kolderal; 184 Martin Llado; 187 Roberto Moiola / Sysaworld; 189 serts; 190 serts; 191 The Washington Post / Contributor; 193 Don Smith; 198-199 Pawel Libera / Contributor; 201 WadeW; 206-207 Stuart Stevenson photography; 208-209b DEA / V. GIANNELLA; 210 Tom Nebbia; 219tl Andrew Bret Wallis; 223 Roberto Moiola / Sysaworld; 225 Eloi_Omella; 236r Artur Debat; 236b Zowy Voeten / Stringer; 237 Mika Volkmann; 241b Alexander Spatari; 242 DavideMottarella; 246-247 Achim Thomae; 252-253 Alex Treadway; 254 Tatyana Aksenova / 500px; 255 Angel Villalba; 256 Cavan Images; 258 Oleh_Slobodeniuk; 259t Sean Gallup / Staff; 266 Cavan Images; 267 Roberto Moiola / Sysaworld; 269 Fibru Photography; 270 Francesco Riccardo Iacomino; 273 Anton Petrus; 274 Circle Creative Studio; 275 Arman Zhenikeyev; 276-277 Adam Jones; 279 Punnawit Suwuttananun; 281 Buena Vista Images; 283 John Rickwood; 288 Edwin Tan; 294 Edwin Remsberg; 295 Roberto Moiola/robertharding; 302 Mark Newman; 306b Martin Harvey; 316 Kieran Stone; 322-323 Pakin Songmor; 324 Andrew Geiger; 328 Qilai Shen / Contributor; 329t acavalli; 331 Kelvin Zhang; 335 Peter Adams; 340 Nancy Brown; 341 FEBRUARY; 342 davidf; 343 Gabriel Perez; 350 Quang Ngoc Nguyen; 354 Jim Purdum; 356 Panya Khamtuy; 361 Bohistock; 368 swissmediavision; 374-375 Sergio Amiti; 376-377 Mike Mackinven; 379 Francesco Riccardo Iacomino; 382-383 Colin Anderson Productions pty ltd; 386-387 Chris Williams Black Box; 388 Chasing Light - Photography by James Stone james-stone.com; 392-393 Moritz Wolf; 394 Reinhard Dirscherl; 395 Whitworth Images; 400-401 Matthew Williams-Ellis; 402 Connect Images; 404 Stephen Frink; 416 Levente Bodo.

iStockphoto: 34 GarysFRP; 143 Delbars; 212-213 NicoElNino; 233b Orbon Alija; 241t Drazen_; 348-349 StefanoZaccaria; 403 MaFelipe.

Shutterstock: 15 Wang Jui-Lin; 29 Vacclav; 32l Sacha van der Veen; 61 Faina Gurevich; 62 Adrinson Yanes Hernandez; 64-65 Barry A Mosley Photography; 80 Tobias.Brahms; 89 fokke baarssen; 95 sarahnev; 97 Andrew Glushchenko; 98-99 f11photo; 105 NayaDadara; 106 Ethan Yetman; 114 Lauren Gregg; 116 finepic; 122 Jam Travels; 126 Leonard Zhukovsky; 133 Kenrick Baksh; 140 J. Abelardo Alvarez S; 146-147 tolobalaguer.com; 149 worldroadtrip; 155 Damsea; 167 Eteri Okrochelidze; 170 David Ionut; 171 Donatas Dabravolskas; 182-183 rayints; 185 Nowaczyk; 196 Stephen William Robinson; 197 Alla Tsyganova; 203 James Mellish; 224 givaga; 227 Javen; 228 fokke baarssen; 235 Stephen Bridger; 245 Tohuwabohu 1976; 249 mikecphoto; 261 Eszter Szadeczky-Kardoss; 262 weniliou; 271 Razbitnov; 280 Altug Galip; 285t abackpacker; 285b Y.am; 287 Ondrej Bucek; 289 Igor Tichonow; 290-291 Joma Barleah; 304 Berwid; 307 Nick Fox; 315 Michail_Vorobyev; 320 fokke baarssen; 321 Vincent Ducheman; 359 y_seki; 360 Pajor Pawel; 364r Rajaraman Arumugam; 371 AA.Apt; 385 Amy Caccamo.

Unsplash: 2-3 allPhoto Bangkok; 12 Roberto Nickson; 27 Pascal Debrunner;

PICTURE CREDITS

32r Sunira Moses; 54 Anna Claire Schellenberg; 76t Aubrey Antles; 77 Nicole Geri; 86 Sandro Gonzalez; 96 Skylar Zilka; 104 Andrew Spencer; 124 Nick Rickert; 128 Aurelly Yollanda; 137 Victoria Bragg; 166 Shreyas Nair; 172 Léo Castro; 194-195 Bjorn Snelders; 204 Zoltan Tasi; 215 Simon Spring; 220 Daniel Zbroja; 221 Clay Banks; 232 threeedil; 239 Raja Sen; 260 Linda Gerbec; 265 Patrick Schneider; 272 Chloé Lefleur; 278 Filippo Cesarini; 284 Kyriacos Georgiou; 312 Bernd M. Schell; 318-319 Matteo Catanese; 329b Daniam Chou; 358 Cosmin Serban; 365 Lily Banse; 384 Kate Trifo; 390 Raelle Gann-Owens.

Dreamstime: 83 © Cvandyke; 230 Evgeniy Parilov.

Also: 10 Inn on The Lake / © Inn on The Lake; 13 Four Seasons Resort and Residences Whistler (https://www.fourseasons.com/whistler/ / © Four Seasons Resort and Residences Whistler; 17 Tourism Saskatchewan www.tourismsaskatchewan.com / © Tourism Saskatchewan; 24 www.hotelarctic.com / © Ulrik Amdi Hotel Arctic A/S; 30 Photographer: Travis Rowan (@travisrowanmedia) / © Hotel Wailea (@hotelwailea); 35 Nicole Freshley @nicolefreshley / © Minam River Lodge; 37 The Donum Estate www.thedonumestate.com / Photo by Robert Berg / © The Donum Estate; 41 Nicole Franzen http://www.nicolefranzen.com / © The Surfrider Malibu; 42t Image courtesy of Calamigos Guest Ranch calamigos.com / © Calamigos Guest Ranch & Beach Club; 42bl Image courtesy of Calamigos Guest Ranch calamigos.com / © Calamigos Guest Ranch & Beach Club; 42br Image courtesy of Calamigos Guest Ranch calamigos.com / © Calamigos Guest Ranch & Beach Club; 47 Courtesy of The Ranch At Rock Creek; @Theranchatrockcreek / © Jennie Schuette; 59 aman.com @aman / © Courtesy of Aman Group SARL; 63 Shortgrass Resort www.shortgrassresort.com / © Candace Gustafson; 69 Laura McReynolds Owner / © New Life lavender; 78 Asleep in the Cyclone, 21c Museum Hotel Louisville / © 21c Museum Hotels; 81 PumpkinSky / Wikimedia; 92 Hayley Renee Studio @Haleytrunkett / © Hayley Renee Studio @Haleytrunkett; 100 Jessica Orlowicz, Emily Repici / © Cape Resorts; 101 Jessica Orlowicz, Emily Repici / © Cape Resorts; 107 Noe DeWitt https://www.noedewitt.com / © Noe DeWitt; 115 The Potlatch Club / Photographer: David Loftus The Potlatch Club, www.thepotlatchclub.com / © The Potlatch Club, photographer: David Loftus; 123 William Thornton / © William Thornton; 127 Nobu Barbuda / © Nobu Barbuda; 132 sandals.com / © Sandals Resorts; 148 ranchosantana.com / © Rancho Santana; 153l Hacienda AltaGracia, Auberge Resorts Collection @altagraciaauberge / © Auberge Resorts Collection; 153r Hacienda AltaGracia, Auberge Resorts Collection @altagraciaauberge / © Auberge Resorts Collection; 154 Nayara Bocas del Toro nayaraboasdeltoro.com / © Nayara Resorts; 162 @pikaialodge / Pikaia Lodge, Galapacific SA; 163 @pikaialodge / Pikaia Lodge, Galapacific SA; 164 700000 heures Impact / © 700000 heures Impact; 186 Sebastian L. Torjusen / Salmon Eye / © Salmon Eye AS; 205 Will Darkin @will.darkin https://www.intonefilms.com/ / © Unyoked; 209tl Ashford Castle / © Ashford Castle; 209tr Ashford Castle / 214 Yann Allègre / Eleven @elevenexperience elevenexperience.com / © Yann Allègre / Eleven; 226 Bruno Bruchi / © Bruno Bruchi; 259b Ciprian Lupan / © Matca Relais & Châteaux; 268t The Rooster / © The Rooster; 268b The Rooster / © The Rooster; 296 Volcanoes Safaris / © Volcanoes Safaris and Black Bean Production; 297 The Safari Collection / © The Safari Collection; 298-299 Crookes&Jackson @crookesandjackson / © Crookes&Jackson; 300 Singita, www.singita.com @https://www.instagram.com/singita_/ / © Singita; 306t Silverless / © Natural Selection; 309b Unless otherwise specified, all image credits to Rovos Rail / @Jos Beltman; 313 The Royal Portfolio @theroyalportfolio / © The Royal Portfolio; 317 Oliver Fly @oliverflyafrica / © Oliver Fly for Miavana by Time + Tide; 332-333 https://www.sixsenses.com/en/hotels-resorts/asia-the-pacific/india/fort-barwara/ / © Six Senses Fort Barwara; 334 Uga Chena Huts - https://www.ugaescapes.com/chenahuts/ / © Uga Resorts; 337 Anantara Kihavah Maldives Villas / © Minor Hotels; 338-339 Photo by: John Athimaritis, Owner is Conrad Maldives Rangali Island (@conrad_maldives or conradmaldives.com) / © Conrad Maldives Rangali Island; 344 Instagram: @anantara_goldentriangle | Website: Anantara.com / © Anantara Golden Triangle Elephant Camp & Resort; 345 Instagram: @anantara_goldentriangle | Website: Anantara.com / © Anantara Golden Triangle Elephant Camp & Resort; 346 Twinpalms Tented Camp Phuket https://www.twinpalmshotelsresorts.com/tented-camp-phuket/ / © Twinpalms Hotels & Resorts; 351 https://www.sixsenses.com/vn/hotels-resorts/asia-the-pacific/vietnam/ninh-van-bay/ / © Six Senses Ninh Van Bay; 352 Ravy / © Shinta Mani Angkor; 353t Ravy / © Shinta Mani Angkor; 353b Ravy / © Shinta Mani Angkor; 357 Courtesy of TRUNK, yoyogipark.trunk-hotel.com/en / © TRUNK; 367 www.tallship.com.sg / © Tall Ship Adventures Pte Ltd; 369 Four Seasons Bali at Sayan / fsbali or fourseasons.com/sayan / © Four Seasons Resort Bali at Sayan; 370 www.bambuindah.com / © Bambu Indah Resort; 372t Tanveer Badal @tanveerbadal (instagram) / © Tanveer Badal; 372b Tanveer Badal @tanveerbadal (instagram) / © Tanveer Badal; 378 capelodge.com.au / © Cape Lodge; 381 www.journeybeyond.com / © Journey Beyond; 389t https://www.saffire-freycinet.com.au/ / © Saffire Freycinet; 389b https://www.saffire-freycinet.com.au/ / © Saffire Freycinet; 391 Wai Ariki Hots Springs and Spa - Rotorua Lakefront / © Wai Ariki Hot Springs and Spa; 397 Nanuku Resort @nanukuresort / © Nanuku Resort; 398 www.kokomoislandfiji.com / © Kokomo Private Island; 399 www.kokomoislandfiji.com / © Kokomo Private Island.

AUTHOR BIOGRAPHIES

KATHRYN ROMEYN

Kathryn Romeyn is an American journalist, editor, and podcast host living and working in Bali, Indonesia. After earning her journalism degree, she decamped to Los Angeles, California, where she spent eight years at luxury lifestyle magazines, working her way up from assistant editor to executive editor. In 2014, she began traveling heartily as a freelance contributor focused on luxury hospitality, honeymoon travel, culture, sustainability, design, and well-being, writing for publications including *Conde Nast Traveler*, *AFAR*, *Travel + Leisure*, *vogue.com*, *Brides*, *Architectural Digest*, *Los Angeles Times*, and *The Hollywood Reporter*. Along with covering exciting hotel openings around the globe and exploring far-flung destinations, Kathryn focuses much of her work on telling stories that excite and motivate travelers to embark on their own journeys.

KELLI ACCIARDO

Kelli Acciardo is a seasoned writer and editor who kicked off her career editing a relationship series for *Seventeen*. Since then, she's covered romantic getaways, luxury hotels, spa treatments, and dining experiences for top-tier outlets that include *Brides*, *The Knot*, *TripSavvy*, *Hotels Above Par*, and *PureWow*. Kelli also pens a popular column for *Parade*, offering a behind-the-scenes look at the meals she creates with her chef husband in their kitchen at home. While she loves a relaxing couples' massage, her favorite amorous activities for duos include cultural exploration and uncovering hidden gems in wanderlust pockets of the world.